Gavin Mortimer is arguab[illegible] wartime special forces. He has [illegible] subject, including *Stirling's Men*, a g[illegible] of the SAS in the Second World War, *Merrill* [illegible] *The Untold Story of Unit Galahad and the Toughest Spe*[illegible]*orces Mission of World War II* and the best-selling *The SBS in World War II*. An award-winning writer whose books have been published on both sides of the Atlantic, Mortimer has previously written for the *Daily Telegraph*, *Sunday Telegraph*, the *Observer* and *Esquire* magazine. He continues to contribute to a wide range of newspapers and magazines from *BBC History* to the *American Military History Quarterly*. In addition he has lectured on the SAS in World War Two at the National Army Museum.

Also by Gavin Mortimer

Fields of Glory (Andre Deutsch, 2001)

Stirling's Men (Weidenfeld, 2004)

The Longest Night (Weidenfeld, 2005)

The Great Swim (Walker & Company, 2007)

Chasing Icarus (Walker & Co, 2008)

Double Death (Walker & Co, (2009)

The Daring Dozen (Osprey 2011)

The History of the Special Air Service in World War II (Osprey, 2012)

The History of the Special Boat Squadron in World War II (Osprey 2013)

Merrill's Marauders (Zenith Press, 2013)

The First Eagles (Zenith Press, 2014)

For Lofty and Barbara,
for their generosity, hospitality and honesty

Acknowledgements

I'd like to thank the SAS Regimental Association for encouraging me to write this book. Last year the Association organized the inauguration of a Long Range Desert Group memorial, alongside that of David Stirling's statue in Scotland, and they have been unstinting in supporting this book, and in keeping alive the memory of the LRDG.

I am also grateful to Grenville Bint for his assistance in my research, particularly in the supply of many wonderful photographs. Similarly, I am indebted to Jonathan Pittaway, author of the excellent history of the Rhodesian members of the LRDG, and to Sarah Johnston at the New Zealand Sound Archives in Christchurch.

I salute the staff at the Imperial War Museum, National Archives and the Churchill Archives in Cambridge (where the copious papers of Ralph Bagnold are housed).

I must thank several relatives of LRDG personnel, notably Barbara Atherton, daughter of Harry Horton, one of the unit's most efficient signallers, who died aged ninety-eight in April 2014, just a few days before I was due to visit him. Although I didn't have the opportunity to meet Harry, Barbara was generous enough to give me his photo album and his complete collection of LRDG Association newsletters, from the inaugural issue in 1945 to the final edition in 2000. I will forever treasure them.

My journey to the home of Rudolf Schneider was a trip I won't forget. Treated royally throughout by Rudolf and his family, it was a memorable experience and a reminder of the courage and honour displayed by so many ordinary German soldiers in the war. Doreen Brade made the initial contact with Rudolph and has provided great assistance during my research in all matters requiring a native German speaker.

Thank you to my agent, Felicity Blunt, and her assistant, Emma Herdman, at Curtis Brown for their diligence on my behalf. Reading small print and such like isn't my strong point so it's reassuing to have two people I can rely on so completely to take care of that side of business!

The whole team at Constable & Robinson must be congratulated for their enthusiasm, efficiency and expert eye in editing the book. From Charlotte Macdonald to Andreas Campomar to Linda Silverman, and Josh Ireland. It was Josh who did such a good job in editing the manuscript, telling me at one point there were one or two places where I needed to 'let my inner *Boy's Own* loose'. So good was that piece of advice I'm trying to apply it to my everyday life.

I'll be in trouble if I forget to mention my mother, Sheila Mortimer, who ferried me across southern England in her car in order that I could spend a wonderful afternoon in the company of Jim Patch. The cheque's in the post for the petrol . . .

Finally to the veterans themselves who allowed me to intrude upon memories that had lain dormant for decades. What can I say, other than thank you for the privilege. This book is for you, and for all who served in the Long Range Desert Group.

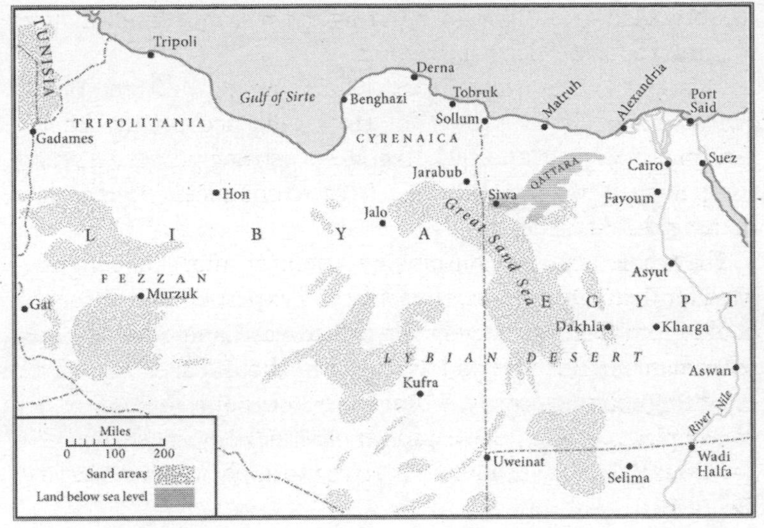
TUNISIA
Tripoli
Derna
Gulf of Sirte
Benghazi
Tobruk
Matruh
Alexandria
Port Said
Sollum
TRIPOLITANIA
Gadames
CYRENAICA
Cairo
Suez
Jarabub
QATTARA
Hon
Siwa
Fayoum
Jalo
Great Sand Sea
L I B Y A
Asyut
FEZZAN
Murzuk
Gat
E G Y P T
Dakhla
Kharga
LYBIAN DESERT
Aswan
Kufra
River Nile
Miles
0 100 200
Sand areas
Land below sea level
Uweinat
Selima
Wadi Halfa

Contents

Prologue

There were few bigger men in the Long Range Desert Group than Lance-Corporal Mike Carr. His mates called him 'Lofty', and at six foot four inches and fifteen stone he had the build of a rugby player. But Carr was much more than just brawn. He was one of the three top navigators in the LRDG, a man capable of finding his way across the flat, featureless, unforgiving expanse of the Libyan Desert.

For the last four days he had navigated a mixed force of LRDG men and soldiers from the Sudan Defence Force hundreds of miles north-east from the Kufra to the outskirts of Jalo Oasis.

It was now nightfall on 15 September 1942. Carr took a star shot and confirmed they were fifteen miles west of Jalo. In his West Country accent he passed the information to the patrol commander, Captain Anthony Hunter, a Lancastrian and former officer in the Royal Scots Fusiliers who at thirty was nine years Carr's senior.

They moved off in their trucks, continuing over the rough desert terrain on a bearing of ninety-five degrees. Four and a half miles from Jalo the column halted. Hunter ordered everyone to dismount and split his force into three. Emphasizing the need for absolute silence, the raiders moved noiselessly on foot towards Jalo.

Carr's armament of choice was a single Vickers K machine gun, a frightening gas-operated weapon that fired 1,200 rounds a minute. A soldier needed to be strong to carry a Vickers, stronger still to fire it. Carr used it like a shotgun, a weapon he'd grown up with in the West Country, and the LRDG armourer had been good enough to fit a handle to the top of the Vickers K to make it easier to carry.

Tonight, however, Carr entrusted his Vickers to a stout-looking soldier of the Sudan Defence Force. Keep close to me, Carr told him, in case I should need it. In the meantime Carr navigated the force the four and a half miles through the darkness using his theodolite.

Their target was the Italian-garrisoned fort at Jalo, a desert oasis approximately 250 miles south of the Mediterranean port of Benghazi on the Libyan coast. It was a godforsaken place, little more than a fort, a few native houses and a perpetual wind that blew soft sand into the faces of the inhabitants. The water was brackish, the flies numerous and the heat unbearable. The LRDG had occupied Jalo at the start of the year, before General Erwin Rommel had driven them out. Now they wanted it back. It might have been a hellhole but it was a hellhole of strategic importance to the British as they prepared to launch their big offensive the following month at El Alamein.

Carr, at the head of the three columns, led the force forward for more than an hour. Suddenly he stopped. He raised a hand. Hunter, at his side, asked what it was. Minefield. Hunter ordered one column to look for a way round the minefield to the left; the other two columns swung to the right.

As Carr steered the force round the minefield it was still impossible to see through the blackness the outskirts of the village just 100 yards up ahead. The absolute stillness was shattered by a cry from an Italian sentry. Carr froze. Hunter froze. Everyone stood motionless. Seconds passed. Total silence. Then the sentry issued a second challenge. Carr's bearded face broke into a faint smile. This soldier was raw, he was going through the Buckingham Palace book of procedures for a sentry.

Hunter leaned into Carr and whispered 'shoot him.' Carr reminded his officer he didn't have his weapon. 'Then get it.' Carr grabbed his Vickers K having first plugged his ears with the two cotton wool balls he always carried in the pocket of his tunic. The Vickers had a double cocking action. Click. Wait. Click again. Fire. Any alert sentry would open fire at the first click, but this Italian wasn't much good at his job.

Carr cocked the Vickers and fired from a sitting position. He was so close to his target he saw the Italian picked up and thrown back, bits of incendiary and tracer sticking all over his uniform. Hunter urged his men onwards. Capture the fort. They had gone only a few yards when the world erupted in a whirlwind of enemy fire. The Sudanese troops panicked. Most turned and fled, chased by the long coloured lines of enemy tracer. Their British officers also set off in pursuit of the Sudanese troops, screaming at them to stop and return to the fight. If they didn't they would shoot them themselves.

Hunter and Carr were on their own. Bullets cracked overhead, others thudded into the ground, sending up small fountains of sand. A mortar round landed close by. Hunter tugged at Carr's sleeve and pointed to his head. His eardrums had been blown out. Carr shouted at his officer to get the hell out of it. Then the young lance corporal raised himself up to one knee and fired a long burst from the Vickers. The tracer illuminated the night sky. Carr jumped up and moved to his left. He had to hook up with the third column.

He gave the Italians another long spurt of fire, and then several shorter bursts. He had to preserve his ammunition. Suddenly the Vickers stopped firing. Carr dropped to his knee and tried to clear the jam. It was no good. The weapon had overheated, the copper firing caps in the base of the .303 cartridges melting inside their brass cases. Liquid copper had jammed everything. Carr discarded the Vickers and ran around the perimeter of the minefield. He could see no sign of the third column but there were voices not too distant. Italian voices, and they were headed his way. Suddenly a stroke of good fortune. Carr almost ran straight into the low stone circular wall of a desert well. He stepped a giant leg over the wall, then another, and eased himself inside the well. He was safe, for the time being. Until daylight at least.

CHAPTER ONE

'Old friends in Cairo'

Ralph Bagnold was already twenty-four years old when Lofty Carr came into this world. A veteran of the Great War, the scholarly Bagnold was reading engineering at Cambridge University when Carr was born in Froome, Somerset, in October 1920. Apart from the proximity of their birthplace – Bagnold, like Carr a West Countryman, was born 100 miles from Froome in Stoke Devonport – the pair had little in common. But for the Second World War their paths would never have crossed. Carr's enquiring mind might have led him to read one of Bagnold's articles in a scientific journal at some point, but the big man with the working-class roots would never have had the opportunity to sit and discuss the vagaries of life with the renowned academic.

Bagnold was born in April 1896. Shy, reserved, possessed of a stutter and an unprepossessing physique, he was neither an artist nor an athlete, Bagnold recoiled at the ethos of 'Muscular Christianity' that he encountered at Malvern College in the years leading up to the First World War. 'Games were greatly overemphasized,' he recalled later of his English public school. 'I resented compulsory football and cricket. I was, however, able to avoid both by joining the engineering school where, as an afternoon alternative, I learned to use metal-working machine tools, lathes, milling and drilling machines.' Another escape was the works of H.G. Wells, which stimulated the boy's mind 'with the idea that there were new, unimagined things still to be discovered'.

It was always expected of Bagnold that he would follow his father, Colonel Arthur Bagnold, into the Royal Engineers, and in the spring of 1914 he passed the army entrance exam for the Royal Military Academy, Woolwich. Bagnold placed fourth in the exam, out of several hundred candidates, but just as he enrolled in the academy, war was declared between Germany and the British Empire.

Bagnold survived the war, though his experience of serving in the trenches was embedded in his memory for the rest of his life. 'Pieces of bodies were everywhere,' he recalled of the July day in 1916 when his battalion marched up to the frontline in the Somme Valley. 'Buried bodies squelched underfoot as one walked . . . green-backed flies swarmed over them under a blazing sun.'

Peace came as a shock to Bagnold. In four years he had matured from a naive teenager to a veteran of trench warfare, a soldier who had seen death on an unimaginable scale. 'When the war ended and the armistice came the bottom seemed to drop out of life altogether,' said Bagnold.

It was his commanding officer, Lieutenant-Colonel Frederick Stratton, who rescued the bewildered young soldier. A former mathematical lecturer at Cambridge University and soon to be one of the leading figures in pre-war astronomy, Stratton encouraged Bagnold to go up to Cambridge to study engineering. He took the advice, reflecting that the period he spent at university 'was the happiest time I ever had in my life'.

After Cambridge Bagnold resumed his military career with the 5th Division Signal Company, then serving in Ireland. In 1925 he was posted to Egypt. As part of his research into his new posting Bagnold digested the work of Dr Alois Musil, a Czech explorer who, at the turn of the century, traversed 13,000 miles of Arabian desert on camel. The doctor was a prodigious writer, churning out more than fifty books (several of which were lavishly illustrated with maps) and 1,000 articles for various academic and scientific journals. Not everyone admired his work. T.E. Lawrence, better known as Lawrence of Arabia, the British officer who helped foment the Arab revolt against the Ottoman Empire in World War

One, expressed his views on a Musil book about North Arabia in an undated letter to Bagnold in the twenties: 'It is difficult to read because Dr Musil is not anxious to convey more than the facts of his observations,' wrote Lawrence in reply to a letter from Bagnold. 'Arabia has been fortunate in attracting so far people who travelled in it, rather than people anxious only to map it. Musil's map seems to me wasted because he does not distinguish between the part which is observed and the part which is hearsay.'

Bagnold was captivated from the moment he set foot in Egypt, its landscape stirring memories of the excitement he'd felt walking across Dartmoor with his father as a boy. 'Both had the strange aura induced by the physical presence of the remote past, and also by the great bare trackless expanses where the careless might well get lost,' he reflected. Where many of his fellow officers saw only danger in the desert, Bagnold beheld beauty, and potential. 'It was rather like yachting at sea, one could go where one liked, never knowing what one would find over the next horizon,' he said, 'which made it very interesting and exciting.'

Bagnold was aware that in the First World War a small band of intrepid Allied soldiers had formed the Light Car Patrol, venturing into Palestine and the Western Desert in Model T Fords with 'oversize three and a half inch tyres'. Yet the unit had been disbanded in 1919 and as Bagnold discovered on arriving in Cairo, 'the general opinion was, even then, that the motor car was meant for roads'.

Bagnold regarded such short-sightedness as nonsense. 'Why shouldn't one use Ford cars to travel across country?' he asked himself. While the married officers idled away leisure hours with their wives at the Gezira Sporting Club, and many of the single men feasted in the fleshpots of Cairo, Bagnold and a small number of kindred spirits from the officers' mess at Abbassia Barracks (the Engineers shared these living quarters with the Royal Corps of Signals and the Royal Tank Corps) procured some Model T Fords and ventured into the desert, tentatively at first, like a child entering the ocean for the first time.

In March 1926 Bagnold and a fellow officer, V.C. Holland, drove along the old caravan road from Cairo to Suez. It was exhilarating. In the months that followed they acquired more experience, learning what they and their vehicles were capable of in the alien environment. A ten-day expedition took them 1,000 miles across Sinai, via Nekhel and Jerusalem, to the Transjordan, and in April 1927 Bagnold led a party from Suez to the southern Sinai.

Eventually, in October 1927, Bagnold – now a major in the Royal Corps of Signals – felt confident enough to tackle the daunting immensity of the Western Desert. His intention was to reach Siwa Oasis, 400 miles to the west, where in 332 BC Alexander the Great had visited the Temple of the Oracle of Amun during his conquest of Egypt. It was said Alexander reached Siwa by following the birds across the desert; for the first fifty miles of his expedition to the oasis Bagnold saw only the occasional gazelle. Then even they vanished from view and the explorers had nothing for company other than each other. There were six of them all told, including a twenty-six-year-old officer in the Royal Tank Corps called Guy Prendergast, sombre and self-contained. They travelled in three Model T Fords, carried forty-two gallons of petrol and had water for ten days.

'Horizon followed pebbly horizon interminably,' wrote Bagnold in an account of the journey. 'No living plant or even insect. The gnarled black trunks of forest trees that lie about for many hundred miles only increase the sense of utter lack of life, for they have ages ago been turned to stone.'

In their first evening in the desert they sheltered 'behind a low bank a hundred miles from the Nile', but it afforded little protection against the wind. Bagnold's scientific mind was aroused by the effect the wind had on the sand. Early the next morning they encountered the Ramak Dunes. Bagnold was entranced. 'They were,' he wrote, 'the most remarkable sand formation in the world – a single ridge of sand reaching down from the north geometrically straight for eighty miles from beneath the inland cliffs that bound the coastal plateau . . . it is as if someone had accurately dumped sand in great hundred foot heaps one on another along a ruled straight line.'

Bagnold's wonderment continued to shine through the prose in his subsequent account of the journey to Siwa. At times he wrote the gravel 'was finer and of a chocolate hue', and yet the further they drove from Cairo the more brutal the desert became, what Bagnold described as 'a terrible tract of white jagged rock'. All the while the explorers were conscious that to their south 'rose the irregular line of thousand-foot cliffs that separate for over five hundred miles the coastal plateau of north east Africa from the low lying inner desert far below sea level'. Before they reached the cliffs the vehicles became ensnared in 'low tongues of soft yellow salt-marsh hardly distinguishable in the glare from the surrounding limestone dust and sand'.

They were looking for the Masrab, or camel track, that led from the Mahashash Desert in the north-east to Siwa but it took them several torturous hours to find it. It was a wretched spot, reflected Bagnold, who now understood why the Ancient Greeks had believed the Libyan Desert harboured the petrifying Gorgons. 'It was a painful crossing,' he wrote. 'The cars creaked and groaned as each wheel climbed independently and fell over the cracked waves of upthrust salt. For nearly an hour we crawled across at walking pace, past here and there the bones of camels who had fallen broken-legged by the way.'

Their reward for navigating a passage over the cliffs was to enter a dense palm forest, its trees guarding 'damp gardens of oranges and pomegranates'. A stream of water ran beside the road, a heavenly vision to the parched explorers. The next day they reached the tiny village of Qara, seventy miles north-east of Siwa, and situated on the western edge of the fearsome Qattara Depression. The few villagers they encountered were poor and forlorn, desperate to sell these strange intruders some dates, the only commodity they had. Bagnold and his companions were relieved to leave the following morning, climbing away from Qara up a precipitous camel track onto an upper plateau where the air was fresh and invigorating. They pressed on, across the ocean of sand, all of them eagerly anticipating their first glimpse of 'land'. By midday they had Siwa in their sights, and the moment overwhelmed them.

Climbing out of their vehicles they looked down upon Siwa, its salty lakes and groves of dark-green palm trees a picturesque scene. With adolescent enthusiasm Bagnold and his companions wondered aloud if it was on this exact same spot that Alexander the Great first saw 'water after his long desert march from the coast on that strange journey of his to the Siwan temple'.

Bagnold had read much about Siwa prior to his expedition but nothing could prepare him for what he discovered upon entering the town. For centuries nomad tribes from the west had plundered Siwa, leading the inhabitants to turn their homes into impregnable fortresses constructed from mud and the trunks of palm trees. The sun had hardened the mud so it was as hard as brick and the colour of dun. Over the years, as the population expanded, the townspeople eschewed building outwards and instead built up upwards, constructing houses on top of existing ones until old Siwa looked like a beehive.

Bagnold discovered, however, that a recent earthquake had prompted the Egyptian government to expel Siwans from their ancient beehive because of fears the mud houses would collapse. A new town was under construction, the western side occupied by the Senussi tribe, and the east by the Medania.

The explorers acted like the tourists they were. First a coffee in a café in the town's market, then a bathe in one of Siwa's numerous springs, and finally a hike out of town to the ruins of the temple of Ammon. The next day, 'after a lazy morning buying bread and dates in the market and wandering through the tunnels of Old Siwa and in the surrounding fruit gardens', Bagnold and his companions bade farewell to Siwa. Their next destination was Jarabub (also spelt Giarabub), sixty miles to the west, the Holy City of the Senussi, with its famous white-domed mosque. Entombed in the mosque are the remains of Sayed Ibn Ali es Senussi, the founder of the Senussi who died in 1859 and was buried in Jarabub by his son and successor, Sidi el Mahdi.

For the first twenty-four hours of their journey west from Siwa, Bagnold was preoccupied with the view south of the Great Sand

Sea and its towering dunes, some as high as 500 feet from trough to crest. On the second day, as they neared Jarabub, the Britons saw the tracks of Italian armed convoys. Then they encountered a small Italian outpost, not much more than a few wooden buildings encircled by thick tangles of barbed wire with a bored sentry slouching in a watchtower. 'It was hard to believe that in all this emptiness a war was going on,' reflected Bagnold, 'and that a sufficient force could rise from nowhere to attack Italian columns of sixty cars and more.'

He decided against pressing on to Jarabub, instead leading his party north-east to pick up the coast road that led back to Cairo. He sympathized with the Arabs and their guerrilla war against the Italian invader, but he and his companions were explorers, they had no place in a war zone. Besides, 'we had to get back quickly for our leave was nearly up.'

In the decade after his expedition to Siwa, Ralph Bagnold had established himself as the pre-eminent desert explorer of his generation. There had been further expeditions, in 1930, when he discovered that a motor car could climb the vertiginous dunes of the Great Sand Sea, and two years later when he and his companions covered 6,000 miles of the Libyan Desert. At one point during that epic voyage, the British came upon a unit of the Italian army only 900 miles south-west of Cairo at Uweinat just on the Libyan side of the Egyptian-Libyan-Sudanese border. The meeting was friendly, the Italians hosting the British for lunch, and as a result no party wished to spoil the atmosphere. 'Both sides left the question of ownership severely alone,' wrote Bagnold. 'Neither were any questions asked as to either party's reasons for being here, or of their future intentions.'

Since the mid-twenties tensions had been simmering between Britain and Italy, with the former increasingly concerned by Benito Mussolini's determination to control the Mediterranean. The fascist Italian dictator held sway in North Africa, and increasingly the British felt their influence in Egypt and the Sudan under threat – with good reason. One Italian officer, Major Orlando

Lorenzini,* had pointed out – in the most charming manner over plates of spaghetti – that Uweinat was only 550 miles from the Aswan dam on the Nile. In the event of a war, joked Lorenzini, 'what fun it would be to take a battalion to Aswan and seize the dam.' Gazing at Bagnold, he had asked with faux jocularity, 'What could you do?'

By 1935 it was a question that no longer concerned Bagnold. Shortly before his fortieth birthday, he retired from the army, put his exploring days behind him, and began building a reputation as a science writer. Ever since his first foray into the Libyan desert in 1927, Bagnold had been intrigued by the behaviour of blown sand and he was 'fascinated by the origin and formation of the desert dunes'. The result was two short papers, published in the *Proceedings of the Royal Society* in 1936 and 1937, followed two years later by the completion of a book, *The Physics of Blown Sand and Desert Dunes*, for which some of the research was conducted at Imperial College London. By 1939 Bagnold's expertise in desert exploration was in great demand. That summer he was commissioned to write a long article for *Scientific American*, entitled 'A Lost World Refound.' He was paid $40 for his time, the journal's editor commending his 'crisp prose'.

It was the last article Bagnold would write for a while. On 15 August he was recalled to the colours and at the end of the month he was posted to Officer Commanding, East Africa Signals. His diary entry for 3 September 1939 was laconic: 'War declared'.

On 28 September, Bagnold was one of several hundred military personnel that sailed from Britain for East Africa on board the Cunard vessel, RMS *Franconia*, requisitioned as a troopship shortly before it was scheduled to depart on a world cruise. 'It was provisioned accordingly,' recalled Bagnold, 'so we had unlimited caviar and other delicacies.'

A week out of port, as the *Franconia* zig-zagged its way through the Mediterranean to avoid enemy submarines, the vessel collided

* Subsequently promoted to general, Lorenzini was killed in action at Keren, Eritrea, in March 1941.

with the merchant cruiser *Alcantara*. Bagnold saw the incident from the deck and surmised that the *Alcantara* 'must have mistaken starboard for port for she ran straight into us'.

Neither ship sank but the damage required the vessels to limp into the nearest port for repairs. The *Franconia* arrived at Malta on 6 October and the following day Bagnold transferred to the *Empress*. The ship was not the only change to Bagnold's schedule: instead of sailing directly to East Africa, he was first heading to North Africa, to Port Said, where he disembarked on 9 October while they waited for the next available troopship to take them onwards to Kenya.

Bagnold was delighted. 'I took this welcome opportunity to look up old friends in Cairo and therefore caught the first available train,' he reminisced.

He found the city much the same. They were still playing polo at the Gezira Sporting Club, still visiting the fleshpots and still drinking champagne on the terrace of the Shepheard's Hotel. Italy had not entered the war and no one imagined they would, at least not in North Africa.

One of the first old friends Bagnold looked up was Colonel Micky Miller, Chief Signals Officer at Headquarters of British troops in Egypt. The pair went for a drink in the Long Bar of the Shepheard's, and Bagnold asked Miller if he could pull a few strings with the War Office; after all, surely his talents could best be employed in North Africa, not East Africa, a region with which he was unfamiliar. Miller promised he would cable London. As the pair talked they were observed by a reporter from the *Egyptian Gazette* who, though not close enough to eavesdrop, assumed that the man he recognized as the great desert explorer Ralph Bagnold was back in town on war business. A day or so later the paper's 'Day In, Day Out' gossip column ran a short piece praising the perspicacity of the British High Command, a welcome change to the obtuseness of the Great War. 'During that war, if a man had made a name for himself as an explorer of the Egyptian desert he would almost certainly have been sent to Jamaica to report on the possibilities of increasing rum production.' The tittle-tattle was picked up by the London *Daily Telegraph*, which applauded the authorities for 'utilizing the services of an expert in the place where his knowledge can be put to use'.

Little did either newspaper know that Bagnold was only killing time in Cairo before continuing on to his original posting in East Africa. But thanks to the item in the *Egyptian Gazette*, General Archibald Wavell, General Officer Commanding-in-Chief of Middle East Command, discovered that he had on his doorstep the foremost expert on the Western Desert. He sent for Bagnold, and the pair met for the first time in 'a tiny office in an attic'. Wavell had been installed in his post in July 1939, but it was a low-key appointment, the British keen not to antagonize the Italians. Wavell remained out of sight in his 'tiny office' at the top of the 'Grey Pillars' HQ. Yet despite the relaxed atmosphere in Cairo among the junior officers and general population, the War Office had been readying itself for conflict in North Africa for years.

Bagnold's reports of his encounters with Italians in the early thirties had been relayed in detail to his superiors, and subsequently the British had discovered through its Middle East Intelligence Service that the Italian secret service were collecting information on Britain's defences in Egypt. The spies' conclusion, which was accurate, was that in the event of an Italian invasion the British would lure their forces to Mersa Matruh – 135 miles west of Cairo – and attack them with fresh reinforcements. Thus the Italian secret service report advised launching any assault on Egypt from Uweinat in the south, up into the Nile Valley, which was precisely the direction Major Orlando Lorenzini had mischievously speculated about to Bagnold during their desert lunch at Uweinat in 1932.

But the British, on receiving this intelligence, scoffed at the idea that any Italian force of significant strength would be able to cover such a route north into the Nile Valley. It was the Italian presence in Mersa Matruh that concerned the British high command, even after the signature in April 1938 of the Anglo–Italian Agreement, designed to bring harmony to North Africa. Neither side trusted the other, and the British were also becoming concerned by the presence of German military and diplomatic personnel in the region. A Germany Military Mission appeared in Benghazi, a Libyan port 675 miles west of Cairo, and German pilots were reported to be conducting training flights in conjunction with their Italian counterparts.

In fact, the German Minister in Cairo, Baron Ow-Wachendorf, had spent several weeks at the end of 1938 cajoling King Farouk, ruler of Egypt, to adopt a neutral stance in the event of a war between Britain and Germany. German attempts to curry favour with the king – which included gifts from Adolf Hitler – might have succeeded had not Germany occupied Czechoslovakia in March 1939 and Italy invaded Albania the following month. Fearing his country could be similarly targeted, King Farouk spurned further German advances and instead put his army on a war footing, even restricting desert exploration by declaring a large section of the desert prohibited territory, including five oases, one of which was Siwa.

The response of the Axis powers was to step up their air patrols over Egypt and the Sudan but the Egyptian Ministry – at the prompting of the British – ruled in the late summer of 1939 that these too were a violation. Italy announced its neutrality when Germany and Britain declared war in September, however this was of little comfort to the British, who knew that the Italian appetite for Africa was insatiable. Having already devoured Libya, Somaliland, Eritrea and Abyssinia, Italy's ravenous eyes were now cast towards Egypt and the Sudan.

CHAPTER TWO

'Piracy on the High Seas'

'Wavell was a short, stocky man with one eye,' recalled Bagnold, 'and one felt there was something about him that made one think here's a very strong personality.' The general, who had lost his other eye to shrapnel in the First World War, impressed Bagnold with what he knew of his career, and asked 'whether I would not rather serve in Egypt'. Bagnold replied in the affirmative, and on 16 October he wrote in his diary:

> Cable from WO [War Office] agreeing to my staying in Egypt. Posted to Armoured Divisions Signals, Matruh.

Before he left for his new posting at Matruh, Bagnold 'called in at HQ, BTE [British Troops in Egypt] to get a map showing the whole country to the west'. All they could offer was a map dating from 1915, 'on which the interior of Libya was an almost medieval guesswork dating from Rohlfs' seventy-year-old notes'.* One can picture Bagnold staring at the map with a mix of dismay and disbelief, shaking his head at the words written to the west of the desert – 'Limit of dunes unknown'.

Bagnold left Cairo alarmed at the 'insular peacetime attitude of

* Gerhard Rohlfs was a German explorer who, in the 1870s, made a series of epic explorations across the Libyan desert. Unfortunately on his second expedition, in 1878, desert tribesmen attacked his party and their notes and equipment were lost, so he was unable to contribute much to the cartography of the region.

the headquarter staff . . . and their total ignorance of the desert country beyond the Nile cultivation.' Much of the blame for this ignorance lay with General Henry 'Jumbo' Wilson, a good tactician, but a traditional one, a soldier who had first seen action in the South African War of 1899–1902 and whose thought processes still travelled along conventional lines.

Fortunately when Bagnold arrived in Matruh he discovered that General Percy Hobart, commander of the 7th Armoured Division, had a more expansive mind. Bagnold had already drafted 'a short note suggesting that we might at least buy a small assortment of desert-worthy American vehicles and train a nucleus of officers and men in the art of cross-country driving, as the Light Car Patrols had been trained in 1916'. He showed it to Hobart on arriving in Matruh. 'I entirely agree,' said Hobart upon reading the document. 'I'll send this on to BTE but I know what will happen. They'll turn it down.' They did, and Hobart was soon forced into retirement by a cabal of senior officers who distrusted his 'unconventional' military ideas.

Nonetheless, Bagnold was encouraged to learn that the army – 'though without a word of acknowledgement' – had adopted many of the techniques and equipment that he and his fellow explorers had perfected on their inter-war expeditions. These included the use of steel channels, about five feet long and eleven inches wide, deployed to extricate trapped vehicles by placing them in the sand in front of the rear wheels; Bagnold's method of water conservation had also been implemented. Having discovered that vital water was lost in the desert when radiators boiled over and blew water off through the overflow, Bagnold came up with an ingenious solution for his vehicles: 'Instead of having a free overflow pipe we led the water into a can half full of water on the side of the car so it would condense in the can,' he explained. 'When that began to boil, too, it would spurt boiling water over the driver who would have to stop. All we had to do was turn into the wind, wait for perhaps a minute, there'd be a gurgling noise, and all the water would be sucked back into the radiator, which was full to the brim.'

The British Army had adopted Bagnold's sun compass, a

navigational device he had invented after his first expedition into the Western Desert, when he had discovered that the magnetic compass was unreliable because of all the metal in their vehicles. This forced the explorers to take a compass bearing some distance away from their vehicle, impractical for long-distance expeditions. The solution was Bagnold's eponymous sun compass, a modification on the sundial that was subsequently manufactured by Watts and Co. of London. 'Simply, it was a knitting needle set vertically in the centre of a horizontal white shadow disc, 3 inches in diameter' wrote Bagnold. 'The face of the disc was graduated in 360 degrees of bearing, and the disc could be rotated in its fixed mounting to follow the sun through the day from east through south to west, according to a card giving the sun's azimuth every 10 minutes of the day.'

Bagnold had the compass mounted on the vehicles' dashboards because the Model T Fords he used in his expeditions had neither windscreens nor roofs. Thus the sun's shadow was always visible, even on overcast days, except at midday when the sun was directly overhead and cast no shadow. Bagnold solution to this predicament was always to stop for lunch at 12.00 p.m. sharp.

At night Bagnold had navigated with a theodolite, using the stars as his guide, much as a sailor relied on a sextant, and this method had also been embraced by the army. Unfortunately, though the army had adopted Bagnold's innovations, no one appeared to have much idea about how to use a sun compass or a sand channel. This had less to do with the 7th Armoured Division's mental agility and more with the fact the division was operating close to the coast, far from the brutal interior of the desert. Therefore they had little opportunity to really test their skills against the desert the way Bagnold had done a decade earlier.

The longer Bagnold spent in Mersa Matruh, the more alarmed he grew that the British could be easily outmanoeuvred by the Italian forces in Libya, estimated to number a quarter of a million men in fifteen divisions under Marshal Rodolfo Graziani. He tried a second time in January 1940 to convince Middle East HQ

(MEHQ) to invest in a small force to patrol the 700-mile frontier with Libya. This time the proposal was backed and submitted by General Michael Creagh, who had replaced Major-General Percy Hobart as commander of the 7th Armoured Division in December. Again the idea was strangled at birth. General Jumbo Wilson's staff sent an 'angry reply' and told Creagh it 'was none of his business'. Wilson even reprimanded Creagh when, in the company of Bagnold, he spent three days exploring some of the Italian forts in the Western Desert. Creagh was incredulous: 'How does Jumbo think I can defend the frontier without having seen it?' he laughingly asked Bagnold.

Perhaps it was no coincidence that in early February Bagnold was despatched to Turkey as a military adviser. The British were fearful that Hitler might order an invasion of Turkey, and so they sent a small reconnaissance party from Egypt; MEHQ would have been glad to get Bagnold and his crackpot scheme out of their hair for a few weeks. His stay in Istanbul was largely uneventful, the highlight being a party he attended at the Germany embassy on 22 February, hosted by Franz von Papen, the ambassador.

It was rather odd to attend a party hosted by your enemy, but Bagnold and his fellow British officers present were as puzzled by the Phoney War as the rest of the army. Six months after the declaration of war, Western Europe had seen little in the way of conflict. Such was the inertia that in early March Bagnold was able to devote several days to proofreading the manuscript of *The Physics of Blown Sand and Desert Dunes*. On the ninth of the month he posted the galley proofs to the publishers and a few days later he too was posted, 'across the snows of Anatolia and Thrace [Turkish regions in the Balkans] collecting technical details about telegraphs and telephone'.

Increasingly resigned to a place in the quiet backwaters of the conflict, Bagnold was saved by events thousands of miles away. Even more so than the German occupation of the Low Countries in May 1940, it was the declaration of war the following month by Italy on Britain that had a profound impact on Bagnold's military career. A direct consequence of this was that now British forces in the Middle East were cut off from their comrades in Europe because Italy controlled the Mediterranean and Red Sea routes. In addition, the collapse of France and the establishment of a puppet government under Marshal Petain deprived General Wavell of a whole army corps of Syrian troops.

There was another threat, too, one that only Bagnold really understood. It came from Kufra, an isolated desert post in the south-east of Libya, and could potentially lead to the fall of Egypt and the Sudan. Surrounded on three sides by depressions, Kufra was of strategic importance because it served as an air base for Italian East Africa, and its topographical location commanded outstanding views of the land traffic.

Had Bagnold been authorized to carry out reconnaissance patrols of the Libyan Desert nine months earlier he would have known the exact strength of the large Italian garrison at Kufra. 'A well timed raid by a party, say 2000 strong, could sever temporarily our only land connection between Egypt and Khartoum,' wrote Bagnold. 'With submarines to obstruct the alternative Red Sea route, this interruption might vitally affect the delicate and precarious adjustment of our pitiful resources between the two theatres of war [North Africa and Western Europe].'

Bagnold's diary entry for 19 June 1940 was characteristically terse: 'Put forward Libya scheme for third time.'

There was, of course, far more to it than that. On 10 June Italy had declared war on Britain and France, exactly a month after the German invasion of the Low Countries began. Belgium, Luxembourg and Holland had all fallen to the Nazis and the speed of France's disintegration had shocked Bagnold to the core. 'Fall of Paris. French collapsing,' he told his diary on 15 June, before digging out the scheme Creagh had submitted on his behalf five months earlier. He added a further paragraph, explaining there would be three patrols:

> Every vehicle of which, with a crew of three and a machine gun, was to carry its own supplies of food and water for 3 weeks,

> and its own petrol for 2500 miles of travel across average soft desert surface – equivalent in petrol consumption to some 2400 miles of road. By the use of 30-cwt [hundredweight] trucks there would be a small margin of load-carrying capacity in each. This margin, if multiplied by a large enough number of trucks would enable the patrol to carry a wireless set, navigating and other equipment, medical stores, spare parts and further tools, and would also allow extra petrol to be carried for another truck mounting a 2-pdr gun with its ammunition, and a light pilot car for the commander.

Satisfied with what he had outlined, Bagnold handed the proposal to Brigadier Dick Baker at MEHQ. Bagnold and Baker went back a long way, they had been cadets together at Woolwich in the summer of 1914, and the latter promised the proposal would end up on Wavell's desk.

It did, though the subsequent chain of events have been romanticized over time. Bagnold claimed years later that Wavell sent for him 'within an hour', listening in rapt attention as the middle-aged major outlined his scheme. At one point Bagnold mentioned his force would carry out some 'piracy on the high seas', at which Wavell's 'grim face suddenly broke into a broad grin'. Romantic, yes, but the reality? Bagnold made no mention of such a meeting in his diary, simply stating that it was 'taken up by the C in C'.

In an unpublished draft of his memoirs, written shortly after the end of the war, Bagnold wrote:

> I had expected interest, a meeting perhaps, discussions as to whether the scheme was practicable, counter-proposals and considerable delay. But instead of this the whole scheme, just as it stood, had been strongly supported by the heads of both the operations and intelligence staffs, and had been read and approved by the C-in-C himself. I was to push on with it at once, under the aegis of Brigadier Shearer, the DMI [Director of Military Intelligence], without waiting for any formal authority.

The clearest indication as what exactly happened lies in the pages of the LRDG War Diary. It states: 'On 19th June, Bagnold who was then serving on the GHQ Staff in Cairo, again put the idea forward. General Wavell having expressed his approval, it was decided on 23rd June to go ahead at once with the formation of one Long Range Patrol [LRP].'

But whatever the truth, Wavell had accepted the proposal and Bagnold was asked to raise his unit within six weeks. Where to start? He needed officers, men, vehicles, equipment, rations . . .

On 24 June (giving further credence to the assertion that Bagnold was authorized to form the unit on 23 June, four days after submitting the proposal), Bagnold cabled his former explorers and invited them to join his scheme. These were members of the Zerzura Club, a club founded by Bagnold on the evening of 5 November 1930 in the Greek Bar of Wadi Halfa during his expedition into the desert that year. The club was named after the mythical oasis that had lured many an adventurer into the heart of the Libyan Desert, and membership was open to all desert explorers. Among the six explorers present at the club's inaugural meeting were Guy Prendergast, Bill Kennedy Shaw and Douglas Newbold. Prendergast, now a major, was in England and unable to accept the invitation – at least for a few months – while Newbold was the political head of the Sudan government (Civil Secretary) and duty-bound to remain in Khartoum.

Kennedy Shaw jumped at the chance, however, as did another of the Zerzura Club, Pat Clayton. Like Bagnold, Clayton was forty-four (only thirteen days separated them in age) but whereas his friend had returned to England after those early desert expeditions, he had remained in the Middle East, accumulating nearly twenty years of experience with the Egyptian Survey Department. Clayton was surveying in Tanganyika when he received Bagnold's cable, which he recalled later as 'a vague message apparently offering a safe chair-borne job in Cairo'. He said yes even though he described himself as a middle-aged 'civil servant of low medical category'.

Kennedy Shaw also accepted, delighted for the opportunity to escape the monotony of censoring newspapers in Palestine in the service of the Colonial Office. He was thirty-eight in the summer of 1940, a man described by his contemporaries as 'utterly charming' with a 'tidy and academic mind' and a gift for describing places so vividly that one could imagine one was actually there. He also spoke Arabic and was an expert in archaeology, botany, entomology and navigation. In fact just about the only flaw Kennedy Shaw possessed, as far as Bagnold's putative unit was concerned, was 'he loathed anything mechanical, particularly the motor-car'. If he'd had his way, Kennedy Shaw would have travelled the desert on a camel.

Invaluable as Clayton and Kennedy Shaw were, neither had any recent experience of soldiering (Clayton had served in the Royal Artillery in the First World War), so Bagnold turned to two other erstwhile desert explorers who did: Rupert Harding-Newman and Teddy Mitford.

Harding-Newman had spent twelve of his thirty-two years in the British Army, serving in the Royal Tank Corps* in the Middle East. He had accompanied Bagnold on his 1932 expedition on the recommendation of his friend Guy Prendergast. Though Harding-Newman had a great respect for Bagnold, their different personalities precluded a close friendship. 'Bagnold was an impetuous person, and he could never sit still,' recalled the phlegmatic tank officer years later of the 1932 expedition. 'Therefore though we had an archaeologist, botanist and a geologist from Oxford, one of the top geologists, he rarely gave them time to pursue their own particular interests when we came to an interesting place . . . Bagnold was always impatient to get on. He could never say "Right we'll camp here for a day or even two days to do what you really want." But he was a brilliant leader and he achieved a vast amount.'

Harding-Newman was in Cairo when Bagnold was granted permission to raise his special force, but he was considered too important by the British Military Mission to go off gallivanting

* In 1939 the RTC became the Royal Tank Regiment.

in the desert, so his assistance was restricted to advice and intelligence. Not so Captain Mitford who, like Harding-Newman was a tank man. He was also a member of the family made infamous by the activities and allegiances of the Mitford Sisters, though he was not, as has been stated in some sources, their brother. Arriving in Cairo in 1932, Mitford 'soon caught the desert motoring disease and bought a Ford car which I fitted with fat desert tyres'. In 1938 Mitford became one of the few Europeans to have travelled by motor car across the desert to Kufra Oasis.

Mitford and Bagnold had never met, but the latter knew enough about Mitford's reputation as a desert explorer to contact him on 24 June. 'I got a telephone message from Major Bagnold, saying "Come and see me" and I thought "This is going to be rather fun."' recalled Mitford. 'He asked me to come into long-range patrols and I said "Yes, love to" . . . I had to get permission from the division I was in, to leave them, to go into this extraordinary thing, this private army, and I was given permission and that was grand.'

Mitford and Kennedy Shaw joined Bagnold in his office in the Grey Pillars building at GHQ in Cairo, the latter receiving a commission as a lieutenant. It took Clayton another month before he arrived from Tanganyika (commissioned as a captain), by which time his brother officers had acquired an impressive array of equipment. Harding-Newman 'wangled' a quantity of sun compasses from the Egyptian army; maps were printed at the Cairo Survey Department; theodolites were charmed from the Physical Department and field glasses were donated by race enthusiasts from the Gezira Sporting Club. Among other items obtained during this period were nautical almanacs (for use with the theodolites), logarithmic tables and trouser clips (to keep maps on their boards). All the while, recalled Kennedy Shaw, 'in half-forgotten shops in the back streets of Cairo we searched for a hundred and one (to the Army) unorthodox needs'.

The most pressing problem remained, however: the vehicles. It was here that Harding-Newman came into his own. Though the army couldn't spare him officially, he was able to devote more and more of his free time to Bagnold's nascent enterprise. In his recollection years later of those heady days in Cairo, Harding-Newman was disarmingly modest. 'I merely had to help in the formation by providing any equipment I had,' he said. 'We knew everything about how we wanted to navigate, we knew the food side . . . basically the whole thing was there.'

Bagnold described Harding-Newman's contribution to the formation of his unit as 'invaluable'. Within twenty-four hours of being asked, he presented Bagnold with four types of truck that he thought suitable for the unit. 'We took them out for test runs over rocks and through soft sand,' remembered Bagnold. 'I decided there and then upon an ordinary commercial pattern of 30-cwt Chevrolet, fast, simple and easy to handle.' Mitford recalled that Bagnold 'produced a camouflage pattern of very broad dark and light stripes, different for each truck, which would help in areas of rock and scrub'. Additionally, the 7th Armoured Division's red rat insignia was painted on each vehicle to further conceal the unit's 'real purpose'.

Choosing the type of vehicle was easy, acquiring them in sufficient numbers was the hard part. But once again Harding-Newman came to the rescue, his charm and influence persuading the Egyptian government to loan them nineteen from their fleet. A further fourteen were supplied by General Motors in Alexandria.

Bagnold relied on men such as Harding-Newman and Shaw to butter up their contacts to the best of their ability. He himself, for all his virtues, was not a man with an easy social air. When Tim Heywood joined the unit as the Signals Officer he recalled his first impression of Bagnold as a 'small wizened figure with piercing eyes and an abrupt manner'. He found the initial encounter 'unnerving', as did another future officer in the unit, David Lloyd Owen, when he was summoned for an interview with Bagnold. 'He received me with courtesy, but he was not particularly ebullient nor forthcoming with pleasantries,' wrote Lloyd Owen. 'He was not that kind of man; there was never any time to waste over trivialities in his life. He lived it to a plan, which was worked out in every detail of efficiency and purpose.'

Bagnold was not one for small talk. He spoke when he had

something to say, not because he liked the sound of his own voice. He disliked verbosity in others, as he did vanity and pretension. That was why Bagnold's milieu as a young man was the desert; sand he found more edifying than society and he felt more at peace in the desert than he did in racy Cairo.

He was not alone in this. Bill Kennedy Shaw alluded to a similar feeling when asked what attracted him to a region most Europeans feared. 'A psychologist would say, perhaps, that to take pleasure in deserts is a form of escapism,' he said, 'a surrender to the same impulses which made hermits of the early Christians, a refusal to face the unpleasant realities of modern life. He may be right.'

While Rupert Harding-Newman instructed the Army Ordnance workshops how best to modify the trucks so they would withstand the rigours of off-road desert travel – including the attachment of water condensers to radiators, the raising of the sides of the normal box body in order to carry the required loads, mountings for machine guns and brackets for compasses – Kennedy Shaw was busy 'adapting our old methods of dead-reckoning, astronomical position-finding and map-making into simple rules we could teach the troops'.

The 'troops' themselves were the domain of Bagnold. He didn't want regular troops or reservists, because they would have to be retrained, and he didn't have the time to do that. Similarly he didn't want the sort of 'tough and knuckle-duster men' that were at that very moment being recruited for the Commandos in Britain. 'We wanted an intelligent, responsible and self-sufficient type who would treat their precious vehicles and apparatus as their own, realizing that their lives might depend on them.'

Bagnold played with the truth in his memoirs in describing this moment, neglecting to mention that his first attempt to recruit men entailed a flight to Palestine on 29 June to see Lieutenant-General Thomas Blamey, commander of the Australian Corps. He went on the advice of Brigadier Arthur Selby, an Australian then on the British staff in Cairo, who said his countrymen should be Bagnold's first choice because, after all, they had manned the

Light Car Patrols of the First World War. Bagnold concurred, confident that a new generation of Australians possessed the requisite ruggedness and resourcefulness to fulfil a similar role a quarter of a century later. But Blamey refused Bagnold's request, explaining that his orders from the Australian government forbade his soldiers being siphoned off on various British schemes.

Bagnold returned to Cairo despondent. He visited General Jumbo Wilson at BTE and realized that 'the C-in-C [Wavell] had clearly talked to him,' because gone was Wilson's earlier disdain for the idea of a long-range desert force. Wilson was now all sunny cooperation. He approached Brigadier Edward Puttick, temporary commander of the New Zealand forces in Egypt in the absence of Major-General Bernard Freyberg, who was in England with the second infantry brigade of the NZ division. Puttick told Wilson he had no objection to Bagnold selecting a small number of New Zealanders from a 'dusty camp in Maadi', and eventually eighty officers, non-commissioned officers and men from the New Zealand Divisional Cavalry Regiment and Machine Gun Battalion volunteered for the Long Range Patrol (LRP).

The selection of the final New Zealanders was left to one of their own, Lieutenant Bruce Ballantyne, but Bagnold approved of what he saw when the Kiwis arrived at Abbassia barracks in Cairo. 'They made an impressive party by English standards,' recalled Bagnold. 'Tougher and more weather-beaten in looks, a sturdy basis of sheep-farmers, leavened by technicians, property-owners and professional men, and including a few Maoris. Shrewd, dry-humoured, curious of every new thing, and quietly thrilled when I told them what we were to do.'

Bagnold explained that the purpose of the unit was primarily reconnaissance, that they were to discover what the Italians were up to in their desert forts behind the Great Sand Sea, the natural barrier roughly the size of Ireland that stretches from Siwa Oasis, in the north-west of Egypt, almost as far south as Sudan.

Before they embarked on their first patrol, however, Bagnold and his officers had to train the New Zealanders. They proved quick learners, gaining a rapid understanding of how to drive across the desert. Soon they were covering 150 miles in fully loaded trucks. Flag signals were deployed to help patrols travel in strict formation and Kennedy Shaw had the task of instructing the men in desert navigation using the sun compass. Within a week the New Zealanders had mastered the art of navigating at night. When Pat Clayton arrived in Cairo 29 July he was astounded at the 'enormous and terrifyingly fit New Zealanders'; he was also somewhat taken back when Bagnold instructed him to draw up plans for the unit's first patrol.

Clayton's recommendation was for 'a small patrol to drive across the Italian routes leading from the coast to Kufra and the South, and see from the traffic and tracks thereon what the Italians were up to'. Just a couple of vehicles would suffice, added Clayton, and no wireless was necessary. Bagnold took the plan to GHQ and returned a few hours later having had it approved by the Chief of Staff. 'Fine,' said Clayton. 'Send me the poor mutt who is to go and I'll put him wise.' Bagnold looked at his old friend with the hint of a smile. 'Oh, you're going,' he said.

Clayton and his small hand-picked party of seven left Cairo on 7 August in two Chevrolet trucks. It was a curious party, comprising the middle-aged, grey-haired Englishman, Ali Fadail his 'old driver friend' from his Desert Survey days, and six New Zealanders. One of the Kiwis was actually an Englishman by birth – Dick Croucher, a former merchant seaman who in his youth had served on twenty-five ships and knew everything there was to know about the art of navigation. Before they departed, recalled Clayton, 'care had to be taken to leave behind nothing to disclose to the Wops [Italians] that the invasion had begun, so army toilet paper was refused and old Italian newspapers garnered from our lady friends in the censorship.' The women asked why Clayton wanted such a substantial quantity of old Italian newspapers. 'If I told you what it was for,' he replied, 'you wouldn't believe me.'

From Cairo the small force drove west to Bagush, a British military camp close to Mersa Matruh, where Clayton checked in with General Richard O'Connor, commander of the Western Desert

Force. They then headed south into the interior, reaching Siwa Oasis on 8 August. They were greeted by Major Tom Bather of the Egyptian Frontiers Administration, who augmented Clayton's two vehicles with seven more crewed by Sudanese with 'a keen young Egyptian officer' in charge. Their job was to help in the carriage of petrol and water through the Sand Sea to 'two mushroom hills'. Here the Frontiers trucks turned back to Siwa as they were now perilously close to the Libyan border. 'The little patrol of two cars then struck due west, exploring, and made the unwelcome discovery of a large strip of sand sea between the frontier and the Jalo–Kufra road,' reported Clayton. 'The Chevrolet clutches began to smell a bit by the time we got across, but the evening saw us near the Kufra track.'

Here they laid-up for three days, taking great care to conceal their presence from the Italians, as they observed the track for signs of activity. Without knowing it, Clayton and his small band of intrepid companions had conducted the unit's first reconnaissance: what would come to be known as a 'road watch', the detailed surveillance of enemy transport that would make such an important contribution to victory in North Africa.

In August 1940, however, the reconnaissance entailed three days of intense boredom under a broiling sun. Unable to drive further westward for fear of leaving tyre tracks that would alert the Italians, thereby losing the British the element of surprise, Clayton despatched a patrol on foot to discover the width of the traffic lane. They returned after a five-mile march reporting that 'no tracks fresher than several months old were seen.'

Satisfied the Italians were nowhere in the vicinity, Clayton decided to return to Cairo with his intelligence.

They were back in time for lunch on 19 August, having covered 1,600 miles in thirteen days, three of which were spent in observation. 'We had, as hoped and intended, not fired a shot or seen the enemy,' reflected Clayton. 'But we had proved that [LRP] could go and come back to a strict timetable.' The patrol had also discovered a hitherto unmapped strip of sand sea, 100 km wide, immediately east of the Jalo–Kufra road, and Clayton had gained an insight into the impish nature of New Zealanders. 'I learnt with surprise that there were at least six unlicensed cameras with the party, and a snap of me, asleep, was used for kindly blackmail, while it was explained to me that British Army orders on photography in the Western Desert of Egypt could not possibly apply to New Zealanders touring in Italian Libya!'

The next day, 20 August, Clayton and Bagnold reported their findings to General Wavell. He listened as Bagnold explained the importance of the fresh tracks found by Clayton's patrol, information he would later share with the wider world. 'Just as the Bedouin can tell the age, breed and condition of every camel in a caravan that has passed by from the footmarks in the desert, so can a European with years of experience extract a wealth of information from the marks of motor traffic,' noted Bagnold. 'For, except over the moving dunes, car tracks persist for many years. In places in the Egyptian desert the old tracks of car patrols from 1916 can still be plainly seen.'

Having heard an account of the unit's first patrol, Wavell 'made up his mind then and there to give us his strongest backing'. A week later the general, accompanied by Brigadier Shearer, inspected the LRP at Abbassia Barracks and told them he had informed the War Office they 'were ready to take the field'.

Not surprisingly, there was a note of triumph in the unit war diary that evening. The entry reflected that in the space of a few weeks, 'equipment had been collected, the unit formed and trained, preliminary reconnaissance had been made into enemy territory and dumps formed in the west, ready for immediate operations'.

CHAPTER THREE

'Not worth the effort to keep alive'

Bagnold split his force into three Patrols, assigning to each a letter of no particular significance. Captain Teddy Mitford commanded 'W' Patrol, Captains Pat Clayton and Bruce Ballantyne were the officers in charge of 'T' Patrol and Captain Don Steele, a New Zealand farmer from Takapu, led 'R' Patrol.

Each patrol consisted of twenty-five other ranks, transported in ten 30-cwt Chevrolet trucks and a light 15-cwt pilot car, and carrying enough rations and equipment to sustain them over 1,500 miles. For armament each patrol had a 3.7 mm Bofors gun, four Boys anti-tank rifles and fifteen Lewis guns.

At the start of September 1940 Bagnold paired Kennedy Shaw, now officially the unit's Intelligence Officer, with Mitford for a reconnaissance of possible landing grounds in the south-west of the desert. By now Mitford had got to know Bagnold well, describing him as 'a very sharp chap, very small, and sharp, with a sense of humour, and . . . he was very meticulous and keen on getting everything absolutely right'.

Together with Bagnold and Kennedy Shaw, Mitford planned their patrol down to the smallest detail, leaving nothing to chance. 'One worked out what the distance was going to be, worked out the amount of petrol you wanted for that distance, and the food you worked out day by day,' recalled Mitford. 'You sat round making a menu for each day, a lunch and evening menu.' He found it all 'great fun', a throwback to the thirties when he had gone off into the desert – once with his wife in tow – seeking out remote oases.

Kennedy Shaw was more circumspect about the perils of the desert, and before the unit embarked on their first patrols proper he lectured the New Zealanders on what awaited them. Likening the Libyan Desert in size to India, 'an area twelve hundred miles by a thousand', Kennedy Shaw explained that it was bordered by the Nile in the east and the Mediterranean in the north. In the south, which was limestone compared to the sandstone in the north, the desert extended as far as the Tibesti Mountains, while the political frontier with Tunisia and Algeria marked its western limits.

In the far north, a coastal strip twenty miles wide at its broadest point, sufficient rain fell to make the region green and fertile, but elsewhere it never rained 'except an occasional local thunderstorm once every ten or twenty years'. Wind erosion over many millennia had made the desert's surface 'as naked and lifeless as the face of the moon', and in some areas blown away so much sand that in deep depressions a water-bearing stratum had been exposed. In some of these depressions the artesian water is in small wells encircled by palm trees, but at the 'great oases of Siwa and Kharga, it gushes out so freely as to support a settled though isolated population and to irrigate gardens and crops, before draining away to evaporate in malarial lakes and treacherous swamps of crusted salt'.

The landscape was also one of sharp contrasts. The gravel desert was called in Arabic *serir*, the stony areas known as *hammada*. Both, in general, were good to travel on because the wind had removed the sand, a process known as 'deflation'. At other times they would encounter a bed of powdered clay, which enveloped intruders with choking, billowing clouds of white dust that were visible for miles around and found their way into every nook and cranny. There were also dunes and escarpments, warned Kennedy Shaw, but these were surmountable – most of the time.

As for the temperature, they had better get used to the sight of the sun. It shines on most days, he told the New Zealanders, 'shrivelling you to a cinder in summer and putting but little warmth into the winter winds. The temperature may reach 120°F in the shade in June and fall a degree or two below freezing in winter.'

On 5 September Mitford and Kennedy Shaw started out from Cairo with 'W' Patrol, accompanied by a small HQ party under Bagnold. They drove 350 miles south-west to Ain Dalla, on the eastern edge of the Great Sand Sea, and replenished their petrol and water supplies from dumps laid earlier in the summer.

Though the New Zealanders had proved quick learners to date, there was still much they had to discover about desert travel. 'In that part of world if you were in soft sand you let the tyres down so they were flatter and then you would pump them up again [once you were on harder ground],' recalled Mitford. 'Our soldiers didn't like doing that and were fed up with pumping up tyres. One chap said to himself "well, I've pumped it enough."'*

When Bagnold came round inspecting all the tyres he told the New Zealander to pump some more air in. The soldier protested, saying it had sufficient air. Bagnold told the man to obey orders and turned on his heel. Mitford watched as the Kiwi began pumping more air into the tyre, muttering under his breath: 'The trouble with that bugger is he's always right.'

Another bewildering trick played by the desert on the unwary was the perception of speed when on the move because of the sun shimmering on the often featureless terrain. New Zealander Peter Garland was travelling in a truck when he saw an object fall from the vehicle 100 yards in front. Garland told his driver to slow down so he could retrieve whatever it was. 'I stepped out but to my surprise hit the ground with a thud and did a few flips,' he recalled. 'Luckily I was OK. My driver said he was still doing 25 mph when I stepped off. I thought it was only about 5.'

* * *

* Kennedy Shaw wrote: 'When we passed out of the stony ground we could let down the tyres so that the lower pressure gave an extra inch or two on the bearing surface of the tread. It was a common belief that the sand was harder in the early morning but the real explanation was that at the time the tyre pressure was lower; in the heat of midday the pressure would rise considerably.'

That night the men slept in the shadow of the Great Sand Sea, Kennedy Shaw marvelling at the 'beauty of those sweeping curves of sand' as the sun sank behind them. The trouble was that he knew that the next day, as they endeavoured to take the first convoy of heavily laden trucks across the Sea, the place would be 'as good an imitation of Hell as one could devise'.

Kennedy Shaw had last voyaged across the Sand Sea in 1935 and he reminded himself of what was required to successfully negotiate the dunes. 'Always keep height so that you can turn downhill when a soft patch comes and profit by the slope to get through it,' he recalled. 'Ribbed sand, butter-yellow, is generally hard and safe; shining purplish patches are usually liquid bogs; never brake hard to stop or the wheels will dig in; change down early before the slope begins and charge it in second gear.'

The dunes they encountered were wondrous in size and span. Some rose as high as 300 feet and the further west they travelled the more numerous were the dunes until they were packed so tightly together 'all traces of solid ground disappear'. The major dune range stretched for 20 km but the total width of the belt was 260 km.

Bagnold led the way over the worst of the dunes, accelerating up the slope, then slowing near the top and stopping on the crest with all four wheels in line. Then it was a question of toppling the truck gently over the edge of the precipice, so the vehicle sailed down the sand in first gear to the bottom. Never, stressed Bagnold, accelerate over a dune because the vehicle will flip over as it flies across the crest and who knows how far the drop might be on the other side.

After two days of strenuous travel the patrol reached the western edge of the Sea on 11 September. Ahead they saw the only feature in an otherwise blank landscape – the five-foot high 'Big Cairn', built by Clayton eight years earlier on a survey expedition.

Clayton soon appeared at the Big Cairn with 'T' Patrol and Don Steele's 'R' Patrol; they had spent the past few days transporting 7,000 gallons of petrol across the Sand Sea from Siwa Oasis. After a brief rest the patrols parted: Clayton headed south towards Chad;

Steele returned to Siwa to ferry more supplies to the Big Cairn, and Mitford and Kennedy Shaw drove east towards the Kalansho Sand Sea for what the latter described as 'the three most unpleasant days of my life'.

The ordeal began on 16 September. At the Big Cairn the thermometer had read 110°F but as 'W' Patrol struggled across the Kalansho Sands the wind speed and the temperature increased still further. They were in the grip of the Libyan *qibli*. Kennedy Shaw had heard about the *qibli*, and he had first-hand experience of the Egyptian equivalent, the *khamsin*, a southerly wind that whipped up a giant wave of hot sand, but that was nothing compared to the furnace they endured for three days. 'You don't merely feel hot, you don't merely feel tired,' he wrote, 'you feel as if every bit of energy had left you, as if your brain was thrusting its way through the top of your head and you want to lie in a stupor till the accursed sun has gone down.'

The men suffered that day but worse was to follow on 17 September. The wind got up, turning into a southerly sandstorm, and the grains felt like thousands of small needles pricking faces, arms, legs, every pore of exposed flesh. The only advantage of such vengeful weather was that it kept the enemy away. No Italians were to be seen on the two landing grounds the patrol visited on the Jalo–Kufra air route, so in their absence the patrol laid waste to the enemy petrol pumps, fuel tanks and wind indicators.

The next day there was no let-up in the weather as the patrol turned south-east towards Wadi Zighen, though they did encounter five shallow wells with drinkable water. They also met an Arab caravan comprising thirteen men and seventy camels, carrying rice, sugar and cloth from Benghazi to Kufra, a distance of approximately 550 miles. Unsure whether to trust the Arabs, Kennedy Shaw convinced them they had driven up from the south and were bound for Jalo.

The Arabs must have wondered what on earth this small band of men were doing out in such weather. So too Kennedy Shaw, who estimated the temperature to be in excess of 120°F. Several of the New Zealanders were suffering from heatstroke and it was decided that 'there was no alternative for the Patrol [other] than to lie in what shade could be made from about 1100 to 1500 hours'. Even the birds migrating for the autumn succumbed to the heat, the patrol finding scores of doves on the track, 'crouched and gasping' when they moved off in the late afternoon. They stopped and offered a couple of birds some of their own precious water but, recalled Kennedy Shaw, 'they seldom drank it . . . they seemed to have decided, rightly, that it was not worth the effort to keep alive.'

The *qibli* eased on 19 September and the next day the temperature was actually tolerable. The Italians began to emerge from the sanctuary of their bases, only to encounter a new foe. Recalled Kennedy Shaw: 'While we were following the track to Kufra near the LG [Landing Ground No. 7] there appeared, churning slowly through the soft sand, two six-ton lorries of the Italian firm of Trucci and Monti, the fortnightly convoy to Kufra.'

Mitford ordered his men to fire a burst from the Vickers K machine gun over the lead truck, thus giving 'W' Patrol the honour of firing the unit's first shots in anger. But that was the extent of the 'battle'. The two vehicles braked hard and out stumbled two Italians, five Arabs and a goat. Mitford dismounted and he and his men took stock of their prisoners. They were a sorry-looking bunch. One of the Italian drivers 'spoke reasonable English', the rest just grinned nervously. It was hard not to feel a smidgen of sympathy for the native Arab soldiers, caught up in somebody else's war and armed with hopelessly inadequate weapons. One of them cheerfully handed his sidearm to Mitford, a 1911 Austrian revolver that the officer kept as a souvenir. There were other spoils of war to be had.

Inside the trucks the New Zealanders discovered 2,500 gallons of petrol, some miscellaneous equipment and, most importantly, a bag of official mail. There was also a carpet, an expensive-looking one, that Mitford imagined was 'destined for the house of the commander of Kufra'. It was duly liberated by the New Zealanders. A few weeks later Mitford was accused of stealing the carpet by an Italian lawyer, employed in Cairo in the office of the Custodian of Enemy Properties. Bagnold asked Mitford for an explanation.

Mitford replied that somewhere between the Landing Ground No.7 and Cairo the carpet had been regrettably lost. Bagnold wrote an apologetic letter to GHQ, explaining that 'owing to the extremely difficult nature of the terrain, the carpet was probably used for un-sticking vehicles and that it was certainly damaged beyond repair.' Privately Bagnold and Mitford agreed that the suggestion the LRDG had stolen the carpet was a 'terrible accusation against our good name'. Years later word reached Mitford that the carpet was 'gracing the floor of a New Zealand farm house'.

Rejoining Bagnold's HQ Patrol with the prisoners (the trucks were hidden at the foot of a plateau), Kennedy Shaw and Bruce Ballantyne escorted their captives and bag of mail back to Cairo, while Mitford and 'W' Patrol set off to reconnoitre the track joining Kufra to Uweinat in the south-east corner of the Libyan Desert.

The departure of Kennedy Shaw left 'W' Patrol perilously unbalanced. The New Zealanders were now under the sole command of Mitford, a man who appeared to embody the very worst traits of the English upper class. 'We were looked upon by Mitford as just bloody scum,' recalled one of the patrol, Corporal Alfred 'Buster' Gibb. 'He sort of lost sight of the fact New Zealanders weren't the rag-tag of the local population. They were educated men . . . farmers, accountants, every conceivable type of occupation and all bright enough people.'

The difficulty lay in Mitford's upbringing. He was an aristocrat, who had grown up on the family's 4,000-acre family estate in Northumberland. From birth he had been taught that his class didn't mix with anyone but their own. This ethos had been reinforced at his public school, then in the officers' mess of the Royal Tank Corps. Even one of his brother officers recalled that Mitford enjoyed 'looking and acting like a classic British nobleman – elegant, weary, bored and vapid'. Yet get to know him, and one discovered under all the affectations was 'a very keen mind and wide range of interests'.

But how could Mitford be expected to suddenly shed his attitude of superiority? Unbeknown to Gibb, Mitford had a great respect for the New Zealanders. They were, in his opinion, 'first-class chaps, very good indeed . . . people who knew how to look after themselves'. Mitford even considered them more capable than the average British soldier; his problem was simply that he treated the New Zealanders in the same aloof manner that he had been taught to display towards the British soldier – and, understandably, the New Zealanders didn't like that.

'As a matter of fact, all the boys were talking about doing him in because of his whole attitude,' said Gibb, who had left school at fifteen and spent the pre-war years working first on a Hawkes Bay sheep farm and then on the railways. At first Gibb didn't believe his comrades were seriously considering murdering Mitford but after dark – under a tarpaulin rigged up between two trucks – they discussed it in whispered tones over their nightly rum ration. Gibb was aghast. 'I have to admit I had a lot of difficulty in turning the blokes away from doing what they wanted to,' he said.

Gibb told the men to give Mitford a chance, and he in turn invited the Englishman the following night to join them under the tarpaulin for a tot of rum and to listen to some of their tall tales from back home. Mitford couldn't bring himself to sit with the Kiwis but he did prop himself up against the rear wheels of a truck so that he was on the edge of the conversation.

Gradually the atmosphere changed, said Gibb, 'and after Mitford got over his English attitude and decided that these Kiwis are good blokes, he was a good soldier. He really turned on and he was good to work with.'

After an extensive reconnaissance of Uweinat, Mitford's patrol reached Cairo on 4 October. Bagnold described them as 'bearded, unwashed but exultant ruffians', the stench from their ragged uniforms so overpowering that most had to be peeled off their bodies and burned. While the men submerged themselves in warm, soapy water to scrub away their second skin of thick grime, Bagnold pored over the intelligence, in particular the new route to Ain Dalla that opened up even more desert to the LRP.

Suddenly the unit was the talk of the town, not just for their 1,300-mile round trip to Kufra, but for seizing a mail truck deep inside enemy territory. 'In clubs and messes the tale became exaggerated,' wrote Kennedy Shaw. 'And so it laid for us the foundation of a reputation which we never lost.'

Wavell sent a personal note to Bagnold, in which he said:

> I should like to convey to the officers and other ranks under your command my congratulations and appreciation of the successful results of the recent patrols carried out by your unit in central Libya.
>
> I am aware of the extreme physical difficulties which had to be overcome, particularly the intense heat. That your operation, involving as it did 150,000 track miles, has been brought to so successful a conclusion indicates a standard of efficiency in preparation and execution, of which you, your officers and men may justly be proud.
>
> A full report of your exploits has already been telegraphed to the War Office and I wish you all the best of luck in your continued operations in which you will be making an important contribution towards keeping Italian forces in back areas on the alert and adding to the anxieties and difficulties of our enemy.*

Bagnold mentioned the 'letter of appreciation' in his diary on 2 October, and three days later he recorded that he'd put in an official request to reconstitute the Long Range Patrol as the Long Range Desert Group (LRDG), which was 'to consist of 2 squadrons of 3 patrols each. More officers to be asked for'. The new name would, Bagnold hoped, reflect that his force was more than just a small reconnaissance patrol.

Such was the burgeoning reputation of the the unit that on

* The mail captured by Kennedy Shaw revealed no intent on the part of the Italians to go on the offensive, so the reinforcement convoy about to sail for the Middle East went the longer but safer route round South Africa rather than the shorter, but more hazardous, route through the Mediterranean. These troops – the 2nd and 7th Royal Tank Regiments – were 'to prove of fundamental importance to the success of Wavell's eventual counterattack against the Italian thrust at Sidi Barrani in December 1940'.

16 October they were inspected by Anthony Eden, Secretary of State for War, during his visit to the Middle East. Only one patrol was in barracks at the time – Mitford's 'W' Patrol. Having only just become accustomed to the free and easy way of the New Zealanders, Mitford was horrified to learn they would have to parade before Eden. 'We thought "God Almighty, we've got to do something!"' recalled Mitford. 'So the soldiers were put into three straight lines and as long as they didn't walk around getting dusty it worked very well.'

Eden was evidently impressed, for he congratulated the men on all they had achieved and asked Bagnold 'for a special report on what had been done'.

Eden's visit to Abbassia Barracks to inspect the LRP was no doubt a result of a request submitted by Bagnold to the War Office on 13 October asking for an expansion of the unit. Wavell was all for it, concluding that with the LRP he could sow seeds of confusion in Italian minds by launching a series of small attacks against them across a wide region. This was the strategy espoused by T.E. Lawrence in the First World War during the Arab revolt he fomented against Turkey, one he expounded on in an article on Guerrilla Warfare published in 1929 in the fourteenth edition of *Encyclopedia Britannica*:

> A casual calculation indicated perhaps 140,000 square miles [of desert]. How would the Turks defend all that – no doubt by a trench line across the bottom, if the Arabs were an army attacking with banners displayed . . . but suppose they were an influence, a thing invulnerable, intangible, without front or back, drifting about like a gas? Armies were like plants, immobile as a whole, firm-rooted, and nourished through long stems to the head. The Arabs might be a vapour, blowing where they listed. It seemed that a regular soldier might be helpless without a target. He would own the ground he sat on, and what he could poke his rifle at. The next step was to estimate how many posts they would need to contain this attack in depth, sedition putting up her head in every

> unoccupied one of these 100,000 square miles. They would have need of a fortified post every four square miles, and a post could not be less than 20 men. The Turks would need 600,000 men to meet the combined ill wills of all the local Arab people. They had 100,000 men available. It seemed that the assets in this sphere were with the Arabs, and climate, railways, deserts, technical weapons could also be attached to their interests. The Turk was stupid and would believe that rebellion was absolute, like war, and deal with it on the analogy of absolute warfare.

Before the LRP could embark upon a similar campaign of insurgency, however, a problem arose. General Freyberg had arrived in Cairo and was displeased to discover that some of his men had been purloined by the LRP. He demanded their immediate return but Wavell refused, a measure of the regard in which he now held the unit. A compromise was reached: the New Zealanders would be 'replaced gradually' by British soldiers but this still presented Bagnold with a problem. As he noted in the war diary: 'Owing to chronic shortages in officers and other ranks in the Middle East, unit and formation commanders were very loath to part with men of the high standard required for the peculiar and exacting work which the Long Range Patrols existed to do.'

While Bagnold and Kennedy Shaw wrestled with the challenge of recruitment, 'W', 'T' and 'R' Patrols ventured once more into the desert to carry out operations at Uweinat and on the main road north of Jalo. Between 24 October and 8 November, they laid mines, attacked vehicles, reconnoitred enemy positions and took prisoners.

Pat Clayton returned after covering 2,100 miles in fifteen days, laying five minefields and capturing a fort at Aujila (west of Jalo). 'No resistance was offered by the garrison,' he wrote in the report. 'After the first burst of Bofors and M.G. fire, the occupants left the fort and ran for the adjacent native village. One Libyan prisoner was captured.'

The petrified Libyan was brought back to Cairo and readily told

Kennedy Shaw everything he knew. Revealing that Jalo was garrisoned by only fifty troops, the prisoner said 1,500 were stationed at Jarabub but that morale was low among the Libyans. They were paid 360 lire a month (140 fewer than their Italian counterparts), a pittance considering a sack of sugar cost 760 lire. He had not eaten meat for months – and was 'delighted' when given some by his captors – and said most of his compatriots had been compelled to take up arms by the Italians. Of most significance, however, was the prisoner's revelation that, thanks to the activities of the LRP 'no vehicles were now allowed to go to Kufra except on convoy with sufficient protection.' The Italians were rattled, and Bagnold was delighted to hear it, boasting 'that mysterious noises out of the desert, possibly imagined but possibly the very real vibrant hooting that the dunes sometimes emit spontaneously began to be reported on all sides as indicating the passage of an enemy patrol. We can picture the commander, poring anxiously over his inaccurate maps – as most Italian maps of the interior have proved to be –and wondering out of which sandy sea one of our ubiquitous little columns would appear.'

On 11 November, three days after the return of the patrols, Wavell wrote to Bagnold telling him the LRP's work 'is most valuable and shows skill and enterprise of a high order'. Wavell sent the latest intelligence back to London, explaining that because of the LRP the Italians were compelled to divert troops and vehicles from the main battlefield in the north to deal with the guerrilla attacks in the south. Also, that because of the LRP's activities between Kufra and Uweinat, the Italians would be increasingly unlikely to launch an attack on the Nile from this area.

The response of the War Office, received on 22 November, was to authorize the expansion of the unit to comprise two squadrons each of three patrols consisting of two officers and twenty-eight other ranks. Bagnold was promoted acting lieutenant colonel, Don Steele upgraded from lieutenant to acting captain and Captain Mitford promoted to major. Finally, the War Office agreed that in future the unit would be known as the Long Range Desert Group.

CHAPTER FOUR

'A dreadful condition of nerves and exhaustion'

The decision to double the size of the Long Range Desert Group obliged Bagnold to find a bigger home for the unit. Hitherto they had been billeted in the Fever Hospital barracks at Abbassia but on 4 December 1940 they relocated to the Citadel, a stunning edifice built by Saladin in 1166 using stone brought from the small pyramids of Gizeh. As the LRDG war diarist commented the move coincided with the cessation of the unit as 'a purely New Zealand family and [it] began to assume a new character with the arrival on December 5th of British personnel to fill the establishment of Unit H.Q. and one complete squadron.'

The squadron was comprised of thirty-six guardsmen, selected from the 3rd Battalion The Coldstream Guards and the 2nd Battalion The Scots Guards. In command of what was designated 'G' Patrol was twenty-five-year-old Captain Michael Crichton-Stuart of the Scots Guards with Lieutenant Martin Gibbs, a Coldstreamer, his second in command. 'We were new to one another,' reflected Crichton-Stuart of Gibbs, 'and to the Citadel and everything in it.'

Crichton-Stuart came from impeccable stock. The grandson of the 3rd Marquess of Bute, his father was Lieutenant-Colonel Lord Ninian Edward Crichton-Stuart, killed fighting on the Western Front in 1915 while the sitting MP for the United Boroughs of Cardiff, Cowbridge and Llantrisant. Educated at Eton and

Cambridge, Crichton-Stuart was everything one expected a Guards officer to be, but he also possessed the breadth of mind to adapt to his new environment. Nonetheless when Pat Clayton appeared to take Crichton-Stuart on a guided tour of the Citadel the new recruit was 'a little surprised' by what he saw. 'A grey-haired Englishman in a rather dishevelled fore-and-aft cap with a General Service badge,' he recalled. Clayton noticed Crichton-Stuart stare and made a joke of the badge, asking if he approved of his 'Crosse & Blackwell' insignia. Having conducted Crichton-Stuart on a tour of the LRDG's new barracks, Clayton took him to meet Bagnold.

Crichton-Stuart was a little in awe of the fabled desert explorer as he sat down in Bagnold's 'pokey little office'. He had read T.E. Lawrence's *Seven Pillars of Wisdom*, as most young Englishmen ardent for adventure had in the thirties, but he had been even more enraptured by Bagnold's *Libyan Sands*, published in 1935, a book which 'was the most up-to-date in pointing the way to modern desert adventure'.

All the same, admitted Crichton-Stuart, it was hard to reconcile the intrepid desert explorer with the middle-aged man before him, busy outlining a plan 'which seemed somehow the more fantastic for the hesitant stutter and matter-of-fact manner of its delivery'.

The plan had been conceived by Bagnold the previous month and promised to be his most audacious operation to date. It entailed an attack against Murzuk, a well-defended Italian fort in south-western Libya set among palm trees with an airfield close by, approximately 1,000 miles west of Cairo as the crow flies. As Bagnold noted, the fort 'was far beyond our self-contained range but a raid on it seemed possible geographically if we could get some extra supplies from the French Army in Chad.' No one in Cairo knew whose side the French forces in Chad were on. Other French dependencies had declared for the Vichy Regime but there had been no announcement from Chad. Bagnold and Wavell thought that an invitation to the French to support a daring raid might be just the sort of escapade to rally them to Britain's cause.

Bagnold flew to Chad at the start of November and met the commander of the French troops, Colonel Jean Colonna d'Ornano, a tall red-headed officer in his mid-forties, described by Bagnold as a 'stately figure' who liked to travel on a camel. Born in Alger, d'Ornano was a decorated veteran of the Great War who in the inter-war years had proved a brilliant administrator in North Africa. But soldiering was his first love and during his time in charge of indigenous affairs in Morocco he had raised and trained a unit of *harka* – native troops loyal to France. D'Ornano demanded to know the purpose of Bagnold's visit. 'I told him frankly what I wanted – petrol, rations and water,' recalled Bagnold of the meeting. D'Ornano agreed to cooperate but with a caveat. 'I'll do all you ask but on one condition,' he told Bagnold. 'You take me with you to Murzuk with one of my junior officers and one NCO and we fly the French flag alongside yours.' Bagnold knew the raid would have no significant impact on the desert war. It was as Crichton-Stuart described it, 'no more than a hit-and-run affair', an operation aimed at weakening the morale of the Italian and Libyan troops, while giving the French cause for pride.

There was much to do before Crichton-Stuart led 'G' Patrol on its first operation at the end of December. 'W' Patrol had 'ceased to exist' with its men distributed between 'R' and 'T' Patrols, perhaps a result of the uneasy atmosphere that continued to exist to a degree between the New Zealanders and Teddy Mitford. 'W' Patrol was 'unhappy and perfunctory' about handing over their Chevrolet trucks to the British guardsmen but Crichton-Stuart had no time to waste on petty rivalries. Dividing the guardsmen into squads to master their new weapons, he then led his patrol 'among the sand dunes near the Bayou oasis when trucks and guns were given a good workout under the benign direction of Pat Clayton'.

As 'G' Patrol readied itself for its inaugural operation, the desert war swung spectacularly the way of the British. In mid-September six divisions of Italian troops had advanced cautiously into the Western Desert, covering sixty miles before calling a halt at Sidi Barrani, some eighty-odd miles west of the British positions at Mersa Matruh. Their commander, Marshal Rodolfo Graziani, ordered the construction of a series of fortified camps that were spaced too far apart to support one another. For nearly two months the desert war came to a halt until Wavell 'decided that, as the Italians did not come on, he would sally forth and strike at them'. The attack was launched by General Richard O'Connor's Western Desert Force early on 9 December, and caught the Italians completely off-guard. The British force of 30,000 – compared to the 80,000 enemy troops – captured thousands of prisoners and 400 guns in the first three days of the assault. The Italians fled in panic to the coastal fortress of Bardia, their rout so complete that if Wavell had pressed the attack he could have advanced into Libya. Instead he stuck to the original plan, which was to recall the 4th Indian Division as soon as Sidi Barrani had fallen and transfer it to the Sudan. In the meantime the British dug in and waited for the arrival from Palestine of the 6th Australian Division before continuing the offensive against the demoralized Italians.

The success of the British strike at Sidi Barrani almost led to a change of plan for the LRDG, 'in which we were to cut the enemy's lines of communication along the coast'. To Crichton-Stuart's relief the operation was cancelled and 'G' Patrol continued preparing for the raid on Murzak. There was still so much for the guardsmen to learn, while the LRDG's new signals section also needed time to find its feet.

For the first few months of the unit's life, wireless communication comprised just one Wireless Set No. 11 and two New Zealand regimental signalers. This proved wholly inadequate because though the wireless sets worked over a range of 800 miles, 'the standard of operating was far too low to meet the exacting needs of continued work behind the enemy's lines where concealment of identity and position was essential.'

During November 1940 the New Zealand signallers were replaced by British radiomen, who were taught 'commercial procedures and various means were devised whereby cipher messages were made to imitate code messages sent between Egyptian inspectors of state wireless services.'*

In the first week of December Second Lieutenant Tim Heywood of the Middlesex Yeomanry arrived at the Citadel to apply for the vacant position of LRDG Signals Officer. Like Crichton-Stuart a product of Eton, the twenty-six-year-old Heywood had spent a large chunk of his education building illicit radios in the group of workshops that pupils there knew as the School of Mechanics. His lively mind needed constant stimulation, something he was not getting in Palestine serving with the Yeomanry, so he jumped at the chance to join the LRDG. Heywood arrived at his interview confident he would impress Bagnold with his signals expertise. Asked if he was familiar with the No. 11 set, Heywood replied:

'Yes, pretty well. We are equipped with them.'

'What is their range?' enquired Bagnold.

'Officially about twenty miles,' said Heywood, adding a touch smugly. 'However, recently, using two of them, I have managed to communicate with our HQ in Haifa from Beersheba, which is about 120 miles.'

'I expect you to manage over 1,000 miles,' replied Bagnold. His face broke into what Heywood recalled was a 'winning smile', and he added: 'Don't worry, I'll show you how.'

The LRDG departed Cairo on 27 December and rendezvoused near Tazerbo, 350 miles east of Murzuk, on 4 January, 1941. In total there were seventy-six raiders in twenty-three vehicles, comprising 'T' and 'G' Patrols under the overall command of Pat Clayton. D'Ornano had, as promised, delivered the supplies requested by Bagnold, and the Frenchman, along with nine of his soldiers, was seconded to the LRDG as they struck out

* Lofty Carr confirmed that the 'LRDG's cover was as an Egyptian company . . . on the radio we used commercial procedure not military procedure, which is completely different, so that if Jerry was listening he would believe it was an Egyptian company and not us.'

west toward Murzuk. They stopped for lunch on 11 January, just a few miles from Murzak, and finalized their plan for the attack: Clayton's 'T' Patrol would attack the airfield that lay in close proximity to the fort while 'G' Patrol targeted the actual garrison. Crichton-Stuart recalled that as they neared the fort they passed a lone cyclist: 'This gentleman, who proved to be the Postmaster, was added to the party with his bicycle. As the convoy approached the fort, above the main central tower of which the Italian flag flew proudly, the Guard turned out. We were rather sorry for them, but they probably never knew what hit them.'

Opening fire 150 yards from the fort's main gates, the LRDG force split, with the six trucks of Clayton's patrol heading towards the airstrip. The terrain was up and down, and the LRDG made use of its undulations to destroy 'a number of pill boxes scattered about, including an anti-aircraft pit'. Clayton, in the vanguard of the assault, circled a hangar and as he turned the corner ran straight into a concealed machine-gun nest. 'Colonel d'Ornano was shot through the throat and died instantly,' recalled one of the New Zealanders. '. . . a round hit the theodolite on the running board; another went through the truck just behind the driver and another through the seat underneath him.' A bullet went through the calf of a French captain, the officer later cauterizing the wound with a cigarette with an air of Gallic sangfroid that impressed the New Zealanders.

The enemy position was silenced and by the time Clayton withdrew, his force had destroyed three light bombers, a sizeable fuel dump and killed or captured all of the twenty guards.

Meanwhile the attack on the fort was well underway, the occupants cowering under a withering mortar barrage. The garrison commander had the misfortune to return from lunch midway through the onslaught and neither his staff car nor the escort vehicle made it through the fort's gates, although the LRDG were dismayed to discover among the shredded wreck of the car the bodies of the commander's wife and two children. After two hours 'a white flag was shown from the hangar and a prisoner was sent to order the occupants to come out with their hands up'. The LRDG selected two prisoners from among their considerable haul – the ones they considered best placed to answer an interrogator's questions – and told the remainder to be on their way. Clayton and his men then withdrew into the vastness of the desert before the inevitable aerial reinforcements arrived from Hon, a large Italian air base 250 miles to the north-east. As the column moved off, the jolt unbalanced one of the prisoners, who fell from the back of the truck. Rather than seize the moment to escape the Italian, his face a mask of animal terror, 'dutifully started running after the truck to avoid being left behind'.

The LRDG paused to bury d'Ornano and Sergeant Cyril Hewson, the only other fatality of the attack, five miles to the north of Murzuk. The next day the unit headed towards the Tibesti Mountains in Chad, overrunning a small outpost at the town of Traghen, whose fifty inhabitants 'marched out en masse to surrender with drums beating and banners flying'. All but two of the prisoners were native troops, under the command of a pair of 'sheepish-looking' Italian *carabinieri*.

Bagnold arrived by aircraft on 20 January and, accompanied by the rest of the LRDG, he drove south to Faya to discuss with the French the impending attack on Kufra. Six days later Clayton's 'T' Patrol crossed back into Libya and was only seventy miles south of Kufra when they were attacked by an Italian motorized patrol on Gebel Sherif on 31 January. The two forces lined up with similar numbers of men and vehicles, but the Italians possessed four 20 mm Breda guns, and the appearance of three of their aircraft further turned the fight in their favour. Nonetheless the LRDG fought gallantly. Trooper Rex Beech, a 33-year-old New Zealander, returned fire with his Vickers as the vehicle he was in jerked over the bumpy terrain. Another Kiwi, Ronald Moore, recalled that 'the noise was terrific and we could see the bullets of the Italians, who were using explosive incendiaries, ripping all around us.' Beech's truck was hit. The driver ordered its abandonment. Beech chose to remain at his post, 'firing his Vickers gun from the running board of his stationary truck', allowing his comrades precious time to escape. Italian bullets ripped through the truck and tore into Beech. The New Zealander fell onto a carpet of spent cartridge cases, one leg wedged under the running board. Also hit was Moore's truck. 'I yelled to the others "Shall we go or surrender?" The reply was unanimous. No surrender.'

With three of their eleven vehicles destroyed and Beech dead, Clayton ordered the rest of the patrol to withdraw from the valley. 'I was shepherding them away to the south and being the last car got full attention from the planes,' wrote Clayton in a letter to his sister-in-law on 10 February. 'The neighbouring trucks failed to see we were hit by the planes' machine guns.'

One Italian bullet had pierced the radiator, two more had blown out the front tyres. Clayton had also suffered a cut to his head from a slither of shrapnel. Ignoring the gushing blood, Clayton and one of his two comrades, Lance-Corporal W.R. Adams, jumped out of the vehicle and set about repairing the damage. The other crew member, Clarrie Roderick, kept the aircraft at bay with the Vickers. 'They kept circling and gunning us while we changed wheels and mounted tyres,' recalled Clayton. One enemy bullet hit the pump connection, causing a further delay, but over the noise of battle, Clayton heard a triumphant yell from Roderick as his bullets shattered the cockpit of one plane. 'We poured in water and started again and did 3 or 4 kilos until the engine dried up,' said Clayton. They jumped out, replenished the water and set off again. But the Italian pilots were in no mood to break off the attack. Another aircraft came in low, its guns raking the ground all around the fleeing vehicle. A bullet tore through Clayton's forearm and another shattered the engine. The three men tumbled out of the truck but this time they knew there was no chance to make running repairs. Approaching through a cloud of dust they saw two Italian trucks. The fight was over.

In his letter to his sister-in-law, who lived in Cairo, Clayton asked her to pass a message to the LRDG asking them to send a note to the families of Roderick and Adams, reassuring them of their wellbeing. Clayton had obviously spent the past ten days ruminating on the engagement, wondering if he was to blame for what happened. 'I don't feel I did at all well,' he reflected. 'But every chance we took turned wrong that day and after 36 days' travel men and vehicles were a long way below par.'

Clayton clung to the comforting thought that at least his good friend, Kennedy Shaw had not been with them. And on further reflection, perhaps he need not be too downcast. 'I had a good run and cannot complain,' he concluded. 'After all I took two forts and an aerodrome and burnt Murzuk fort and blew up lorries north of Aujila – not bad for 44.'

The Italians were delighted. Finally, they had scored a victory against the British guerrillas, and more to the point they had captured 'Major Klayton [*sic*] . . . well-known explorer of the desert'. The unit that surprised the British was the Auto-Saharan Company, the nearest force the Italians had to the LRDG. Most of the men were experienced desert travellers and many knew of Clayton's reputation; some were even acquaintances of Teddy Mitford from his pre-war days of exploration.

An article in *Il Popolo D'Italia*, the fascist newspaper founded by Benito Mussolini in 1914, crowed:

> The capture of Klayton [*sic*] was a master-stroke, the enemy had lost an irreplaceable element for its experiences of the desert, and with him many precious documents had fallen into our hands. Klayton tried to keep his spirits up in this unhappy situation but from this day was forced to give up his studies of 'Desert Geology' that had caused him to explore the country.

So triumphant were the Italians at having captured Clayton and two of his men that they neglected to conduct a thorough search of the hills, missing the opportunity to bag four more enemy soldiers. The quartet – Trooper Ronald Moore; Private

Alfred Tighe, a fitter from Manchester who had recently joined the LRDG from the Royal Ordnance Army Corps; and two Scots Guardsmen, Alexander Winchester and John Easton of Edinburgh – hid among the rocks after the destruction of their truck.

After the Italian motorized unit left the Jebel Winchester and his three comrades had a decision to make: walk the seventy miles to Kufra and surrender to the Italian garrison or head south, following the tracks of their comrades in the hope of encountering an LRDG or Free French patrol. They chose the latter, setting off south on 1 February, even though Easton had a wound to his throat and Tighe was suffering from the recurrence of a stomach condition that had troubled him previously in the desert campaign.

What followed became part of British Army folklore, an epic tale of stoic endurance and selfless courage that was soon being recounted in newspapers, bars and restaurants, from Cairo to Cambridge. For a few weeks Moore became the most talked about private soldier in Allied uniform, decorated with a Distinguished Conduct Medal and invited to describe his story to wide-eyed war correspondents.

They walked south, covering forty miles in the first twenty-four hours, a blistering pace but one they could never maintain. Soon thirst and hunger were stalking their every step. 'We were nearly mad with thirst and decided to give up,' said Moore. Their chance came when they saw a vehicle in the distance. A brief conflab and they were all in agreement: they would surrender. 'But we got closer and closer with nothing happening,' remarked Moore. 'When finally we reached the car we found it had been abandoned – shot to pieces, evidently by one of our patrols.'

The vehicle's chassis resembled a 'cheese grater' and the sand was dark with blood. The water had leaked out from the radiator and there was no food to be found inside, only some empty condensed milk cans. 'We scraped the remains of the milk with our finger nails from the insides of the cans, but it was hard and full of sand,' said Moore. And then suddenly there was a shout. One of the men had discovered 'a water tank among the debris of the car that had about a gallon and a half of water left in it'.

On they marched, less parched but still hungry, and dressed only in shirts and shorts. At night it was so cold 'we dug a hole in the sand and lay with our arms round each other.' The first to weaken was Tighe, whose stomach condition deteriorated to such an extent he told his comrades to go without him. 'There was not much water left by now, but we divided what little there was, putting Tighe's share in an empty lentil bottle we found,' said Moore. He, Winchester and Easton pressed on but two mornings later the wounded Guardsman couldn't stand up. 'Winchester and I rubbed his legs to start the circulation and, finally, got him to his feet,' explained Moore. 'But he could not stand for long, just stumbled a few paces and dropped in the sand.'

Winchester and Moore helped their comrade back to his feet but again he collapsed onto the sand after just a few paces. They tried again, but the strength in Easton's legs had gone. 'I knew, somehow, by the staring look in his eyes, that he was done,' recalled Moore. 'He asked for water and I gave him half of what was left, but it was no good, and in a few moments he died.'*

Moore and Winchester buried Easton and continued south but by now even these two hard men were suffering untold agonies. With barely any water left, their boots had worn through and they tramped barefoot over the liquid sand. 'I don't remember very clearly what happened after that,' admitted Moore, 'except plodding hour after hour through the hot sand. I didn't dare drink the last few drops of water I had, so I just swilled

---

* The death of Easton was subsequently romanticized, presumably for propaganda purposes by the Ministry of Information. According to versions of the story released to the press, when found by the French Easton was still alive and temporarily revived by a cup of sweet tea. 'With a little smile he was heard to say 'I don't usually take sugar with my tea.' He died shortly afterwards.

my mouth out with it and spat it back into the bottle to use again.'

By 10 February Winchester had dredged the last of his endurance from his withered body. 'He could go no farther,' said Moore. 'I just scraped a hollow in the sand for him to lie in.' There was no more water to share out so the New Zealander had nothing to give the Scot but a whispered 'good luck', before continuing on his torturous way. 'By this time I could only go a mile or so without resting but I went as far as I could each time before sitting down in the sand,' said Moore.

The next day Moore staggered on, aware that on either side of him were 'bones, bones everywhere'. They were the bleached white detritus of camels, and their sight dismayed Moore; if camels couldn't make it, what chance he? Then from somewhere in the distance Moore heard a sound that didn't belong to the desert. Turning, he imagined the truck must be a mirage, the heat playing one last ghastly trick on him. 'I couldn't believe my eyes,' he confessed. But the truck was not a mirage, it was real.

The French soldiers who eased Moore into their truck told him about the fate of his comrades. Tighe had decided to plod on and die in his tracks rather than sit on the sand and wait for death to reach him. His cussedness was rewarded by two incredible strokes of good fortune. First, he encountered a deserted hut, and secondly, inside the hut he found a match and a small quantity of oil. With extreme care Tighe crafted a fire from what flammable materials he could muster. He now had shelter, warmth and water. But would they ensure his survival or simply prolong his demise? Three days later Tighe was nearing the end, slipping in and out of consciousness, 'in a dreadful condition of nerves and exhaustion'. Suddenly the door to the hut swung open. Tighe's eyes burned at the sunlight's intrusion into his tomb. The Free Frenchmen could barely believe their eyes as they helped Tighe out of the hut. Tighe tried to explain to his rescuers about his comrades. But he didn't speak French and they didn't speak English. Only when Tighe reached hospital could he finally explain that there were still three of his comrades out in the desert.

The Frenchmen set off at once, discovering Winchester close to death and not far ahead Moore still on the march having covered around 200 miles.

CHAPTER FIVE

'Bagnold's Blue-eyed Boys'

The loss of Clayton was a grievous blow to Bagnold. He learned of his friend's capture on 1 February, and the following day received another signal in which he was furnished with details of the attack. As well as three men captured, five had been killed and three more slightly wounded. Four of the five 'dead' men were Moore's party but the thought of five fatalities left Bagnold deeply troubled. Equally concerning was the news that the 'cipher and all Clayton's papers were captured'. On 3 February the Italians used the cipher to send a series of bogus messages to the LRDG, which raised a smile if nothing else.

General Wavell commiserated with Bagnold and, to raise his spirits, requested that he 'write up [the] LRDG' for the newspapers. The nation needed a lift, what with the Blitz on London and other cities. Bagnold obliged and his account appeared in newspapers across the Empire a few days later.

'A remarkable story of exploits in the vast Libyan Desert during the last six months by a small body of motor commandos, known as the "Long-range Desert Group", has just been revealed,' ran the article on page four of *The Times* on 14 February. 'Going out in small patrols, usually of three cars, they have consistently and successfully harassed Italian outposts, reduced isolated forts, interrupted communications, and generally kept the Italian Command guessing, playing a small but very important part in the eventual British sweep to Benghazi.'

The piece continued in a similar vein, describing a war 'which frayed the nerves of Italian commanders and gave garrisons the "jitters".' The BBC joined in the adulation and the LRDG swiftly became the most famous, the most romantic, unit in North Africa: made instantly recognizable by the Arab headdress – *keffiyeh*, in Arabic – they wore on patrol. (In reality, however, once the photographers and the movie reel cameraman had departed, most of the LRDG removed the headdress and reverted to their cap comforter. 'The headdress was good in a sandstorm or as a dishcloth,' said one soldier. 'But most of us wore the cap comforter, which looked like a short scarf but could be worn as woollen hat.')

Bagnold did not just commit his thoughts to print. He was also recorded – as were several of the Kiwi soldiers – in an interview that was broadcast on the wireless in New Zealand in late February. It was carefully stage-managed, the soldiers all reading from prepared scripts, some more wooden than others, but it was an exercise in boosting the spirits of those on the home front thousands of miles away.

The announcer introduced the LRDG to listeners by likening their exploits with those of Lawrence of Arabia, 'the main difference being that whereas Lawrence lived with the Arabs, as one of themselves, the LRDG operated for many months through countless thousands of square miles behind and within the Italian outposts.' He then handed the microphone to Bagnold.

'Hello New Zealand,' began Bagnold's address, his clipped accent good enough to have earned him a job reading the news on the BBC. Identifying himself only as the 'officer commanding LRDG or the Long Range Patrol as it's sometimes called', he continued:

> I have worked, surveyed, explored, raided and fought in the company of a carefully selected band of New Zealand and British troops. Your men did their work competently and well and probably as a result of their upbringing in faraway New Zealand, seemed to have the flair and the self-reliance that quickly accustomed them to the strange and difficult conditions

> of life in the real desert. It was no easy life out there, literally hundreds of miles from civilization. It was no life for weaklings and I think it can be safely said that judging by results we achieved the rigorous examination through which every applicant had to undergo certainly proved very worthwhile.

One of the New Zealand soldiers, Cyril Aire, from Te Awamutu in the North Islands, reassured their families that they had plenty to eat and drink. In addition, added Aire, 'we had a rum ration at night, two joules per man and it was as good as a good three nips in New Zealand.'

Despite the blaze of publicity, the LRDG was still far from the finished article. The loss of Clayton prompted Bagnold to submit a request that Major Guy Prendergast be posted to Cairo as his replacement. Prendergast arrived in Cairo on 16 February a couple of weeks after the latest batch of volunteers had arrived at the Citadel. Designated 'Y' Patrol, so called because its members had been drawn from the Yeomanry regiments comprising the 1st Cavalry Division in Palestine, thirty-two recruits had reported to Bagnold in late January having been selected by Captain Pat McCraith, the officer in charge. Bagnold was not impressed by what he encountered. 'It was found that many of the personnel were unsuitable,' commented the LRDG war diary, 'being ex-cavalry reservists of bad character whom their units wanted to get rid of.' Of the thirty-two recruits, twenty-four were soon on their way back to their regiments. Among the eight who remained were Lofty Carr, Anthony Cave and Arthur Arger.

Arger, from Middlesbrough, was a Yorkshire Hussar who had never heard of the Long Range Desert Group, despite their recent repute. Instead he was motivated by the chance to escape the monotony of regular army life. Interviewed by McCraith, Arger was asked about his hobbies. 'I said that I used to breed budgerigars and he said: "Oh, you'll do for me."' Arger was issued with a travel warrant and told to present himself at the Citadel in Cairo. He did as instructed, believing he was probably 'going to be in charge of a pigeon loft somewhere'.

From the other end of England came Anthony Cave, who had enlisted in the Wiltshire Yeomanry in 1935 aged sixteen. His father had died when he was a boy and he was the apple of his mother's eye. He was a trumpeter nicknamed 'Tich'* because he stood only five foot two inches. 'I was pretty fed up,' said Cave. 'We were in Palestine and the weather was awful . . . We were all fed up. I just happened to see this notice on the board asking for men of initiative and integrity and half a dozen words that I had to go and look up in the dictionary to find out what they were talking about. Anyway nothing ventured, nothing gained. I wrote out in my most illiterate hand that I would like to be transferred to this new desert unit.' On arriving at the Citadel Cave could hardly believe his eyes: beds, mattresses, clean sheets, even clean pillowcases. Luxuries practically unheard of in his army experience.

Cave's pal was Les Coombs, known to his friends as 'Mickey', another West Countryman, who had sold shoes before the outbreak of war. Coombs was of medium height with a fresh complexion, fine features and a neat moustache which leant a dashing touch to his appearance. Not only good-looking, Coombs was silver-tongued, and his success with the opposite sex earned him another sobriquet – 'Ram'. It was his boast that he didn't need a compass to find his way across the desert: all he need do was follow his erection to Cairo and all its exotic women.

Arger was recruited as a gunner, Cave and Coombs as drivers. What McCraith craved above all else, however, were soldiers who could navigate. They were thin on the ground in Palestine; navigation was not a skill taught to cavalrymen and when McCraith returned to Cairo with his haul of recruits the most prized among them was probably Lofty Carr.

Bagnold had mentioned the shortage of skilled navigators a while earlier to Brigadier John Chrystall, commander of the 6th Cavalry Brigade, comprising the Warwickshire, Staffordshire and

---

* Cave spelt his nickname 'Tich' although in some histories of the LRDG it has been written as 'Titch'.

Cheshire Yeomanry GHQ. Chrystall replied that he had just the man. 'A navigator?' enquired Bagnold. The brigadier replied that the trooper he had in mind was currently 'mucking out horses in Palestine'. But he was also a self-taught navigator, and a skilled one at that. Only recently he had guided the brigadier to the buffer zone between Syria and Palestine for the purpose of reconnoitring an area that the British feared was soon to be attacked by the Vichy French. A signal was sent to the headquarters of the Staffordshire Yeomanry instructing Carr's release. When there was no response from the regiment's commanding officer, Lieutenant-Colonel Gordon Cox-Cox, Chrystall despatched two military policemen with instructions to escort Carr to Cairo.

When Stuart Carr arrived at the Citadel he was interviewed by Prendergast. It was a perfunctory interrogation. Carr, who at six foot four inches towered above Prendergast, was asked if he had a driving licence. Yes, he replied. What car did he drive? His father's. What colour was the uphostelry? Carr answered all the questions, a little baffled, but correctly assuming Prendergast was making sure he was not in the habit of telling lies. In return Prendergast informed Carr that they knew all about his prowess in navigation; what he did not tell the twenty-year-old was that they also knew of his reputation within the Staffordshire Yeomanry.

Carr came from a family of Anglo-Irish soldiers. His grandfather and father had served in the army, the latter leaving in 1908 with a First-Class Certificate of Education that, in time, allowed the family to move up in the world. Carr's father became an accountant, then a brewer, relocating his family to Stone in Staffordshire where he managed a brewery. His younger son was a talented sportsman in his early adolescence, captaining the school rugby and cricket teams. Then Carr changed school, and it was football not cricket that was played at his new seat of learning. He didn't much like football, and anyway, as Carr matured his interests became more cerebral. Books weren't so boring after all, he decided, and he developed a particular passion for astronomy, a hobby inherited from his grandfather who, after leaving the army, took a job on the passenger ships to Australia. He taught his grandson about the stars and how to use them to navigate, giving him star charts for birthday presents. The young Carr was hooked, even constructing a theodolite from Meccano in order to feed his obsession.

But for the outbreak of war, Carr would have spent 1939 training to become a surveyor for the pottery industry. Instead, on 26 April 1939, aged eighteen, he enlisted in the Staffordshire Yeomanry territorials, and on 1 September Carr was mobilized for war.

His independent mind soon began to chaff at the petty regulations of army life, while his intelligence allied to his outspokenness antagonized his officers. Carr despised many of them, regarding the officers' mess of the Staffs Yeomanry as an extension of the North Staffordshire Hunt. To the port-faced officers, war was a jape. Lieutenant-Colonel Gordon Cox-Cox in particular took a strong dislike to the massive Carr, who was head and shoulders above the rest of the regiment in both size and intellect. It was Cox-Cox who had ignored the signal from Cairo requesting Carr's release; he was damned if he was going to give Carr a metaphorical leg-up. Then the two military policemen arrived and Carr and Cox-Cox parted company.

Guy Prendergast took an instant shine to Carr. 'You're ready-made,' he told him at the end of their brief interview. Carr and the other seven members of 'Y' Patrol who had avoided being returned to their units were addressed by Pat McCraith. 'He called us Bagnold's Blue-eyed Boys,' recalled Carr. 'And he also told us to forget everything we had learnt up to now because we were no longer in the regular army.' This was harder for some than for others. The day after arriving at the Citadel one of the eight appeared on parade 'in full riding breeches, puttees, bandolier and shiny boots'. McCraith looked the soldier up and down in mocking silence. Eventually he said in the tone of a father addressing his wilful adolescent son: 'You're not in the cavalry now. I suggest you go and change.'

Carr also remembered that McCraith 'went on to give us each a document which we signed and returned. It was our oath that we would never, for the whole of our lives, reveal what we had been up to in the LRDG.'

Arthur Arger remembered that they were introduced also to Bagnold, who told them: 'I'm looking for people who can live together under adverse conditions in close proximity over long periods of time.' He said they had been selected because they had certain skills but also because it was believed they possessed the right temperament for the LRDG. Bagnold said he 'wasn't looking for bruisers, or thugs, he was looking for ordinary people who could do this sort of thing.'

Nevertheless 'Y' Patrol contained some hard men, most reared in the country, capable of combining animal cunning with swift ferocity. Tich Cave was a case in point, so too Carr, who was soon answering to 'Lofty'. To everyone's great amusement Carr and Cave became best pals, despite the fourteen inches that separated them. 'I was hot-headed as a young man,' admitted Carr. 'I never tolerated being pushed around.'

Carr's size, and his reputation, soon came to the attention of another of the new recruits. 'We were at the Citadel taking stock of each other, as young men do, when Bert Woolley came up to me and said "I hear you're a bit of a scrapper."' Woolley had heard about Carr, and Carr had heard about Woolley, a talented boxer who had sparred with the World Heavyweight Champion Primo Carnera in the thirties. 'Oh no, I'm not!' retorted Carr, prudence replacing pride.

Carr encountered other strong characters among the eight 'Blue-eyed Boys' in the Citadel: Alf Withers and Joe McPike, both regular soldiers, selected by Bagnold to 'stiffen' their younger, less experienced comrades in 'Y' Patrol. McPike was the quieter of the pair but more conscientious in looking out for youngsters like Carr and Cave. Withers, on the other hand, was even more of a ladykiller than Coombs. 'He could find women where there weren't any,' recalled Carr.

The other two 'Blue-eyed Boys' were Bill Bullock, who kept himself to himself, and Alan Denniff, an intrepid Yorkshireman with an extravagant handlebar moustache and a calm, cheerful demeanour.

While the eight volunteers began their training Captain Pat McCraith went off in search of more men with the qualities to impress Bagnold. He eventually found them and by March 1941 'Y' Patrol had its full complement of thirty-two NCOs and men, with Second Lieutenant Jake Easonsmith his second in command. Among those recruited in the second wave were Harry Chard, a former bus conductor in Bristol, who came from the North Somerset Yeomanry; Leonard 'Ginger' Sharratt, at eighteen the youngest recruit, a draughtsman in Wolverhampton before enlisting in the Staffordshire Yeomanry. Also accepted from the Yorkshire Hussars was Gordon Harrison. He and his comrades had 'spent twelve happy months galloping and cantering around Palestine, but rather felt we were wasting our time because there was a war being fought'. He recalled that at his interview McCraith 'didn't want to know if you were good at strangling people, that sort of thing, it was getting an impression of you as a type of fellow, if you would get on with your fellow human beings.'

With the expansion of the LRDG now complete, Bagnold moved 'Y' and 'G' Patrols into A Squadron, under the command of Major Mitford, with an additional patrol, 'S', formed of soldiers from Southern Rhodesia. B Squadron consisted of two New Zealand patrols, 'T' and 'R', after General Freyberg had relented and allowed the LRDG to continue employing his soldiers.

There were also changes in transport in the early months of 1941 with most of the 30-cwt Chevrolets no longer fit for purpose after thousands of miles of tough desert travel. Unfortunately it was not possible to replace like with like, so Bagnold reluctantly took ownership of a consignment of Ford 30-cwt four-wheeled drive trucks. Seventy of these vehicles were given to the LRDG in February and it took nearly a month of modification, notably camouflaging them in colours that included pink – effective because it blended in with the haze of the sun at dawn and dusk – before they were considered desert-worthy. Even then, Bagnold harboured doubts as to the Ford's suitability because of 'their greater weight . . . and the complications introduced by the front wheel drive'.

Nearly all the men preferred the Chevrolets because they were easier to handle and because they had a bonnet. 'On the Fords you had a blast of hot air hitting you in the face all the time from the engine because the bonnet was taken off,' said Lofty Carr. 'The Chev was a wonderful vehicle, very tough, with the chassis specially shortened for us so we could get over obstacles, such as rocks.'

The members of 'Y' Patrol trained on these new trucks, driving a short distance out of Cairo on the old military road. 'It sort of cut across the desert, past the pyramids and there were the sand dunes where you could try your luck,' recalled Arthur Arger. 'That's where the real fun and games came in – how to negotiate sand dunes.' Some of the men followed the example of the New Zealand patrol and humanized their trucks with nicknames. Coombs called his 'Aramis', and the other two Musketeers were adopted by Harry Chard and Brian Springford for their vehicles.

The men soon learned that the dunes also had names. 'Some were called whalebacks and as you went over the top it was like being on a rollercoaster, up and down,' recalled Carr. 'If it was a razorback, the other side of it was sheer and as you came over you left the ground completely for twenty or thirty feet.' They noticed, too, the way the dunes changed colour the higher they rose, from butter yellow at the base to 'white with yellow depths – not the blue-white of snow' at the crest.

Bagnold taught the recruits how to tame a 'razorback' by driving fast up the side, slowing and then going over the crest straight on and not an angle. Or, as Bagnold's Blue-Eyed Boys liked to call it, going for a 'flying fuck'.

Lofty Carr received some navigational training from Bill Kennedy Shaw, a man he found hard to like. 'He knew his stuff, and the sort of material we needed,' he reflected. 'But he talked down to you all the time.' Most of what Carr learned was imparted by John Stocker, a self-possessed and self-deprecating figure who was immensely popular with everyone. In the thirties he had been a master mariner in the Merchant Navy but the war offered the opportunity for a fresh challenge, so Stocker enlisted in the army and was posted to the Middle East with the Royal Tank Corps. Then he answered a call from the LRDG for expert navigators and subsequently wrote the navigation notes that became the bible for all aspirant navigators in the unit.

'John was a wonderful man,' remembered Carr. 'But because he had been a deck hand in the merchant navy, that followed him everywhere in the war, and he wasn't considered "toffee nosed" enough for an officer.'

Some of the 'stuff' imparted by the LRDG's intelligence officer to the new recruits concerned the natives that they might encounter in Cyrenaica (the name by which the eastern coastal region of Libya was known). They were the Senussi: desert nomads who had been brutally repressed by the Italians for years and were therefore willing to provide what support they could to the Allies. Nevertheless Kennedy Shaw had drawn up some 'points of conduct when meeting the Arabs in the desert' to lessen the chances of any misunderstandings:

> Remove footwear on entering their tents.
> Completely ignore their women.
> If thirsty drink the water they offer but DO NOT fill your water bottle from personal supply. Go to their well and fetch what you want.
> Do not expect breakfast if you sleep the night. Arabs will give you a midday or evening meal.

Kennedy Shaw, who had a deep respect and admiration for the Senussi, then taught 'Y' Patrol a few basic words of Arabic in case they should ever need to seek their help in the desert. Friend was *sahib;* water was *moya;* food was *akl;* how far? (how many kilometres?) was *kam kilo* and *Taliani/Siziliani* was Italian/enemy.

Kennedy Shaw explained that another reason the Senussi hated the Italians was because 'Mussolini had put iron lids on the wells and sold off the water to Italian businessmen.' If the LRDG came across any such wells they were to blow off the lids. In return the Senussi provided the British with intelligence on enemy troop movements. It was a risk to do so. Carr recalled hearing that if 'the Italians caught any Arabs working for the British they took them up in an aeroplane and threw them out as they flew over their village. Others were found hanging from trees with a meat hook under their chin.'

CHAPTER SIX

'We obliterated these Germans'

On 1 March 1941, ten years and forty days after they had first occupied the Libyan oasis, the Italians were swept out of Kufra by General Philippe Leclerc's Free French. That was just one of the triumphs in North Africa in the spring of 1941, a series of successes that imbued the British with much needed self-belief. As one officer in Egypt – Brigadier Desmond Young – wrote, 'fat pashas invited senior British officers to the Mohamed Ali Club. There were garden-parties in the gardens of the rich around Gezireh. Cairo society ceased to practise its Italian.'

In two months General Richard O'Connor's Western Desert Force (later expanded to form the Eighth Army) had advanced 500 miles and 'beaten and destroyed an Italian army of four corps, comprising nine divisions and part of a tenth. It had captured 13,000 prisoners, 400 tanks and 1,290 guns, besides vast quantities of other material.' The Allies' advanced west along the coast, seizing Bardia (4 January), Tobruk (22 January) and Benghazi (5–6 February). The enemy retreated to El Agheila, a bottleneck where they hoped to block an advance from Cyrenaica into Tripolitania (the western region of Libya). O'Connor wanted to press the attack and throw the Italians out of North Africa once and for all, but on 12 February Winston Churchill sent a telegram to Wavell, congratulating the Western Desert Force on capturing Benghazi 'three weeks ahead of expectation'. Believing that their advances in North Africa were irreversible, Churchill instructed Wavell to transfer the bulk of his troops to Greece (under the command of Jumbo Wilson) in readiness for a German invasion. The desert air force was removed en masse almost entirely, leaving behind just one squadron of fighters, and plans were drawn up to send the Long Range Desert Group into El Agheila to harass the Italians and make them believe there was still a large-scale Allied presence in Cyrenaica.

When Adolf Hitler learned of Italy's humiliation he was initially indifferent. North Africa was a sideshow, inconsequential in comparison to his ambitions in the Balkans and Russia. It was Grand Admiral Erich Raeder, head of the Germany navy, who did most to turn Hitler's attention towards events in the region. What, Raeder asked of his Führer, would happen to Germany if the British maintained their iron grip on the Mediterranean? It would seriously jeopardize Hitler's plans for conquest in the East. Nonetheless, it was with reluctance that on 11 January 1941, Hitler issued 'Führer Directive No. 22', authorizing the raising of a force to be sent to North Africa to support Germany's Italian allies. Codenamed Operation Sunflower, the force was designated 5 Light Division though it was not until 6 February that Hitler appointed as the unit commander Erwin Rommel, a dashing 49-year-old general who had led the 7th Panzer Division, 'The Ghost Division', during the invasion of the Low Countries the previous year.

In late February 1941, by which time its vanguard had already reached Tripoli in Libya, the force was formally reconstituted as the Afrika Korps. Rommel rushed them up to the front, augmenting their strength with a number of dummy tanks mounted on Volkswagens, and the Afrika Korps dug in around the El Agheila bottleneck. With just one squadron of RAF fighters ranged against them, the Germans controlled the sky in North Africa and used their numerical advantage to prevent the British discovering how few troops they had on the ground. Other factors worked in Rommel's favour: not only had the battle-hardened 6th Australian Division been sent to Greece but the 7th Armoured Division was back in Egypt resting and refitting. Their replacements, the British

2nd Armoured Division and 9th Australian Division, were inexperienced and under-equipped and their commander, General Philip Neame, was callow in desert warfare compared to his predecessor, O'Connor.

The intuitive and audacious Rommel sensed this and on 2 April – 'disregarding higher orders to wait until the end of May' – advanced east. The British withdrew, evacuating Benghazi on 3 April, prompting Wavell to order O'Connor to leave Cairo and assist Neame. Three days later the pair were captured when they drove into the vanguard of the German advance. On 11 April the British had been pushed out of Cyrenaica and back into Egypt, right where they had been in 1940. The only difference was that now they were facing not just Italians, but also the Germans.

In fact the Allies had not been swept entirely out of Cyrenaica. The port of Tobruk remained in their hands, besieged by German troops. And 500 miles south the oasis of Kufra was also in their possession. Now, instead of harassing the Italians around El Agheila, the Long Range Desert Group (minus A Squadron) was ordered to Kufra on 9 April and Bagnold appointed commander of the mixed British and French garrison.*

It was a short-sighted decision by the top brass, one that resulted in a frustrating summer in general for Bagnold and the LRDG who were oppressed by the passivity of their existence. At least Bagnold had time to school his men in some of the more primitive ways of the desert, such as how to suck a desert snail out of its shell for a snack, and how to bathe without water. The latter intrigued the men, as Les Sullivan, an LRDG fitter, recalled: 'He taught us to bath in the sand. He said that washing does not get you clean because we don't normally get dirty. He reckoned you washed and bathed to get rid of dead cells of skin. So in deep desert we bathed in the sand. We were not allowed water to wash,

* In May General Charles de Gaulle, who had arrived in Egypt on 1 April, demanded a French commander for Kufra. On 29 May Bagnold met de Gaulle and Wavell in Kufra and the following day wrote in his diary: 'Gen de Gaulle withdraws his demand for French commander at Kufra.'

shower or clean teeth. All water was very precious and was necessary for cooking and drinking and so that was rationed.'

Each man was permitted eight pints (a gallon) of water a day with two issued at breakfast, two in the evening as tea and two at midday. The outstanding two pints were drawn by the men in the evening and were used to fill water bottles for the following day. 'The men,' wrote Bagnold, 'are trained to use their water bottles during the day at their own discretion for sipping from time to time to moisten their lips.'

Rations (which were packed in wooden petrol cases when the LRDG was on a patrol) were considered of the utmost importance by Bagnold and he issued his unit with a sample menu (with recipes) based on the food available. This consisted of:

Breakfast suggestions
Porridge (no milk or sugar)
Fried bacon with oatmeal fritter
Bacon and oatmeal cake
Bacon stuffed with cooked oatmeal
Bacon with oatmeal chappatis
Tiffin
Lentil soup
Various sandwich spreads on biscuits
Cheese and oatmeal savoury
Cheese and oatmeal cake
Oatmeal and date cookies
Dinner
Stewed mutton with dumplings
Meat pudding

Occasionally the men would supplement their rations with a gazelle, the swift, small antelope native to the desert that often appeared in large herds. Some officers saw nothing wrong with this and sanctioned indiscriminate slaughter but others, those more familiar with the animal, insisted on a 'one shot, one kill', rule explaining that otherwise the terrified gazelle would keep running until its heart burst. A few men were outraged at the idea of killing defenceless animals for extra meat when they had all the rations they needed.

Not all of the LRDG spent the spring of 1941 garrisoning Kufra. A Squadron, comprising the Guards and Yeomanry patrols, had found itself caught up in the withdrawal east from Cyrenaica. Having been ordered to Barce – about seventy miles north-east of Benghazi – on 25 March to reconnoitre enemy positions, half of 'G' Patrol under the command of Crichton-Stuart became cut off from the rest of the squadron. Unable to raise Mitford on the wireless, their only source of information came from the BBC on the radio. The news, remembered Crichton-Stuart, 'became ominously vaguer' in the first week of April. 'After Agedabia had fallen to the enemy, the announcer would only say that the situation was "fluid".'

Finally, in the late afternoon of 5 April, Crichton-Stuart's signaller made contact with Mitford, who said he was at Mekili, 'surrounded by the enemy'. He advised 'G' Patrol to head to Jarabub, 215 miles to the east. The news dismayed Crichton-Stuart. 'It was an ugly situation, for Mekili was the last stop before Tobruk, and it meant that not only it and Bardia were threatened, but also Jarabub and Siwa.' 'G' Patrol arrived at Jarabub on the morning of 10 April, welcomed at the town's fort by a 'platoon of Senussi Arabs recruited in Egypt and commanded by a Frenchman'.

Living up to the gastronomic reputation of his countrymen, the French officer treated Crichton-Stuart's patrol to a lavish meal but towards its end the alarm was sounded. 'Seizing our weapons we rushed to man the battlements in the best Western style and grimly covered a number of vehicles approaching from the north,' recalled Crichton-Stuart. 'The strength of my field glasses alone prevented internecine warfare, as just in time I identified the remainder of A Squadron.'

The squadron, commanded by Mitford, and consisting of 'Y' Patrol and the other half of 'G' Patrol, were tired, grimy and hungry when they drove into Jarabub. Crichton-Stuart said the squadron 'celebrated our reunion in Chianti', before listening to an account of their operation.

They had left Barce on 1 April, heading south towards Msus, approximately sixty miles inland from the coast. The terrain was rough and progress slow, so that by the late afternoon they were still ten miles east of Msus. Suddenly, through the heat haze, a number of vehicles were sighted coming their way. 'Earlier McCraith had given us all a talk,' recalled Lofty Carr. 'He reminded us that we were no longer in the cavalry, and we weren't to charge the enemy. Well, when we came across the enemy McCraith immediately shouted "Charge!"'

The vehicles – six trucks in total – turned and fled, and the LRDG gave chase. 'They were too far away to identify but Captain McCraith decided they were Jerries and took off after them,' remembered Tich Cave, who was driving the captain in a V8 Ford pick-up. 'He kept saying, "Faster, Cave, faster" . . . I was going faster and faster – I had my foot through the floorboards and the old bus was doing about eight-five.'

The gunner – Trooper Graham, known as 'jungle', British Army slang for mad – opened fire with his Vickers machine gun from his position on top of the truck. The noise was so great that Cave didn't hear McCraith scream 'Stop!' Nor did he spot the 'little red flags marking the minefield' because of the swirling dust.

From the vehicle behind Carr saw McCraith stand up and wave his arms. Suddenly the 'vehicle took off into the air and crashed down'. Cave had driven over what the British called a thermos bomb, an AR-4 anti-personnel mine used by the Italians that resembled a thermos flask in size and shape. 'The only harm to the truck was a blown rear tyre,' said Cave. 'It was unfortunate for the Skipper because he was standing up and caught the blast and it broke his arm and hand in several places, knocked out some teeth and peppered his face with shrapnel.'

As McCraith's wounds were dressed, Mitford approached Carr. 'He asked me what our position was,' remembered Carr. 'I replied, "I don't know, I stopped checking nine miles ago when we started giving chase and I got the Lewis gun going." He shouted and screamed at me, and told me I had to keep my head as a navigator, and not join in the fighting.'

Mitford had calmed down by the time the LRDG camped for the night, about eight miles from Msus. He called up Cyrenaica Command on the wireless and was informed that the patrol they had chased belonged to an Indian cavalry regiment. The following day Mitford led his men into Msus (in the hands of the Free French) and arranged for the evacuation of McCraith. Rather than appoint Jake Easonsmith 'Y' Patrol's commander, Mitford instructed Martin Gibbs to take charge of the Yeomanry patrol, while he himself assumed command of 'G' Patrol.

It was an error in judgement from Mitford, one that might have been down to his breeding. Everyone in 'Y' Patrol liked Easonsmith, a 32-year-old with the build of a middleweight boxer and a face that belonged on the set of Ealing Studios. Handsome, athletic and erudite, Easonsmith's speech was 'deliberate', his words usually accompanied by a slow smile. The combination, recalled a fellow army officer, 'reflected an inner sureness, a perfect balance, and a mature consideration of life and death . . . if he ever had doubts, he never showed any; with him all was secure.'

Carr remembered Easonsmith as a 'lovely man who used to flog cigars and booze out of the back of a truck in Bristol'. His job entailed a little more than just that. Upon leaving Clifton College, Easonsmith worked first for a tobacco importer and cigarette manufacturer in Bristol, and then as a salesman for the Australian Emu Wine Company. He married in 1935 and captained Clifton rugby club where he first showed signs of his charismatic leadership qualities. Easonsmith came from a well-off family but there was a maverick streak in him that liked to rattle the cage of middle-class convention. He caused 'mild amazement' among his friends when 'instead of peddling around his case of [wine] samples in the ordinary way of commercial travellers he got himself a caravan in which he lived with his wife'.

It was a life of 'comfortable mediocrity', but a fulfilling one all the same for Easonsmith, who was content with his caravan, his wife, Topsy, and his rugby. In time he became a father and, upon the outbreak of war, Easonsmith enlisted in the 66th Searchlight

Regiment as a private. Within a year he was promoted to sergeant, and by the end of 1940 he had been commissioned in the Royal Tank Regiment and was in the Middle East.

Easonsmith was a natural leader of men but in Mitford's eyes he was still a commercial traveller. Gibbs, on the other hand, was a product of Eton and Sandhurst, whose family owned Sheldon Manor, a historic house in Wiltshire. A regular officer before the war, Gibbs had joined 'G' Patrol from the Coldstream Guards and it didn't take 'Y' Patrol long to realize he was still a Guards officer at heart. 'They made some funny decisions on social matters,' said Carr. 'Gibbs was not LRDG in temperament . . . he never mixed or spoke to anybody, he was an officer apart.'

On 4 April Mitford moved the squadron south-east to the Trigh el-Abd (the 'Road of the Slave'), a camel track running through Cyrenaica in a north-easterly direction that was ten miles wide in places. They camped for the night about eighty miles east of Msus and the following day moved north towards Mekili. Informed of the enemy advance, Mitford's squadron spotted no signs of ground troops even though the Axis forces had swept through Msus along the Trigh el-Abd.

By sundown on the 5th, Mitford had lost contact with Cyrenaica Command. Their last communication had ordered the squadron to Mekili so Mitford did as instructed, placing himself under the command of the brigadier in charge of the Indian motorized brigade defending the town from a force of Italians attacking from the south. Mitford was asked to attack the enemy on their western flank so, splitting the squadron, they 'went off hunting'.

Mitford's unit captured an Italian officer, while Gibbs had a brief skirmish with an enemy HQ. They rendezvoused on the night of 6 April four miles south-west of Mekili. 'The following morning found us on top of a small plateau,' recalled Tich Cave. 'It wasn't very high, maybe a couple of hundred feet, and you could see Mekili quite clearly.'

Admiring the view alongside Cave was Robert 'Nobby' Hall, one of the squadron's anti-tank gunners. The Boys was ineffectual at a range of more than about 100 yards but Hall decided it might be fun to fire at a tank he could see in the distance. 'You fire that toy at that tank, don't be surprised if you get a bloody great shell come back at you,' Cave told Hall. The gunner laughed and told Cave they were concealed from the enemy. Cave didn't share his gunner's confidence. 'If we can see them, I'm bloody certain they can see us.'

Ignoring Cave's advice, Hall fired two rounds at the tank. 'There was a bit of a pause,' said Cave. 'Then there's a "whoosh-crump" and a ruddy great shell came over and landed somewhere. Where the hell it landed I don't know but Nobby . . . decided discretion was the better part of valour.'

Mitford meanwhile had been busy on the wireless, communicating his whereabouts to the brigadier inside Mekili. It was agreed the squadron would continue harassing the Italian flanks. 'We hadn't gone 100 or 200 yards when a stone went through my radiator and the whole thing came to a grinding halt,' remembered Cave. 'Major Mitford had to decide what he was going to do about it. He could abandon the truck or take it in tow. He decided not to do this. He decided to send me back to Mekili and get the damn thing repaired.' Mitford told Carr to help Cave tow the truck into Mekili where Cave would remain while it was mended. Carr would return the following day to collect him.

Carr did as instructed and was soon back with the squadron while Cave remained inside Mekili waiting for the fitters from the Indian motorized brigade to fix the damaged vehicle.

Throughout 7 April the squadron skirmished with the Italians, at one point opening fire on a forty-strong column of vehicles that turned out to be German. Two trucks were destroyed and four prisoners taken. That evening the squadron laid up for the night in an escarpment six miles west of Mekili.

The next morning at 0600 hours the Germans attacked the town in force from the south, east and north. Carr could only look on at the enemy assault, despondent at the fate of Tich Cave. Knowing where Cave was, Carr suggested to Mickey Coombs that they could slip into Mekili and rescue him. Coombs was willing to give it a try. 'I went towards Mitford and started to say that we would go and get Cave,' recalled Carr. 'Mitford yelled "Get off that fucking skyline!" And that was the end of our rescue plan.'

It was the second time Carr had been bawled out by Mitford but it didn't diminish the respect in which he held his commander. As the New Zealanders had discovered, Mitford might have been brusque in his attitude but there were few better practitioners of desert warfare. 'He was a tough man, hard to work with, but I liked him,' reflected Carr. 'You knew where you stood with him. I had a lot of time for him. He always swore at me and, yes, he could be aloof, but Mitford taught me more about tactics than anybody. He taught me such clever tricks.'

One of the tricks was known as 'dragging the wing'. 'If a predator comes close to a partridge's nest, the mother partridge will act like she has a broken wing. So the predator follows her and the mother leads it further away from nest,' explained Carr. 'We did the broken wing on anyone daft enough to follow us into the desert, and they were never seen again. One time we were being chased and we left one vehicle looking like it was trouble, that was the partridge, and the other four vehicles went ahead.'

The truck that was feigning trouble crested a dune and then stopped. Joe McPike was waiting behind the Bofors gun when the enemy appeared at the top of the dune. Opening fire at point blank range, McPike destroyed their pursuer.

It was Mitford's skill that enabled the squadron to escape unseen from their ominous predicament. By clever use of the terrain, and aided by a sudden dust storm that had sprung up, A Squadron withdrew to the east and by sundown on 8 April were forty miles clear of Mekili, where they found themselves three miles from a column of German artillery.

At first light on 9 April Mitford set out to investigate the column. It was encamped in a depression, and composed of nearly fifty vehicles and artillery pieces, their occupants asleep and oblivious to the danger. 'He hid us down behind a ridge and then moved us very cleverly off the ridge and we got behind a number of German artillery pieces with their backs and guns to us,' said Lofty Carr. The LRDG moved noiselessly into position and on a hand signal from Mitford opened fire. 'We obliterated these Germans,' remembered Carr, 'and then hopped it.'

The squadron headed south-east towards the oasis of Siwa but late in the day received orders directing them to Jarabub, where they arrived on 10 April, to be welcomed by Crichton-Stuart and his bottles of Chianti.

Tich Cave had been left by Lofty Carr with some Indian fitters commanded by an English captain. It took them less than two hours to repair the truck. 'I thought about just driving back to the patrol because I've always had a good eye for country and it didn't seem any trouble as far as I could see,' reflected Cave. 'Then I thought "well, if they've moved off I might have difficulty finding them again." So I decided to stay where I was.'

Any lingering indecision was dispelled by the hospitality of the fitters, who produced food and some tea and told Cave to make himself comfortable while he waited for his friend to return. He even managed to have a shower. 'I'd just got my shorts back on and that was all and a salvo of shells came over,' said Cave. 'I didn't bother to stop and put anything on. I dived into the nearest slit trench. The Captain landed on top of me along with a small Indian.'

A despatch rider roared up to the unit shortly after the shelling had finished, informing the captain the brigade was pulling out of Mekili. However they were too late and, before they could escape, their convoy of trucks was intercepted by a force of Italians. Cave, who had been given an overcoat by one of the fitters, was searched and herded with the rest of the prisoners into a temporary holding centre. 'I decided to have a look round to see what sort of place we were going to be locked up in,' remembered Cave. 'I took a walk round . . . I should say the area was about 150 yards long by 100 yards wide – a couple of football pitches. We were guarded on the four compass points by seven-ton Fiat trucks with two machine guns on each truck and a crew of four Eyeties. There was no other way of enclosing us and, in any case, who was going to run away from a place like Mekili – where the devil could you go to? But I'd already worked out what I was going to do. I know this sounds silly but from the moment I was captured I started planning how to get out of it.'

CHAPTER SEVEN

'Forget everything the army ever taught you'

Michael Crichton-Stuart remembered Jarabub as a 'little walled village huddled round the mosque, dominated by its white dome'. Nearby was a fort and a small palm grove. One's first impression, from a distance, was of quaint desert charm. But a few hours in Jarabub was enough to change most people's opinion. The air was heavy, the stench ghastly and the flies and mosquitoes unbearable. When the Allies had driven out the Italians they found waste everywhere as well as the unburied corpses of animals and soldiers. The Senussi had done their best to restore order but Lofty Carr remembered the 'great big shallow grave with arms and legs sticking out, donkeys and cats, etcetera, all killed and then set alight. It was a horrible sight.'

The LRDG didn't outstay their welcome, departing on 12 April for Siwa. Mitford, however, detailed a small party to remain at Jarabub. 'They left five of us,' explained Carr. 'We were told to stop there and give the impression to the Germans that there was a garrison.' Like creatures of the night, the soldiers remained hidden during the day, emerging only when it was dark. 'We had found an old tractor and one of the boys had made it so we could tow it,' said Carr. 'So the tractor went round all night leaving what looked like tank tracks to the [German] reconnaissance planes that came over during the day.'

When Carr and his comrades received instructions to withdraw to Siwa they arrived at the oasis to discover two small WACO aircraft, purchased from their Egyptian owners by the army after the RAF had refused to loan any of their own aircraft. WACOs were biplanes whose names derived from the original American manufacturer, the Weaver Aircraft Company of Ohio. The WACOs comprised the LRDG's aerial wing, the brainchild of Major Guy Prendergast, and he himself flew one with the other piloted by sergeant Trevor Barker, an experienced New Zealander. Prendergast had selected the two WACOs having 'nosed about in Almaza Airport, Cairo'. The more powerful of the two had a Jacobs 285 horsepower engine and was nicknamed 'Big Waco', while 'Small Waco' possessed a Jacobs 225 horsepower engine. Once Prendergast had secured the services of Barker, who had been taught to fly by the celebrated Australian aviator Charles Kingsford Smith, famed in 1928 for making the first Trans-Pacific flight from the USA to Australia, the pair familiarized themselves with the machine at Almaza. Prendergast then 'had the back seats removed and a fold-up canvas seat put in in their place, so that we could carry a wounded man and junk which had to be transported'.

Compact and sturdy, the two aircraft had a small take-off and it was Prendergast's intention to use them to maintain lifelines between Cairo, Siwa and Kufra.

Hampered by the loss of several vehicles in the withdrawal from Mekili, the LRDG was temporarily reorganized by Prendergast into three patrols, commanded by Mitford, Crichton-Stuart and Martin Gibbs. Crichton-Stuart commented later that 'during the month that followed the operational employment of "G" Patrol could be summed up as a) passive misuse and b) active misuse.'

First Crichton-Stuart set off west with his patrol (comprising four 'G' Patrol and two 'Y' Patrol trucks) to try and salvage some of his abandoned vehicles. He was too late, however, and aborted the mission because of the large enemy presence in the area. Next Crichton-Stuart's patrol spent a week observing enemy movements on the track that led from Aujila to Jarabub. The men suffered from heat and tedium, their surveillance 'enlivened only by a football'.

Gibbs' patrol, meanwhile, comprising an equal number of guardsmen and yeomanry, was maintaining a similar watch on the northern approach to Jarabub. The two patrols returned to Siwa in late April, around the time Rommel's Afrika Korps seized the coastal town of Sollum, just inside the Egyptian border and approximately 130 miles north of Jarabub.

Gibbs was therefore detailed to take his patrol and guard 'the immediate approaches to Jarabub'. This mission coincided with what Bill Kennedy Shaw described as the 'worst *qibli* in LRDG history', a heat storm far more merciless than the one his patrol had endured the previous September. For Gibbs and his patrol it was made all the worse by the fact there was no water to be had from the wells around Jarabub: they had been polluted by the Italians during their occupation.

On 10 May Crichton-Stuart was in Jarabub with a unit of Australian engineers. They had already demolished the polluted wells and salvaged a quantity of Italian ammunition. The Australians were all for blowing up the town's white-domed mosque but Crichton-Stuart dissuaded them, pointing out that the Senussi would be outraged at such sacrilege. Towards the evening of the tenth, Crichton-Stuart received a message from Martin Gibbs in which he said his patrol 'was in distress and coming into Jarabub'. They arrived at noon the following day, a pitiful sight, weakened and exhausted by the *qibli*.

Gibbs assured Crichton-Stuart that he had adhered to the principles of their water ration but the heat was too great, their minds and bodies unable to function in the desert furnace. He added: 'The guardsmen couldn't guard, the fitter became unable to fit and the navigator went right off his head and became very violent when asked to navigate. He is a big man and started knocking people about. When he did consent to navigate he was 180 degrees out exactly. Luckily I realized.'

The 'big' navigator in the account given by Gibbs to

Crichton-Stuart was Lofty Carr, who revealed what actually happened. 'It was a terrible heatwave, even by desert standards' he recalled. 'We ran out of water and just had to sit there. We even drank the radiator water, we were really absolutely done.'

The heat was so intense that all the men could do was cower under their trucks, like the terrified birds that Kennedy Shaw had seen the previous year gasping for air by the marker posts. Carr recalled that they called up headquarters on the wireless and reported the situation but the message came back 'Sorry, you can't come back, somebody's got to be there to see if there's any movement.' Gibbs should have ignored the order, used his initiative, but he was a Guards officer and they never disobeyed a command no matter how nonsensical. 'We were lying under the trucks and Gibbs suddenly decided he wanted to be friendly,' recalled Carr. 'Mickey [Coombs] and I were lying under the truck and he crawled under the truck and put his head on Mickey's leg. Mickey just took his leg away. He was too late to try and pal up with us.'

As the situation grew critical and the men began to shrivel in mind and body, Gibbs radioed Crichton-Stuart and 'begged' to come in. 'We were all in a state,' admitted Carr, who was helped into his vehicle by Joe McPike, one of the few men still capable of functioning. 'The navigation was difficult because I was delirious and I said if I've got the bearings right when we come over that ridge we'll be looking down on somewhere . . . recognizable, can't remember where exactly. And I remember coming over the ridge in the vehicle and the next thing I remembered is Sandle and McPike looking after me.'

By an extraordinary force of will, Carr had kept navigating until he saw the white dome of Jarabub away in the distance. When he came to, he was tended by Stan Sandle, 'Y' Patrol's medical orderly. 'Sandle was built like the side of a house, an enormous bloke and the kindest bloke you ever met,' said Carr. 'I woke up and I was in Sandle's lap and he was bathing my lips with salt water, and he was telling me "I have a beautiful sister in Bristol and after the war I'm going to introduce you." He never did.'

Crichton-Stuart saw the state of the patrol and ordered their evacuation to Siwa. He suggested to Gibbs that it might be an idea to stop at 'the salt lake at the eastern end of the Jarabub depression' and bathe their bodies. The lake was called Melfa, and Carr recalled: 'We couldn't drink the water of course, but we were up to our necks in it, it was four to five feet deep in places. We were floating little paper boats on it.' They didn't stay long at the lake, driven away by flies as big as wasps that hovered over their heads in their thousands.

When they arrived at Siwa the patrol was examined by a medical officer and several were evacuated to hospital in Cairo. 'I was put in a mental ward under observation for a fortnight,' recalled Gibbs, 'in the next bed to an old man who was under the impression that he had lost three Mobile Bath Units.'

Upon discharge from hospital, Gibbs spent another six weeks convalescing and then rejoined the Coldstream Guards. One of his fellow LRDG officers reflected: 'Poor Martin Gibbs. Heat exhaustion can be a very nasty experience . . . [he] may have left things a little too long before he realized what had struck them.'

Gibbs was an excellent army officer, but his milieu was the Guards, not a unit such as the LRDG. 'We were regarded by some as an undisciplined, wild rabble,' recalled Carr, who rejoined the unit after a short spell of leave. 'But anyone who didn't fit in, didn't meet the LRDG etiquette, was gone. They just went at a moment's notice. We had discipline but it was LRDG discipline, not the Army's. We didn't think much of Army discipline because the self-discipline that we needed in the LRDG was a lot more demanding.'

Gordon Harrison, who had also survived the patrol, never forgot the words of Ralph Bagnold not long after arriving at the Citadel in 1941. 'He told us, "I have a most difficult job for you to do. You must forget everything the army ever taught you and learn to use your own initiative."' It's a very difficult thing to do. In the Yorkshire Hussars, or many regular units in the British Army, you nearly ask permission to blow your nose. In the LRDG you didn't, you used your own initiative.'

Harrison recalled that there were one or two soldiers who

couldn't rise to the challenge and who, at their own request, returned to their regiment and a more regulated life where they simply followed the orders of their officers. 'But few were forcibly returned,' said Harrison, 'which indicates they selected the right people.'

CHAPTER EIGHT

'I just kept going'

May had been a trying month for the LRDG, as it had been for the Allied army as a whole. On 27 May three Afrika Korps assault groups had driven the British out of the Halfaya Pass, the strategically important escarpment just inside the Egyptian border with Libya. The enemy, noted General Rommel, 'fled in panic to the east, leaving considerable booty and material of all kinds in our hands'.

The next day, 28 May, a gloomy General Wavell lamented the fact that his 'infantry tanks are really too slow for a battle in the desert'. Easy prey for the German 88 mm anti-tank guns, the British armoured corps had suffered heavy casualties since the arrival of the Afrika Korps but Wavell nonetheless retained his belief that he would 'succeed in driving the enemy west of Tobruk'.

As Wavell prepared to launch Operation Battleaxe in mid-June, he received a complaint from Ralph Bagnold 'as to the misuse of the LRDG patrols' in the preceding weeks. Teddy Mitford in particular had agitated for a more 'active employment' rather than acting as garrison troops in Jarabub and fetching and carrying supplies to Mersa Matruh. Additionally, an outbreak of malaria among the LRDG patrols stationed at Siwa brought the unit to its knees. 'It must have been just about the most malarial place in North Africa,' recalled Gordon Harrison. Eventually a doctor, described by General Wavell as a 'malariologist', was dispatched to Siwa and he brought with him a large jar of quinine. 'The dosage was to drink as much from the jar before being sick,' said Harrison.

In June 1941 the LRDG published its inaugural magazine. It was called *Tracks*, and provided the unit with a timely fillip. Illustrated by Signalman John Maxfield, designed by trooper B.F. Shepherd and edited by sergeant N.A. Moore, Bagnold's clerk, *Tracks* enlightened, entertained and amused in equal measure. There were jokes, cartoons, puzzles, poems, a short story by Moore, and an article by Bill Kennedy Shaw on the history of Kufra. There were two things, however, that stood out in the magazine. The first was the sketch on the cover of the unit's new badge, depicting a scorpion beneath which was the inscription '*Non Vi Sed Arte*' (Not by Strength by Guile).

Confusion surrounds the origin of the badge. A legend arose that it was the creation of 'Bluey' Grimsey, the New Zealand navigator of 'R2' Patrol, who was stung by a scorpion while resting on patrol at Taiserbo, 157 miles north-west of Kufra. 'I was rudely awakened by an extremely sharp stabbing pain in my right shoulder blade, in my elbow and again on the back of my hand,' recalled Grimsey. 'In the morning I found a dead scorpion in my blankets.' Grimsey called over his mates who all roared with laughter, finding it hilarious that the scorpion had come off worse in their duel.

'This became quite a joke and the scorpion was taken back to Kufra in spirit,' said Grimsey. 'Time passed and then again at Kufra I received a note from HQ in Cairo with a scorpion, which I think was mine, asking me to design a badge. This I did and this is how the official badge came to be designed by me.'

But Grimsey was adamant he was bitten by the scorpion on 9 June 1941, just days before the publication of the LRDG magazine with the sketch of the scorpion on its front cover. A more feasible explanation as to the badge's creation came from Teddy Mitford. During his pre-war expedition to Kufra Mitford encountered some Fiat CR.32 fighter biplanes that were part of the Italian air force that flew between East Africa and Libya. The aircraft belonging to 93 Squadron had painted on their fuselage a black scorpion within a blue wheel. 'When I joined the LRDG I thought what a good idea to have a badge like that. So I said to Bagnold 'what about having a badge, a scorpion inside a wheel?' He said "good idea, let's do that." Then I got one of my soldiers, Bluey Grimsey, a New Zealander, to draw the thing properly, which he did, and it worked very well . . . this was accepted by GHQ.' Mitford's story was corroborated by Bill Kennedy Shaw who credited Grimsey with 'some hand in the design'.

The second eye-catching feature of the LRDG magazine was the editorial, written, naturally, by the unit's commander.

> It is just one year ago that my ideas for the formation of Long Range Patrols were approved by General Wavell. Within the space of six weeks the original patrols were collected and equipped, forward dumps were made and the Sand Sea was crossed for the first time by a military party. Since then the unit has more than achieved the purpose for which it was designed. It has in fact become famous, not only for the exploits of individual patrols but for its ability to exist and to move about over a desert and in a climate both of which had been thought impossible for any military force.

Bagnold – 'Bags' or 'Baggers' to most of his men – praised the unit for the work, singling out their patrols from Kufra for particular acclaim, and asked for forbearance in their current predicament. 'We are at the moment doing jobs both in the north and the south, for which the unit was not designed, but which, on the other hand, no other unit in the British Army could have done.'

It was Bagnold's final two paragraphs that caused a collective intake of breath from his men, for he had an announcement to make. 'I now leave the LRDG with the knowledge that it has more action and useful work in front of it, against an enemy for whom new methods must be evolved,' he wrote. 'May I thank all ranks for their hard work and ready cooperation, and wish the unit the best of luck for the future.'

It was a typical Bagnold gesture. Though he might have detested organized sport at school, he was a quintessential 'team player', and by the early summer of 1941 recognized he was no longer the man to lead the LRDG. Selfless, dutiful and devoid of egoism, Bagnold stepped aside. To his close associates he blamed the heat, 'which was terrific' and as a consequence of which his health 'was beginning to suffer, so I thought it was time to quit'.

But there was another reason for leaving, to which Bagnold alluded in his resignation letter to his men. The LRDG was now confronted by 'an enemy for whom new methods must be evolved'; in other words, the Afrika Korps. Bagnold suspected he was too old and worn out, so he decided to hand the baton to Guy Prendergast. He had already shown he had the ingenuity in raising an aerial wing and Bagnold had no doubt he was leaving the unit in the best possible hands.

Prendergast was punctilious in all he did, be it planning a military operation or combing his hair. He was rarely seen unshaven and his one concession to the idiosyncratic nature of the LRDG was a pair of round sunglasses. He was not a demonstrative man and, like most Britons of his class and generation he disapproved of any man who was. At least one officer who encountered Prendergast in the North Africa war found him 'unapproachable', and he was certainly not a commanding officer who courted affection. He wasn't interested in what his men thought of him, only in ensuring that as many of them as possible survived the war. One LRDG officer, Alastair Timpson, said that Prendergast's 'painstaking precision' was his overriding contribution to the success of the LRDG. 'He felt it was necessary to be in a position at all times to give and receive orders. That meant being next to a wireless set or telephone night and day.' Another, David Lloyd Owen, described Prendergast as a 'man of high ideals and puritan steadfastness'. Yet he was no killjoy. It often appeared that he got a vicarious thrill from hearing about the escapades of some of his more dissolute men on leave in Cairo.

* * *

On 6 June Captain Pat McCraith rejoined the LRDG at Siwa, arriving from Cairo with a batch of new trucks to replace the ones lost in recent patrols. The following day 'Y' Patrol returned from Jarabub and the unit underwent another reorganization: 'Y', 'G' and a new temporary patrol, 'H', were equiped with McCraith leading 'Y', Crichton-Stuart 'G' and Jake Easonsmith 'H'. All three patrols comprised six trucks and were issued with similar instructions, 'the conveyance of agents to the interior of Cyrenaica and the collection of their reports, and with gathering geographical information about the country south of the Jebel-el-Akhdar'. Additionally, in June 1941, the unit's Survey Section was raised under the instruction of Bill Kennedy Shaw. Ken Lawrence was recruited into the section by Bagnold, having just spent four months mapping in the Northern District of Kenya. Lawrence was informed that the LRDG intended to survey five desert expanses: Calansho Serir, Calansho Sand Sea, Big Cairn, Kufra and El Riquba, a total area of approximately 95,000 square miles. His task was to map Kufra. 'An Arab accompanied me in the hope that he could recognize the country and name some of the topographical features which were prominent,' remembered Lawrence. 'It turned out the Arab was of no use at all . . . he was an old man used to walking with camels at two miles an hour and sitting up in the back of an old truck travelling at 35–40 mph, I think he just lost all conception of distance, time and became thoroughly confused.'

McCraith's orders were to take a British agent up into the Jebel south-east of Slonta, approximately 200 miles inside Axis territory. The spy, known to McCraith as Captain Taranto, was then to head off in his own 'light van' to a rendezvous with a pro-British Arab sheik.

'The outward journey of over 350 miles took two and a half days of hard driving,' recalled McCraith. 'In crossing an unavoidable and notoriously difficult area of rock and stone we broke five or six mainsprings and thus all the spares we carried.' On the first night they laagered, Taranto surprised McCraith by producing a bottle of Weasel Brand Gin. It was firewater and McCraith began to have doubts about the agent's suitability.

They arrived in the Gebel without incident and then Taranto, accompanied by the patrol fitter, drove on with a promise he would return in three days. In fact it was four days before the pair returned, Taranto confessing it had taken a bit of 'time to find the sheik due to the fact that he lost his way soon after leaving me'.

McCraith ordered his men to break camp and they set off for Siwa. Two of his men were delirious with malaria and the captain feared they had already stayed too long behind enemy lines. An hour into their journey McCraith's truck broke a mainspring. There were no more spare parts so McCraith ordered the vehicle's abandonment. His sergeant had other ideas. Jock Carningham was a fitter of great ingenuity, a thirty-year-old Scot regarded by Lofty Carr and other younger members of 'Y' Patrol as a surrogate uncle. Using leather bootlaces, wire, metal and wood he bound and wedged the spring and confidently asserted it would see them back to base. McCraith demurred so Carningham bet him a bottle of whiskey. 'We duly arrived safely in Siwa and my sergeant received his bottle of whisky,' recalled McCraith.

There was a surprise waiting for the patrol when they drove into Siwa, their clothes so rancid that McCraith burned his within the hour. There to greet them was Tich Cave. After the handshakes and congratulatory slaps, the men gathered round to hear his tale.

For the first four days of his capture he and the other British prisoners were loosely corralled by the Italians at Mekili. On the fourth day the Germans arrived, bringing some organization to Cave's imprisonment. The prisoners were loaded into a convoy of seven trucks and transported north-west, in the direction of the coastal town of Derna. After a while the convoy halted and they were told to dismount, stretch their legs, and answer the call of nature. To Cave's unbridled joy they had halted close to what had once been a British dump. 'There were boots all over the place, socks, shirts, odd tins of food, ammo, guns, and all sorts of things lying around,' recalled Cave. 'I hunted around and eventually found a pair of boots because I only had my chaplis, those Indian sandals, and I thought, if I was going to do a lot of walking, boots would be necessary.'*

Once in Derna the prisoners – 1,500 in total – were locked up in an old Italian army barracks, close to which was a standpipe that the men used as a shower. Bathed and fed, and generally more content with life, Cave spent the rest of the day reconnoitring the camp for a means of escape. It was a standard army camp, a lot of low buildings and high fences. He soon identified a means of escape, a corner of the camp next to the cookhouse where an RAF bomb had blown a hole in the fence. The hole had been repaired but Cave reckoned it was possible for a small man like him to squeeze through the gap. Once outside he estimated it would take five days to walk the 100 miles to Tobruk provided he had two full water bottles, some biscuits and a few tins of bully beef.

Cave glanced at the faces of his LRDG comrades as he broke off from his story. 'How naive can you be!' he exclaimed.

Cave knew it was foolhardy to escape into the desert alone. He needed an accomplice, someone with whom he could share the privations of what would surely be an epic trek. Unfortunately, Cave explained, nobody was willing to risk an escape. 'I started touting and hawking myself round the camp,' he said. 'I started with the privates, I went to the sergeants, the senior NCOs and eventually I went down to see this captain who had been captured alongside me and asked him whether he would like to escape with me. He said "No way."' After ten days Cave gave up, angry and disappointed with what he regarded as the pusillanimous attitude of his compatriots.

He decided he would have to go on his own. The next night he slipped out of his barrack and made his way across the camp towards the cookhouse. Turning a corner he bumped into a sentry. Cave reacted first, felling the Italian soldier with a blow to the

* Chaplis were another innovation brought by Bagnold to the LRDG from his desert exploration days. 'If you were in sand it was nice to wear Chaplis because the sand went in and out,' recalled Lofty Carr.

head. He ran off into the night not knowing where he was headed. 'As I shot round the corner to open the door, a large hand grabbed me by the scruff of the neck and I was picked up and dumped through a doorway into this small room,' Cave squinted up into the faces of 'six very large, angry-looking Australians'.

The leader of the Australians was Alfred Potter. He listened as Cave explained what had just happened. He also wanted to hear more of the Englishman's escape plan. It was not long before Potter signed up to the idea. They spent ten days husbanding food and then set out one evening, slipping through the fence without detection. Cave and Potter turned south and headed for a steep cliff that took them till daylight to climb. 'Morning found us close to the top but unfortunately the vegetation we had been able to haul ourselves up with finished about fifteen feet from the top and the rest was bare rock, slightly concave,' said Cave. The pair slithered to the top and spent an hour recovering their strength. From their vantage point they could see 'Gazala airfield covered with aircraft and men'. This was no time to admire the view, however, they had to cover as much ground as possible while they still had a plentiful supply of water.

For two days and nights they continued towards Tobruk, but by sundown on 26 May they were down to their last few drops of water. There was a German camp away in the distance, close to the sea. They would have water. Cave and Potter drew lots to see who would steal it. Cave lost. He infiltrated the camp unseen, sliding under a truck and edging his way towards a four-gallon jerrycan of water (It was well known in the LRDG that if a German jerrycan had a white cross daubed on its side it contained water, otherwise petrol). Just as Cave reached for the can a face appeared under the truck and a voice said '*Was ist das?*'

'To say I was scared was to put it mild,' Cave exclaimed. 'So I did the first thing which came into my head. I had Alf's empty water bottle in my hand and I hurled it at this figure's head and at the same time I let out a screech which would have done justice to a Comanche warrior, and I shot out from under the truck like a bullet.'

Cave ran for his life. He heard a shout, the bark of a dog and the crack of a rifle shot. His boots, already coming apart, disintegrated as he sprinted across the beach towards the surf he could see breaking in the moonlight. 'I just kept going,' explained Cave. 'I ran until I could run no longer.' Then he walked, stumbled, reeled along the beach until, exhausted, he lay down on the sand and slept. 'When I awoke the sun was shining on my face, otherwise I would probably have carried on sleeping. I sat up in a hurry and looked to the west and there was nothing but the sandy shore stretching away as far as I could see. I turned to the east and there again the beach stretched away as far as I could see.'

Cave struck out east. By now his water was gone and his tongue was cracked and swollen, too big, it felt, for his mouth. Shortly after sundown he came to a mass of wire entanglements stretching from the land into the sea. With the same bloody-minded defiance that had carried him so far, Cave stripped off the rags of his uniform and 'wriggled my way through the wire', emerging the other side cut and bleeding. He crawled on his hands and knees to a large rock and sat for a few moments with his back to it, recovering. A light wind was blowing along the beach but suddenly Cave thought he heard another sound. 'I was aware of voices and I began to wonder whether I was really hearing them or imagining them,' said Cave. He strained to hear the accent. It wasn't German, definitely not, nor Italian. But it wasn't English. Then the voices stopped. Cave told himself he was going mad. Then they started again. 'I thought the only thing I can do is to shout,' he said. 'So I tried to shout but nothing came out. I tried again and a grunt came out. I thought this really won't do, you really must shout, shout. I tried again and something like a scream came out and the voices stopped and there was a clatter of rifle bolts and a voice said in English, "Come up with your hands up."'

Cave had reached Tobruk. The Indian soldiers gave him a mug of hot tea, wrapped him in hot blankets, and listened in amazement as Cave recounted how he had simply wriggled through their wire entanglements and escaped unscathed through the minefield either side. A few hours later the Indians brought in Alf

Potter, who explained to an overjoyed Cave how he too had made it to Tobruk after they had split up.

The next morning the two men were taken to Army HQ in Tobruk and debriefed by Military Intelligence, who were anxious to learn about the enemy positions between them and Derna. The officer in charge was Henry Frederick Thynne, the Viscount of Weymouth, who had been Cave's squadron commander in the Wiltshire Yeomanry. 'He obviously didn't recognize me,' recalled Cave. 'I doubt if my own mother would have recognized me. My hair was down to my shoulders. I had a straggly sort of a beard and a very tattered and torn shirt and pair of shorts, bare feet and my water bottle – I still hung on to my water bottle which was now full and I intended it to stay full.'

Satisfied that he had gleaned all the intelligence he could from the pair, Viscount Weymouth asked Cave what he wanted to do. 'I want to get back to my unit,' replied Cave. A week later Cave boarded a vessel to Alexandria and from there he cadged a lift to Siwa. He arrived wearing an Australian bush hat, a parting gift from Alfred Potter.

CHAPTER NINE

'Courage was a word none of us liked'

General Wavell launched his offensive – codenamed Operation Battleaxe – on 15 June, with the intention of pushing the Axis forces out of Cyrenaica and relieving the pressure on the besieged port of Tobruk. The assault failed, the British armour destroyed by the German 88 mm guns in Halfaya Pass, renamed 'Hellfire Pass' by the Allies. 'The three-day battle has ended in complete victory,' wrote Rommel to his wife on 18 June. 'I'm going to go round the troops today to thank them and issue orders.'

Despite his success at repelling the British attack, Rommel was unable to capitalize on his triumph by pushing into Egypt. His lines of supply and communication were now stretched precariously thin and the Allied garrison still holding out in Tobruk – to his rear – caused him concern. Nevertheless, a week after the victory Rommel wrote again to his wife, declaring the 'joy of the Afrika troops over this latest victory is tremendous . . . now the enemy can come, he'll get an even bigger beating.'

The failure of Operation Battleaxe cost General Wavell his job. He was replaced as commander-in-chief by Claude Auchinleck with Lieutenant General William Gott succeeding O'Creagh as commander of the 7th Armoured Division. The Allied defeat at Halfaya Pass also had repercussions for the Long Range Desert Group. Michael Crichton-Stuart was recalled to the 2nd Battalion Scots Guards, who had suffered heavy casualties during the failed offensive, and Major Teddy Mitford posted to the 1st Battalion

Royal Tank Regiment. Carr was dismayed to learn of Mitford's departure and rumours circulated among 'Y' Patrol that he had been removed because the antics of his infamous cousins (Diana Mitford was married to Oswald Mosley, leader of the British Union of Fascists, while Unity counted Adolf Hitler among her friends) had left him tainted by association. That seemed unlikely, given Mitford's posting to the Tank Regiment. More probably, concluded Carr, was the fact that 'Mitford was a wonderful tactician but a hopeless administrator . . . When we arrived at Jarabub he did nothing about sanitation, nothing about anything, and half the unit went down with dysentery.' He'd also managed to ruin the 'Going Maps' that Carr had painstakingly produced during the preceding six months. 'These were maps we made as we traversed the desert,' explained Carr. 'I noted down everything. There was a lot of invaluable information on them. I handed them to Mitford and he just stuck them in a map case and allowed the silverfish to eat them. Silverfish were little insects in the desert that liked to eat paper. We'd been warned about them.'

British reverses elsewhere in the war with Germany also had deleterious consequences for the LRDG. Pat McCraith's regiment, the Sherwood Rangers Yeomanry, had lost several officers in the battle for Crete so he too was recalled.

His loss was a particular blow for 'Y' Patrol. 'A lot of officers in the army were resentful of soldiers who displayed any intelligence or initiative, but not McCraith,' reflected Carr. 'He was a fussy fellow, a solicitor before the war, who would spend the whole night before any operation checking every item personally so that the QM [quartermaster] would be at his wit's end.'

Everyone in the LRDG was a specialist, and McCraith's expertise lay in logistics. 'He was the sort of officer who is just right for starting a unit rather than going on to run it,' said Carr. But McCraith's diligence exacted a toll. He suffered from the 'loneliness of the patrol commander', the strain of responsibility eating away at his peace of mind. He later confided to Mickey Coombs that this was a factor in his having offered no objection when summoned by his parent unit.

The description of McCraith's character could, perhaps, be applied also to Bagnold, whom Carr had got to know well in June and July.

Although he had announced his departure from the LRDG in June, Bagnold was to remain in command until Prendergast officially took over on 1 August. Throughout July Prendergast spent much of his time in Siwa and Kufra, as the LRDG continued to ferry agents across the desert and carry out reconnaissance of the Axis positions.

Bagnold in contrast remained in Egypt, interviewing candidates to fill the gaps in the LRDG's ranks, and also exploiting contacts from his days as a desert explorer. On these missions he took Lofty Carr with him as his driver and navigator. 'The bond I formed with Bagnold was spontaneous, we just got on together,' recalled Carr. Approximately 375 miles south of Cairo lies the town of Kharga, the most southerly of Egypt's five desert oases, and a hotbed of espionage for both sides during the war. 'Bagnold had a lot of contacts with the Senussi headmen there but he couldn't be seen to talk to them or as soon as he left they would be bumped off,' recalled Carr. 'So I would drive Bagnold in a truck to a point in the desert where we would meet the headmen. Then once the meeting was over I would drive him back.'

Bagnold was twenty-four years Carr's senior, old enough to be his father, and so on their long journeys to and from Kharga he imparted some of his knowledge and experience to the young navigator. 'He told me that when you're faced with a problem, you begin by discarding the first three solutions and then you start thinking of ways to solve the problem. You do that because the first three solutions will always be anticipated [by the enemy] but not those ones when you've been thinking hard.'

Bagnold had other little mottos that stuck in Carr's head: 'A plan is something to stick to unless something unless turns up'; 'Always be the master of your plan not the plan be your master'; 'Make sure you're running to something and not away from something.'

For his part, Bagnold was amused by Carr's youth, and its

accompanying characteristics. 'He liked my callowness,' reflected Carr. 'Once we were having a discussion about whether navigation was art or science, and I described it as "the art of getting lost scientifically." He liked that.'

Sometimes the pair 'mused'. Carr remembered one particular discussion about the word that has haunted every soldier of every army since time immemorial. '"Courage" was a word none of us liked,' said Carr. 'One of the things I speculated with Bagnold about was whether people started with a reservoir of courage and then, as they were put under stress, it gradually went down until it was extinguished. Or did your courage increase with the more action you saw and the more experienced you became? Bagnold never offered a solution, he offered examples that made me think.'

One of the men interviewed by Bagnold in the late summer of 1941 as a potential LRDG officer was David Lloyd Owen. Well-educated, well-connected and well-bred, the twenty-three-year-old had served with the Queen's Royal Regiment in the Western Desert, commanding a company during the destruction of the Italian army in December 1940. Lloyd Owen's reward for leading his men so ably was, in the best traditions of the British Army, baffling. He was posted to the Officer Cadet Training Unit (OCTU) in Cairo in charge of administration. 'I was about at my wits' end and loathing every minute of it all,' recalled Lloyd Owen. Fortunately his connections intervened. He had first heard of the LRDG from Martin Gibbs, convalescing in Cairo having returned from the desert 'rather stricken with the effect of the sun'. Intrigued by the unit's exploits, Lloyd Owen used his friendship with Joan Wavell, the youngest of the general's three daughters, to arrange an interview with Ralph Bagnold.

Lloyd Owen was a self-confessed 'dreamer' when it came to the desert, a young man reared on the stories he'd read in P.C. Wren's *Beau Geste* and the thrilling tales recounted by T.E. Lawrence in *Seven Pillars of Wisdom*. 'It was in this frame of mind, determined to be chosen for the LRDG, that I went off to see Colonel Bagnold in his office in GHQ,' wrote Lloyd Owen. 'I knew practically nothing of him save that he was said to be a bit remote, austere and somewhat of a mystic.'

Lloyd Owen dressed up for the occasion, immaculate in his 'best tunic with a Sam Browne belt'. Bagnold's response was a withering look and the first of many cold, stammered questions.

'Why do you want to come to us?'

'Well, sir,' replied Lloyd Owen. 'I have heard a lot about you from various friends and I am keen to come and have a crack at the kind of life.'

Bagnold was not impressed. Nor was he when Lloyd Owen admitted he couldn't speak Arabic, knew nothing about Ford trucks and had never fired a Lewis gun.

'What *do* you know?' he asked.

The disdain in Bagnold's voice was unmistakable. Lloyd Owen felt he was on the brink of bursting into tears. Now he was the one stammering.

'Not much, sir. But I am dreadfully keen and sure I can learn.'

Bagnold got to his feet and disappeared into an adjoining room. Lloyd Owen could hear the low murmur of his voices. The other voice was that of Guy Prendergast (recently promoted to lieutenant colonel) who, as the commanding-officer elect, was listening in on the interview. After a few minutes Bagnold reappeared and curtly informed Lloyd Owen that 'he wanted me to take over the Yeomanry patrol from Pat McCraith and he bade me goodbye'.

Bagnold and Prendergast also toured transit camps and infantry depots in search of new recruits to the ranks of the LRDG, but not all the men in the Middle East were as thrilled at the prospect of a Lawrence of Arabia lifestyle as David Lloyd Owen. Alexander Stewart was a bored twenty-one-year-old in the Armoured Troops Workshop of the Royal Army Ordnance Corps when Bagnold and Prendergast arrived one morning at his depot. 'As we listened in a big marquee the bulk of the troops walked out,' recalled Stewart, a Scot from Banffshire. But he was attracted to what he heard and what he envisaged. 'It would be a minimum of discipline, army discipline, and free from parades and drills and so on.'

Guardsman Spencer Seardon was recovering from a leg infection at a Left Out of Battle camp when Bagnold arrived in search of recruits. 'A notice came up asking for volunteers,' recalled Seardon, who shared a ridge tent with eight other convalescing soldiers. 'So we said we would all go up and join the LRDG [because] we were fed up in this camp, there was nothing much to do . . . we went up and one by one they came out and they said, "Blimey Spence, we're not joining that mob, they're a suicide squad."'

Seardon's attitude was different. 'I wanted to fight the war and get on with it,' he reflected. For their part, the LRDG were in search of men skilled in the use of the Lewis Gun, so Seardon was accepted, as was Jim Patch, a slightly built twenty-one-year-old Londoner with a young, inquisitive face. Before the war Patch had worked for the Post Office and on being called-up in May 1940 he was sent to Scarborough to train as a wireless operator. From there his unit was posted to the Middle East in May 1941 (Patch using the voyage out to learn German) where he was billeted in a tent full of bugs, waiting for something to happen. 'One morning a little officer turned up on the parade and said he was calling for volunteers for the LRDG,' said Patch. 'We'd never heard of but it sounded all right so my friend, Bill Morrison and I, volunteered.'

The 'little officer' was a South African, Second-Lieutenant Paul Eitzen, or 'Blitz', as he was better known. Having recruited Patch and Morrison to his artillery section he escorted them to Kufra and upon arriving they were interviewed by Prendergast. He asked Eitzen why he required two signallers in his gun crew. Eitzen explained it was necessary to communicate between the observation post and gun. 'The colonel accepted that,' recalled Patch, 'and we were introduced to the gun, which was a 25-pounder, mounted on the back of a 10-ton lorry, a Mack.' The artillery section had been Bagnold's idea, an innovation bequeathed to Prendergast. It was thought 'that it would be attractive to be able to knock holes in any Italian fort'.

On 24 September the Western Desert Force was reformed as the Eighth Army under the command of Lieutenant General Sir Alan Cunningham. The LRDG was placed under his authority, and a decision was taken to abandon the raising of any other specialist units to undertake similar roles to the Desert Group, save for a small sixty-strong force, L Detachment, currently training at Kabrit under the command of Captain David Stirling.*

The reasoning behind this was that (a) there was a shortage of suitable men willing to volunteer and (b) Cunningham and his superior, General Claude Auchinleck, were confident that with a large-scale offensive planned for November, victory in North Africa would soon be theirs.

On the same day that the Eighth Army came into being, Bagnold wrote from Cairo to Prendergast, whose headquarters were at Kufra. He began by reassuring his successor that the transfer of the LRDG to the Eighth Army 'is quite all right as far as you are concerned'. He continued:

> Cunningham now understands perfectly well that he was a bit hasty in his first reaction to the news that he was getting the unit under him. And the C-in-C [Auchinleck] went out of his way to assure me that he would personally see that the unit was not mishandled and that we could count on him as a friend.

However, cautioned Bagnold, a 're-orientation of outlook will be necessary'. He advised Prendergast to seek advice from Bagush, the British military camp close to Mersa Matruh, rather than Cairo, which, as far as intelligence went, 'was completely out of it'.

Bagnold then offered his thoughts on what Prendergast should do about administration, supplies, the mobile medical unit and the signal section. He mentioned Eitzen's artillery section but warned it would be a further two weeks before it was anywhere near fully trained. There were problems once more with General Freyberg, commander of the New Zealand forces in Egypt, and

---

* Known initially as L Detachment, Special Air Service Brigade, in order to fool the enemy into believing an airborne brigade had arrived in the Middle East, Stirling's force became better known from 1942 onwards as the SAS. For the sake of clarity I will refer to them hereafter as the SAS.

Bagnold informed Prendergast that 'things are such in a muddle with the NZ people between what they say and what they write that I really think you should never rely or act on any more verbal arrangements with them.'

Five days later, on 29 September, a conference was held at Eighth Army HQ, attended by both Prendergast and Bagnold, in which the role of the LRDG was discussed. A major operation was brewing, and the LRDG were told they would have a small but significant part to play. Their tasks, as laid out in the conference minutes, would be as follows:

(a) To obtain information as to enemy movements on certain tracks, and in certain areas, and to watch his reactions to any offensive by us.
(b) To provide further information of the state of the going [the desert surface] in certain areas.
(c) At all times the LRDG should try and harass the enemy as far as possible, and in any way they liked provided they do not get too involved themselves. The army commander realizes that the LRDG should not deliberately court trouble, and is in no way armoured.
(d) Any tactical information obtained would be required as early as possible. During and before offensive operations, LRDG would be justified in taking more risks than usual in order to send back up-to-date information.

CHAPTER TEN

'Just be natural'

The Guards and Yeomanry patrols had returned to Cairo at the end of August for a rest and refit. 'Y' Patrol met their new officers, David Lloyd Owen and an older man called Frank Simms, formerly of the Royal Warwickshire Regiment. Simms was thirty-two and not a particularly imposing figure at first glance. Nor was Lloyd Owen, and the men of 'Y' Patrol looked at both with initial disdain. 'Lloyd Owen was a pretty boy,' recalled Lofty Carr. 'Effeminate, with a high voice. Simms had a voice like someone pretending to be homosexual. But talk about appearances belying the truth.'

Born into a military family, Lloyd Owen's early years had followed a similar trajectory to many young men of his background – in his case Winchester and Sandhurst before being commission into the prestigious Queen's Royal Regiment. He had dark good looks, the sort of face some women would yearn to mother, and often his eyes glinted with a look of schoolboy mischief. But already in his brief military career, Lloyd Owen had proved himself a more than able soldier.

Initially 'Y' Patrol feared that neither would be up to the job. Lloyd Owen sensed their scepticism. 'At first, they rather frightened me because they looked so bronzed, so fit, so purposeful,' he admitted. 'They were mostly countrymen, and thus knew how to move silently and how to outwit their enemy, for they had done it often enough as poachers. They were the salt of the English earth.'

The Guards Patrol also had a couple of new officers in Captain

Tony Hay, recently arrived from the Coldstream Guards to replace Michael Stuart-Crichton, and Lieutenant Alastair Timpson of the Scots Guards. Upon arriving in Cairo a few weeks earlier Timpson had been summoned to see Guy Prendergast in his room at the Shepheard's Hotel. That evening over dinner Prendergast briefed Timpson on the LRDG, and what would be expected of him as a patrol commander. Timpson listened intently before Prendergast broke off momentarily as a tall, slim young officer presented himself at the table. The officer introduced himself as Captain David Stirling. It was the first time the pair had met. Prendergast listened impassively as Stirling 'told him of his plans for forming a new parachute unit'.

Timpson recalled that the 'business of refitting in Cairo dragged on interminably'. The Rhodesian Patrol was also undergoing an overhaul, turning Abbassia barracks into a hive of activity. 'Trucks cluttered up the main square and crowded the alleyways by the storerooms, but not like an orderly vehicle park, for few were stationary for long,' recalled Timpson. 'Certain trucks needed adaptation to carry wireless sets and for the contrivance which enabled them to recharge wireless batteries by their own locomotion. Other workshops had not finished the gun mountings . . . or the chronometers and theodolites had not returned from overhaul by the experts of precision instruments.'

Time dragged. Everyone wanted to be out of Cairo and on their way to Kufra. Finally, on 9 October 1941, they were all ready to depart. One of the new recruits to 'G' Patrol was Cyril Richardson, a tall, strong-jawed native of Horsham in Sussex, who had joined the 3rd Battalion Coldstream Guards in 1936 at the age of eighteen. The following year he had sailed with his battalion to the Middle East, spending more than two years in policing duties in Egypt and Palestine. Boredom had led him to the Long Range Desert Group, and so excited was he at the prospect of what awaited he opened a log, beginning:

> We left Cairo about four o'clock in the afternoon, camping for the night outside of Mena [a few miles south-west of the

> Egyptian capital]. We were up at dawn the next day, the 10-10-41, and started on our thousand-odd-mile journey.
>
> The trip along the Nile Valley to me, who was making the journey for the first time, was a wonderful never-to-be-forgotten experience. The big cumbersome barges loaded with huge bales of cotton sail down the Nile in a never ending stream. Our trucks, about thirty in all, consisting of 'Y' Patrol, HQ and our own 'G' Patrol, created quite a lot of excitement while passing through the little native villages, which are strung along the banks of this historic river along its entire length.
>
> Tins of any sort are prized among the villagers. We amused ourselves by throwing them into the Nile and watching the lads swim out for them.

The column halted for the night at Minya, a city approximately 150 miles south of Cairo, parking up on a racecourse. There was a cinema nearby and many soldiers ambled off to take in a movie. Cyril Richardson stayed on the racecourse. 'When I left Cairo I was prepared to forget cinemas, bar and the luxuries of town life for at least a month,' he wrote in his log. 'And I did not wish to go back so early on my resolutions.'

The column moved off at seven the next morning and the following day reached Kharga where the men had the opportunity to bathe in a swimming pool and barter for eggs and watermelons with the locals. Richardson soon discovered Kharga was not the picture book idyll it looked at first glance. 'I would like to spend four or five pages describing the tortures we endured from flies and mosquitoes at night,' he wrote. 'After the first night we had to move ten miles from the village owing to mosquitoes, but even then we could not sleep so we moved even further away.'

The column was obliged to remain outside Kharga for several days while repairs were made to some vehicles. Eventually they continued on their journey, crossing 450 miles of desert to Kufra. 'We arrived at Kufra rather a dirty, unshaven crowd,' recorded

Richardson in his log. 'But nevertheless happy, on the morning of 19-10-41.' Going without a daily shave was a novel experience for the guardsmen and some found the habit hard to break. The desert soon punished their fastidiousness. First the sun beat down on the freshly shaved faces and then fine particles of sand, whipped across the desert by the wind, combined to 'nearly tear your skin off'.

Prendergast was there to meet them, so too Bill Kennedy Shaw and Tim Heywood, the officer in charge of the signal section. David Lloyd Owen was smitten by what he found in his new home. 'It was so unbelievably peaceful,' he wrote. 'The Arabs with their donkeys padded silently across the sand and only the slight rustle of the palm trees in the breeze would disturb the silence.'

Lloyd Owen's 'Y' Patrol parked their trucks in the shade of some palm trees and were permitted to go for a dip in the two salt lakes close by. Here it was possible 'to lie floating on your back and contemplate the perfection of the blue sky above'.

Lloyd Owen and the other LRDG officers were invited into the officers' mess that Kennedy Shaw had designed the previous April. After formal introductions Prendergast informed the officers that he had reorganized the patrols: from now on they would be split into two, for example 'Y1' and 'Y2', each comprising five 30-cwt trucks with one smaller pick-up truck. This was because a ten-vehicle patrol was too unwieldy, explained Kennedy Shaw, and too conspicuous from the air.

Prendergast was unable to enlighten his officers as to the precise nature of their role in the forthcoming offensive. He did not know himself, and on 21 October, Prendergast wrote to Rupert Harding-Newman requesting information. The response was apologetic, Harding-Newman explaining that GHQ had drawn up instructions for the LRDG 'but they were not at the moment prepared to issue them'. However his personal opinion was that the offensive would not start for at least another three weeks.

The Yeomanry and Guards Patrols spent a further week at Kufra, training and becoming acquainted with their new officers. 'Y' Patrol was split into two with Frank Simms leading 'Y1' and

Lloyd Owen 'Y2', a division that was not without its teething problems. Lofty Carr recalled that Simms 'pulled rank' on the younger officer when he discovered Lloyd Owen had divided the patrol to his advantage. In front of the men, Simms 'rubbed Lloyd Owen's nose in the dirt' by overruling him on several selections of personnel and equipment.

On 6 November the unit left Kufra and travelled 350 miles north-east to Siwa, assembling at the oasis in their entirety three days later. The HQ established by Prendergast at Siwa was called the Rest House, a stone building built on a rocky outcrop close to the oasis's landing strip – a levelled area of sand strong enough to withstand light aircraft. It was here, recalled David Lloyd Owen, that 'Guy controlled and planned all the movements of the patrols and there was room, too, for the small Group HQ Mess'.

The NCOs and men were billeted elsewhere, some in the former barrack house of the Egyptian army close to the airstrip, where there was also a storeroom and a small hospital. 'Siwa was actually quite a big place,' said Lofty Carr. 'So we would be spread out and we barely met the other patrols, the Rhodesians or Kiwis, because of all the comings and goings.'

Though the men were dispersed throughout Siwa a communal meeting place was one of the oasis's many pools. 'At Siwa we had such magnificent pools that we gave them names,' said Gordon Harrison. '[There was] Cleopatra's, there was the Figure of Eight pool and the bubbly pool which had bubbles rising in the middle . . . They had crystal clear water, about eight to ten feet deep. We would pull up beside them in lorry and just fall out of the lorry into the pool. Oh, it was a feeling!'

On the evening of their arrival at Siwa, Prendergast revealed to his officers over dinner what the LRDG's role would be in the imminent offensive. Present at the table were Lloyd Owen, Simms, Timpson, Hay, Jake Easonsmith, Tim Heywood and Bruce Ballantyne. Most of the talking was done by Bill Kennedy Shaw. He explained that their job was purely reconnaissance, and to each officer he allotted an area in which to operate and 'report in detail on what the enemy does behind his front line'. On no account, emphasized Kennedy Shaw, was any patrol to go looking for trouble. 'It will only give the game away if you do,' he said. 'Your job is to watch and tell me what you see and you can't do that if you are seen yourselves.'

Lloyd Owen's operational area was Bir Tengeder, 'a point in the desert about 150 miles behind our front line on the Egyptian frontier where a number of tracks converged'. It was forty miles south of the coast and on the main route that ran south of the Jebel Akhdar. Frank Simms' instructions were to take Y1 Patrol and observe the Garet Meriem area, thirty-five miles south-west of Gazala and sixty miles west by south of Tobruk.

With dinner finished, and after a brief chat with Tim Heywood, Lloyd Owen drove across the landing strip to brief his patrol. He was apprehensive, in need of some reassurance from the old hands. He found Tich Cave loading cases of petrol onto the trucks. There was no other man he would have wished to see more. Already in the short time he had been with the unit, Lloyd Owen had come to regard Cave as the sort of solid, dependable, perpetually cheerful soldier that every officer needs. 'Tich had the phlegmatic calm of a boy born and bred in the country,' wrote Lloyd Owen. '[He] was often silent and happy with his thoughts for hours on end . . . [but] he had a positive lust for action and loved nothing better than a fight.'

Lloyd Owen gathered his patrol around, including Mickey Coombs, Sergeant Jock Carningham and Alan Denniff, his navigator, and explained their orders. He would leave Denniff to work out the route. He had faith in his ability. Similarly he trusted his patrol to be ready to move off at tomorrow morning at 0800 hours.

Not far away Frank Simms was briefing 'Y1' Patrol. He had selected Lofty Carr as his navigator and the pair had developed a cordial working relationship. 'Simms wasn't a friendly bloke,' recalled Carr. 'But I think we got on with each other because we both liked being left to ourselves, except for a small group of friends. He would talk a lot to me when we were mooching around together behind the lines. It was one way to get to know your officers, miles behind enemy lines, because there's no escaping each other. He had his catchphrase, "Stop the War," and that amused him. One morning after we'd set off Simms realized we had left behind our tin of curry powder so he said "Stop the War, we have to find the curry powder." So I broke all the rules by going back on my own for this 7 lb tin of curry powder.'

Simms was a model of sangfroid as he explained their orders, unlike Lloyd Owen who left his patrol and drove back to the officers' mess in search of Jake Easonsmith. He had questions to ask, advice to seek, and there was no better officer in the LRDG than Easonsmith to calm the nerves of an inexperienced young officer on the eve of his first major test. 'Not only was he a natural leader of men, because he understood men in the kind of way which few others have done, but he was also a master at the art of craft and guile,' reflected Lloyd Owen.

Carr had navigated Easonsmith on several patrols and the pair, both with strong West Country connections, enjoyed each other's company. 'I suffered a lot from desert sores and was often yellow from Acriflavine [a topical antiseptic] and dotted with dirty dressings,' said Carr, 'Jake would always greet me with "Ah, Lofty, in your usual state of decomposition, I see." He had a very good dry sense of humour but he was a man you wouldn't want to tangle with. One time we stopped a German lorry and Jake told them to climb out of the cab. He had a Tommy Gun – most of us didn't like the Tommy, but Jake did – and as the German stepped down he stuck the muzzle in his stomach. Suddenly this German dropped a grenade at his feet. Jake threw him on it and stepped out of the way.'

Easonsmith belonged to that rare breed of men who, having being thrust into the army, realized they had found their true vocation. Regular soldiers might have had years more experience but they lacked the traits that cannot be taught on the parade ground: intuition, instinct, alacrity and an iron self-discipline. Easonsmith had all these, as well as a patient wisdom that was a balm to Lloyd Owen in Siwa. 'I coveted his advice for it was always so willingly given and so eminently wise,' he remembered.

On this occasion Easonsmith answered all Lloyd Owen's questions: what to do in the event of being spotted by enemy aircraft; whether to post sentries at night; when to stop for lunch.

Lloyd Owen worried some of the questions were mundane, silly even, and that Easonsmith might think he was in a flap. But he thought about each one, answered it in detail and gave no impression he found the interrogation tiresome. When Lloyd Owen had no more questions, Easonsmith offered one last piece of advice: 'Just be natural; they'll never suspect you.'

Lofty Carr was offering Frank Simms a similar kind of reassurance, in the form of wisdom handed down from Teddy Mitford. 'The further behind enemy lines that you went the safer you were,' recalled Carr. 'If you go 500 miles behind the lines, though it sounds spectacular, you're as safe as houses because nobody's going to suspect you. It's when you're only fifty miles behind the frontline that everyone is trigger happy.'

The four Guards and Yeomanry patrols, along with a New Zealand patrol under Bruce Ballantyne, left Siwa on the morning of 15 November 1941, three days before General Claude Auchinleck launched his grand offensive, codenamed Operation Crusader. Its aim was to retake Cyrenaica and seize the Libyan airfields from the enemy, thereby enabling the RAF to increase their supplies to Malta, the Mediterranean island that was of such strategic importance to the British.

To achieve these aims Auchinleck intended his 13th Corps to launch a frontal attack against the Axis forces holding the frontline, while the 30th Corps would swing round the flanks and annihilate Rommel's armoured force of 174 tanks, markedly inferior in number to the 710 tanks at Auchinleck's disposal. Meanwhile the besieged garrison at Tobruk, 70 miles behind the German frontline, would break out and meet the 30th Corps as they advanced west across Cyrenaica.

The LRDG's role was observing and reporting enemy troop movements, alerting GHQ to what Rommel might be planning in response to the offensive. They did have an additional responsibility, however, one that entailed Easonsmith's 'R1' Patrol collecting a party of fifty-five paratroopers – 'Parashots', as the LRDG called them – once they had carried out a daring raid on a string of enemy airfields at Gazala and Tmimi.

The two Yeomanry patrols, each comprising fifteen men in five trucks, drove for seventy miles and then veered west towards the frontier wire that ran 170 miles along the border that separated Egypt from Libya. Constructed by the Italians in the early 1930s, the demarcation line consisted of four rows of 5 ft 5 in. high stakes with barbed wire in between. It was easy to breach and the LRDG did so at Weshka, close to the ruins of an Italian lookout post. They were now about 100 miles south of Sollum and the two Yeomanry patrols split and went their separate ways.

Shortly before lunch on the next day, 16 November, just as Lloyd Owen was turning his mind towards lunch, Tich Cave shouted 'Aircraft!' Lloyd Owen looked north and saw a small speck on the horizon. Ordering the patrol to stop, he felt 'terribly naked out there in the desert' as they watched the aircraft approach.

It came in fast from the north, its pilot peering down at the trucks that were spaced out 200 yards apart, trying to work out if they were friend or foe. There were no markings on the vehicles and the dust and dirt of the desert made split-second identification virtually impossible as they roared overhead.

'Y' Patrol didn't have the same problem. They could clearly see it was an Italian aircraft, but for a moment Lloyd Owen thought 'we had fooled him.' As the aircraft climbed away the patrol breathed a collective sigh of relief. Then to their dismay the aircraft turned, dived and dropped two small bombs in their direction. The bombs landed some distance from their intended target but the pilot evidently thought he had done his duty. He flew off, leaving the LRDG to laugh at his feeble efforts.

Not so many miles away, and only a couple of hours later, Frank Simms' Patrol was bumping over the desert towards Garet Meriem when up went the shout of 'Aircraft!' Lofty Carr, navigating the patrol from the back truck, looked up from his map and spotted three aircraft coming in low. One of the patrol confidently asserted there was nothing to worry about, they were theirs, RAF Beaufighters. Carr returned to his navigating. Then someone yelled a warning as the three aircraft began firing. 'The ground shook as their cannon shells shattered around us,' remembered Carr. He leapt from the truck, terrified, suddenly a small boy once more, remembering the times he had trespassed on railway lines and watched the express trains go thundering by so close he could almost have touched them.

The three aircraft came in again, concentrating their fire on Carr's vehicle, 'probably because my navigation truck had a radio aerial alongside it.' The aerial was unmistakable, 30 feet of wire suspended between two 20-foot poles. Carr, Simms and Ginger Sharratt took cover as the Beaufighters made another pass. Cannon fire burst all around them. Simms tried to fire the pre-arranged identification flares that would alert the RAF but the ring pull broke in his hand. Matches, he screamed, who's got some matches? Carr pointed to the patrol cook, who was trying to force himself into a small fissure in the ground nearby.*

'Bring me matches,' yelled Simms.

'Fuck you and your matches!' shouted the cook. 'I'm staying down here.'

The Beaufighters came at the patrol from different directions on their third run. Carr, Simms and Sharratt circled the vehicle like men trying to avoid a punch from the pub drunk, a step to their right, one to their left, duck, weave. Carr was amazed by how low they flew, 'as if the tips of their propellers were being polished by the desert'.

A burst of cannon fire came under the truck, ripping up the ground between Sharratt's legs. The truck caught fire. The three men ran for their lives. The Beaufighters broke off the attack and returned to their base at Jarabub but the damage had been done, and the cost was more than just the material loss of one truck. It was, recalled Carr, a 'demoralizing' experience to be attacked by

* According to Cyril Richardson's log, 'the recognition signals for our own planes was at the time that they should fly with their wheels down.'

your own side. Ginger Sharratt in particular had been unnerved by his narrow escape. 'Fuck this, mate,' he said in a quiet voice to Carr as they climbed onto another vehicle. 'I'm not coming out on a job again.'* The following day 'Y' Patrol was spotted by two German fighters. Carr and the rest of the men braced themselves but as the aircraft came in low they suddenly 'waggled their wings, waved to us and cleared off'. They laughed coldly at the irony.

On the same day, 17 November, Simms took two of his trucks in search of Lloyd Owen's patrol. When they found them, not too far from Bir Tengeder, Simms asked if he could use the 'Y2' wireless as his own had been destroyed by the RAF. Having sent through a message to Siwa, Simms sat down with Lloyd Owen and drank tea while he awaited Prendergast's reply. It came an hour later, ordering 'Y1' Patrol to return to base and instructing 'Y2' Patrol to proceed to a new area called Gadd-el-Ahmar.

---

* Sharratt was true to his word, requesting a transfer back to the Staffordshire Yeomanry. He was killed in action in March 1943, aged twenty, and is commemorated on the Medjez-El-Bab Memorial in Tunisia.

CHAPTER ELEVEN

'Act with the utmost vigour'

Gadd-el-Ahmar proved to be a disappointment for Lloyd Owen and 'Y2' Patrol. They had found a wadi in which to conceal the vehicles and for five days they observed a track along which it was presumed the enemy would move.. They saw nothing, and most of the time was spent listening to Mickey Coombs talk about his various 'conquests in Cairo'. Another member of the patrol, Brian Springford, also knew how to spin a good yarn, and Lloyd Owen enjoyed the close proximity to a class of men he had hitherto barely encountered. They, in turn, adhered to LRDG tradition by calling Lloyd Owen 'skipper' and not 'sir'. The only source of friction between the men and their officer concerned breakfast; Lloyd Owen was in the habit of eating the first meal of the day after the patrol had travelled a few miles from their camp of the previous night. Cave and Springford suffered from pangs of early morning hunger, the pair agreeing that Lloyd Owen had 'got no heart and no stomach'.

But despite the tall tales, Lloyd Owen found the five-day surveillance a frustrating experience, though it was enlivened by the search for the fifty-five British paratroopers who had dropped into the area on the night of 17 November. Led by Captain David Stirling, the young officer who had interrupted Lieutenant-Colonel Prendergast's dinner at the Shepheard's a few weeks earlier, the SAS raiders had had the misfortune to parachute into Cyrenaica during what the noted war correspondent Alexander

Clifford described as 'the most spectacular thunderstorm within local memory'.

The raiding party, split into five sticks, descended nowhere near the target area, many men injuring themselves on landing and several dropping straight into the hands of the enemy. The survivors, wandering across the desert, had to endure torrential rain and freezing temperatures as they attempted to reach the pre-arranged rendezvous with Jake Easonsmith's 'R1' Patrol in the Wadi-el-Mra.

Easonsmith encountered Lloyd Owen as he moved between the wadi and a second rendezvous to the north-north-east close to the Gadd-el-Ahmar crossroads. Between them the LRDG patrols collected all twenty-one survivors of the raid, a sorry total from the fifty-five who had embarked on the operation. David Stirling and his sergeant, Bob Tait, were picked up by 'Y2' Patrol early on the morning of 20 November. Stirling didn't seem too depressed by the disastrous failure of his unit's inaugural operation, accepting the offer from Tich Cave of a mug of tea liberally laced with whisky. 'David told me the story of his drop and of all that had gone wrong,' recalled Lloyd Owen. 'He had had rotten bad luck and any lesser men would have had his ardour completely damped. Not so David. He was already trying to analyse what had gone wrong and deciding how it would go right next time.'

As the LRDG transported Stirling and his twenty SAS survivors to Jarabub, further north the Germans were fighting back after their initial surprise at the British offensive. The launch of Operation Crusader on 18 November over a 65-mile front from Sollum to Jarabub had gone as well as Auchinleck had hoped. Armoured troops advanced steadily, reaching the escarpment at Sidi Rezegh (thirty-two miles south-east of Tobruk) and capturing its airfield on the nineteenth. The next day Rommel seized the initiative with a bold counter-thrust that caught the Allies off-guard. There were a series of tank battles, 'long and confused', as both sides sought the decisive victory.

Learning of the Allied breakout at Tobruk, Rommel decided to strike south-east into his enemy's rear at Sidi Omar. It was a brilliant manoeuvre, outfoxing the Allies and costing General Cunningham his job (he was replaced by Neil Ritchie).

Rommel's thrust towards Sidi Omar also led to a change in the LRDG's role with Lieutenant-Colonel Prendergast receiving fresh instructions from Eighth Army HQ on 24 November. No longer were they to be passive observers of the assault, the LRDG were told to 'act with the utmost vigour offensively against any enemy targets or communications within reach'. In particular the patrols were ordered to focus on Mekili, Gadd-el-Ahmar and the coastal road in the vicinity of Jedabia.

Prendergast and Bill Kennedy Shaw studied the map and then directed each patrol to an area within the target zone.

Frank Simms was instructed to take his 'Y1' Patrol – comprising eleven men including himself – and attack convoys travelling between Mekili and Derna. They reached the area on 29 November but for two days had no joy in locating suitable targets. Then, on the late afternoon of 1 December, they discovered a large camp at a road junction twenty miles south-west of Derne.

They spent the night concealed in a wadi and at first light on 2 December Simms and Carr went forward to reconnoitre the camp, the huge muscular Carr and the small, bespectacled Simms making a strange couple. 'He was a hero of mine,' said Carr of his officer, 'one of the few men I have met who appeared to have no fear, or certainly he was able to control his fear.' Simms 'frightened the pants' off Carr. 'He just loved bumping people off. It's part of war but he didn't feel the need to kill because there was a war, he just quite liked the idea.' There was a story about Simms that seemed to confirm this. On one patrol he crawled up to a tent containing two Italians and, being fluent in the language, listened to their conversation. At length one of the Italians came out for a crap. Simms watched the man squat over the desert and whispered to the LRDG soldier next to him: 'I'll wait until he's finished and then kill him, so he can die happy.' As the Italian buttoned up his trousers, Simms crept forward and silently disposed of the soldier.

Carr had witnessed Simms' brutality but he had also seen the other side of his nature; this was a man who once diverted a patrol so he could admire some wild flowers in a wadi. Another time he was overcome with emotion when he discovered a small bird that had succumbed to the heat. Carr found it hard to tally the man weeping over a dead bird with the officer who found amusement in killing enemy soldiers.

Having reconnoitred the enemy camp, Simms and Carr returned to the patrol and told the men it was a motor transport park approximately 800 yards off the main road to Gazala. There were around thirty vehicles in total and Simms said they would attack at sundown, approaching in their trucks before going in on foot. In his perfunctory report of the attack Simms described how they split into two raiding parties and in the attack '15 vehicles were damaged and [the] patrol withdrew'. It was only when he arrived back at the two trucks that Simms realized Carr was missing. 'Patrol waited an hour at first rendezvous for him,' wrote Simms in the report. Concluding that his navigator had been captured, Simms set off for Siwa by the Gadd-el-Ahmar crossroads.

But Carr had not been captured. 'As a navigator I had the problem of being with one party or the other,' recalled Carr. 'I had got back to the trucks and then realized the other half had not got to us and so I went back to look for them.'

As Carr padded silently among the enemy vehicles a figure suddenly leapt at him from out of the rear of a lorry. 'I don't know if he was attacking me or just jumping down from the vehicle thinking the raid was over,' said Carr. It was no time for hesitation. Carr reacted instinctively, raising his rifle and firing a shot from his hip. The man was hit in mid-air and crashed to the ground dead.

Dodging in and out of the enemy trucks Carr searched for his comrades but it was fruitless. Disappointment turned to dismay when he returned to the rendezvous to discover the patrol had moved off. 'I wasn't scared, I was apt to be a cool sort of person,' reflected Carr. 'I knew where the next job was and all I thought was "I'll walk it, I'll get there."'

Carr struck out for the proposed scene of the next night's raid, close to the main road near to Ahmar, and at dawn was two miles from his destination. Then, as he recounted in his subsequent operational report: 'I heard noises of animals which I associated with a Senussi settlement and, with due caution approached, and finding it to be indeed a Bedouin camp I asked for food and water and was provided with camel's milk, macaroni and coffee by the natives.'

What Carr omitted to include in his report was that the camel's milk also contained a handful of camel droppings, 'marbles' in LRDG vernacular. There was a reason why the Senussi laced their milk with camel droppings: the faeces contain *Bacillus subtilis*, a bacteria that combats dysentery-causing germs. Carr didn't know this, but he remembered what Bagnold and Kennedy Shaw had told them all about Arab hospitality. To refuse the milk would have been a grave slight to his hosts. So he drank the milk, droppings and all, and accepted the offer of a blanket and somewhere to sleep, scraping out a small hole in the ground for his hips as was the LRDG custom. 'On waking I found myself to be unwell and unable to carry on,' wrote Carr in his report, 'and the hospitable Senussi took me to their Sheikh's smaller tent and put me to bed on sheepskins.'

Carr remained poorly for the next twenty-four hours, a sickness he attributed to the camel droppings. The Senussi fussed and fretted over him, and on 5 December, one of their number gave Carr some medicine – or what he thought was medicine. 'They brought me some shoe polish which had written on it the word *Medicina*,' said Carr. 'They'd obviously got it from some Italians and thought it was some sort of medicine.'

It might have been stolen from the Italians or, more likely, the Senussi had been duped into accepting the shoe polish in return for dates, eggs or some other commodity required by a passing unit of Italian soldiers earlier in the war.

Slowly, one day at a time, Carr felt his strength returning. On 7 December he 'went to the wadi and scalded myself to kill bugs, fleas, etcetera.' The next day he observed Italians digging positions in the distance. The following day, 9 December, the Italians withdrew and Carr saw artillery explosions to the east.

Enemy patrols were now in the area and on a couple of occasions Carr had to rush from the Senussi village and hide up in a cave in the wadi. Then on 12 December he had his narrowest escape yet. 'I was lying under some camel saddles when six tanks came into the village,' recalled Carr. 'I wasn't sure whose they were so I started walking towards them. On their forage caps the soldiers had a roundel like the RAF. I remember thinking 'I didn't know the British tanks had those. They were German. Fortunately I was dressed as an Arab so I very quietly turned round and ducked into a tent.'

By now the Senussi had accepted Carr into their fold, feeding and sheltering him even though he had, strictly speaking, outstayed his welcome. 'The Senussi have a four-day rule,' explained Carr. 'They will take in any fugitive for four days and at end of the four days they can do what the hell they want with you, turn you in or anything.'

The Senussi liked this huge bearded Englishman with a fragile stomach. So they let him stay and the women no longer wore their veils in his presence. He even had the honour of drinking tea with the village headman. 'There is a whole ceremony to having a cup of tea with the Senussi,' said Carr. 'Everyone sits cross-legged in a circle while the headman puts the little brass container with tea leaves on a little brushwood fire. There were little cups thick with sugar – their currency was sugar and tea, and Prendergast would send a whole lorry-load of tea and sugar to them, which for them was the equivalent of winning the pools, and in return they gave us information – and the headman would pour the tea into these little cups. No one would touch the tea, you just looked at it, and after a time you all poured the tea back into the container. Then the headman poured it out again, and you could do this two or three times. Then the headman would finally drink and that was the signal for everyone to drink.'

Carr remained in the village in the days that followed, committing anything he thought might be of interest to British intelligence to memory:

December 13: Was taken to cave early. Artillery and auto cannon active all day. 30 enemy motorcycle combinations passed through village.

December 14: Cave at dawn. Artillery, bombs and auto-cannon. Senussi shepherd [Mohamed] brought news of crashed RAAF [Royal Australia Air Force] officer.

December 15: Wounded RAAF officer arrived. Goat ate my map.

December 16: Patrols around and artillery and small arms fire to east.

December 17: Note reached 31st regt (Field) RA [Royal Artillery] and was acknowledged. RAAF officer and self went on donkeys and were picked up in truck and taken forward.

Relieved at being rescued, Carr nevertheless was sorrowful to leave the Senussi. For two weeks they had nursed, protected and educated him in their ways. They were an austere people but – as Bagnold, Kennedy Shaw, Clayton and Prendergast had realized before him – Carr saw there was much in their spartan way of life that was superior to Western culture. 'They are a strict sect and I know Bagnold had huge respect for them. We all did,' reflected Carr. 'They are such a dignified people, pure and highly refined.'

The Senussi treated men equally, provided they shared their hardships and their code of honour. Within a day of leaving his Arab saviours, Carr was exposed to the pettiness of his own people. He and the Australian pilot, a flying officer who had been slightly burned when his plane crashed in the desert, were taken to Mersa Matruh by a Scots Guards officer, the Honourable Bernard Bruce, son of the Earl of Elgin. Bruce refused to allow Lance-Corporal Carr to travel in the back of the pick-up truck alongside two officers. So Carr had to sit on top of the vehicle. 'He was a hopeless driver,' remembered Carr. 'There are a lot of little wadis in the desert and when you hit them with a vehicle you must go over them diagonally, a wheel at a time. He didn't. He went very fast over this wadi and smashed all the steering.'

Bruce flagged down another vehicle and together with the pilot officer continued to Mersa Matruh. Carr was ordered to stay with the pick-up until a salvage truck arrived. Don't worry, Bruce told Carr, there is some bully beef if you get hungry. 'In fact when I searched the vehicle I found he had every delicacy under the sun,' recalled Carr. 'So I ate all the delicacies and left the bully for him.'

Carr eventually reached the HQ of the 4th Indian Division on 20 December, where he was 'suspected of being a fifth columnist'. He was cross-examined at a field maintenance centre while a signal was sent to Lieutenant-Colonel Prendergast asking for confirmation that he was missing one of his lance corporals. The following day he was flown to Mersa Matruh and on 23 December Carr was back at Siwa, regaling his comrades with his extraordinary escapade.

CHAPTER TWELVE

'The lead was flying in all directions'

While Carr had been living with the Senussi, his comrades in the LRDG were continuing to take the fight to the enemy. David Lloyd Owen's 'Y2' patrol had overrun a small Italian fort near El Ezzeiat, capturing ten Italians and two Libyans, from whom they extracted enemy troop dispositions in Derna and Mekili. Lloyd Owen had also amused himself by leaving lewd rhymes on any Italian marker cairns he encountered. One such poem ran:

If your fucking truck is stuck
Like our fucking truck is stuck
Then you're fucking stuck
Like we're fucking stuck.

Frank Simms' 'Y1' Patrol drove into the village of Soluk, thirty-five miles south-south-east of Benghazi opening fire on the Axis soldiers lounging about in the belief the enemy was hundreds of miles to the east.

The Guards patrol – 'G1' – under the command of Captain Tony Hay had been blooded in late November east of Beda Fomm, approximately fifty miles south of Benghazi. They hid up behind a small hill fifty yards from the road that led from Benghazi to Jedabia, waiting for a suitable target to present itself. Shortly before sunset a column of vehicles was spotted trundling down the road. 'Much to our disappointment the trucks were at least two miles apart,' wrote Guardsman Cyril Richardson in his log. 'It was useless for us to fire at just one truck, so our officer had a brainwave.'

Captain Hay's 'brainwave' was to follow the advice of Jake Easonsmith and 'Be Natural.' And what could be more natural than to drive along the coastal road in orderly single file as if they were just another column of vehicles? 'After going for about five or six miles down the road passing odd lorries we saw our prey,' recorded Richardson in his log. 'It was a house on the side of the road with lorries parked all around it.'

'G1' Patrol had found an Italian motor transport park, the 'house' accommodating weary drivers taking a break from the monotony of transporting supplies up and down the coast road. The LRDG patrol 'let fly with everything', raking the building and lorries with machine gun fire from each of their five trucks. 'What effect we had on those lorry drivers we did not stop to see,' wrote Richardson. 'But seeing as it took place some six hundred miles behind their lines it must have upset them rather.'

The patrol vanished into the twilight, Hay calling a halt after eight miles. While he and his signaller contacted Prendergast – receiving orders to 'do [the] same again tomorrow night' – the men enjoyed their nightly ration of rum, a treat unique to the LRDG in North Africa, but one that could induce carelessness. One or two men on patrols became lost after straying too far from the trucks in search of a place to empty their bowels. 'People could walk fifteen yards away in poor visibility and never be seen again,' said Lofty Carr. 'So we introduced a drill: when you went for a crap at night, you walked a measured number of steps, fifty, then stopped and did a 180 degrees turn so you were facing the starting point. Then after, they walked the fifty steps back. If they didn't find the trucks for any reason they were to sit down and shout, and we would hear them. It's when people start blundering around that you get lost.'

The LRDG had little sympathy for any man who did wander off and get lost in the desert. It showed a lack of respect for their environment: fatal human conceit. 'We all think we've got a sense of direction,' said Carr. 'But often in the desert you came across a pile of bones. We'd say "Look, here's another guy who thought he had a sense of direction."'

Hay and his men lay up in a wadi during the daylight hours, hidden from the enemy aircraft overhead that were scouring the desert for the men responsible for attacking the transport park.

They left their hiding place at sundown and drove to a small rise close to the road, further south than their vantage point the previous evening. Richardson estimated they were no more than twenty-five yards from the road, so close they could hear the drivers talk to their passengers as vehicles passed. Hay decided to alter tactics, instructing his men to mount their machine guns along the top of the rise. The first unfortunate vehicle to hove into sight was an oil tanker towing a trailer. Richardson described in his log how they 'let him have it good'. The tanker swerved off the road, the two occupants of the vehicle shot dead as they leapt from the cab.

Hay's 'G1' Patrol returned to Siwa in the first week of December. They were met by Prendergast, who was delighted with what they had accomplished. Richardson wrote that their commanding officer 'gave us a lecture telling us our raids had a terrific effect on demoralizing the enemy and that the traffic on the Benghazi road had stopped for twenty-four hours after the second raid. He said we had to repeat our attacks in the near future and that he wished us luck, hoping he would be able to give us an easier job after this one'.

'G1' had little time at Siwa in which to savour the praise of their commanding officer. On 10 December they were off again, instructed to attack more traffic on the Benghazi to Jedabia road. David Lloyd Owen's 'Y2' Patrol were dispatched to harass enemy vehicles on the road that led from Derna to Tobruk. A day after leaving Siwa, however, Lloyd Owen received fresh instructions because of the progress achieved by the Eighth Army in the battle to their north. The vanguard of the British forces were some forty miles west of Tobruk, so Lloyd Owen was told to operate in the same area as Hay, attacking the enemy as they withdrew towards Benghazi.

The two patrols rendezvoused on 14 December, and Lloyd Owen and Hay 'decided to attack the road at roughly the same time in the early evening but at places a few miles apart from each other'. They moved off in the late afternoon and drove west for sixty miles before the two patrols split up and headed for their target areas. 'By the time we reached the road it was quite dark,' recalled Richardson. 'In fact the leading truck which I was on almost had its front wheels on the road before the driver saw it.'

They backed up forty yards, turning the vehicles so that their rears faced the road. Then Richardson and a couple of other Lewis gunners, together with Sergeant Harry Roebuck and Captain Hay, who had a Tommy Gun, returned to the road on foot and settled down to wait. It was a cold night, they could see their breath in front of their faces, and patience as well as control was required. Several vehicles passed, tempting, but not what Hay wanted. Finally 'a decent-sized catch came along.' It was a large truck towing a trailer. Hay whispered instructions to his men and then, on his command, they opened fire. 'The fireworks were soon over,' wrote Richardson. Or so they all thought. Hay leapt up from the verge and running up to the lorry threw a Lewes bomb into its rear where boxes of ordnance were stacked.*

Hay believed there was a three-minute fuse on the bomb. He was mistaken. 'It turned out to be three seconds and before we knew what was happening the whole area was lit up like daylight,' wrote Richardson. The raiders sprinted back towards their vehicles and hardly had they clambered aboard when there was 'a terrific explosion'. Richardson looked round and 'saw the lorry or

* Designed by an SAS officer called Jock Lewes, the eponymous bomb was a mixture of plastic explosive and thermite, rolled in diesel oil with a detonator, instantaneous fuse and a time pencil. The time pencil, a glass tube with a spring-loaded striker held in place by a strip of copper wire, resembled a biro pen. At the top was a glass phial containing acid that you squeezed gently to break. The acid ate through the wire and released the striker. Obviously the thicker the wire the longer the delay before the striker was triggered (the pencils were colour-coded according to the length of fuse). The thermite caused a flash that ignited the petrol.

rather what was left of it burning furiously [and] for the next hour we heard a series of explosions'.

Lloyd Owen's Yeomanry patrol also had the opportunity to use their Lewes bombs. First he had manouevred his four vehicles east of a road, each truck fifteen yards from its neighbour, their bonnets facing into the desert ready for a quick getaway. The four machine guns faced in the other direction, barrels trained on the road, gunners wrapped up well against the black, bitter cold of the night. Lloyd Owen positioned himself in the middle of the row of trucks, a whistle resting between his lips. The wait seemed interminable. Tich Cave took it upon himself to kill some time by shinning up a telegraph pole and cutting the wires. The sudden 'twang' of the wires nearly made Lloyd Owen swallow his whistle.

Eventually a couple of vehicles appeared on the road. The first was a petrol tanker carrying a trailer. The driver was killed in the first burst of fire, his passenger died as he leapt from the cab into a swarm of bullets. The second vehicle screeched to a halt and out leapt several soldiers. One or two returned fire but none were in the mood to die on a lonely stretch of desert road. They vanished into the night 'with a fusillade of bullets to speed them on their way'.

The two LRDG patrols hid up until mid-afternoon on 16 December when they rendezvoused about twenty miles south of Antelat. They swapped stories from the previous night and Hay warned Lloyd Owen that he had noticed an increased enemy presence in the area as a result of their actions – not just aircraft but armoured cars that were evidently searching for them. They agreed it would be prudent to head twenty-five miles north-west and attack the road five miles south of Magrun.

The two officers shook hands and wished each other luck. Though neither voiced any concerns, Lloyd Owen sensed that he and Hay 'felt that it was not going to be quite so easy as it had been the night before'.

Cyril Richardson shared his officers' apprehension. 'We moved off just after five o'clock but not feeling so cheerful as last night,' he wrote. 'The thought of running into armoured cars in our ordinary soft Ford V8 trucks did not appeal to me, or any of us.'

Lloyd Owen's patrol found a suitable spot close to the road from which they could observe enemy traffic. They felt like 'highwaymen' as they waited to waylay whoever should be so foolish as to venture out. Suddenly they heard firing to their south. 'Tony Hay had beaten us to it,' recalled Lloyd Owen. They hung about for an hour, hoping that some stray German vehicle might not have been alerted by the firing. But the road was deserted and finally Lloyd Owen decided he must leave now and put many miles between themselves and the road before dawn diluted the darkness.

'Y2' Patrol covered seventy-five miles that night, lying up in 'some thickish bushes on the edge of a swamp to the south of Msus'. There they remained on 16 and 17 December, being eaten alive by mosquitoes but safe from the enemy aircraft that buzzed overhead. The next day, Lloyd Owen received a signal from Lieutenant-Colonel Prendergast: Tony Hay had been captured and 'Y2' Patrol was to return to Siwa before they too fell into the hands of the enemy.

Captain Hay had led his Guards Patrol to a point on the Jedabia to Benghazi road about ten miles south of where Lloyd Owen and his men were positioned. The traffic was thicker than the previous night, many vehicles heading west or, as Hay told his men, 'retreating west' from the British advance. But as well as the soft-skinned vehicles carrying men and equipment out of Cyrenaica there were also visible some armoured cars patrolling at regular intervals.

Cyril Richardson considered that 'things were definitely getting too warm for us in this area' but nevertheless 'we decided to have one last crack at them before finding fresh hunting grounds.'

Hay led his Lewis gunners on foot close to the roadside, the men stealing forward in the darkness and positioning themselves beside the road. 'We had to be very careful owing to the armoured cars,' recalled Richardson. They did not have to wait for long. Into view came a truck towing a staff car. On Hay's command the guardsmen opened fire, destroying both vehicles and racing back to their trucks before the armoured cars appeared.

They fled the scene of the attack without incident and Hay called a halt after twelve miles. Over dinner Hay told his men it would be prudent to 'get right back out of it', to head due south where they would encounter 'a force of Indians'.

This force was probably the 5th Indian Brigade, operating on the southern flank of the Eighth Army advance, and which had been engaged in heavy fighting during the preceding days against Rommel's 15th Panzer Division and the Italian Ariete Armoured Division. Both sides had suffered many casualties and while the British paused to await resupply, Rommel decided to stage a gradual withdrawal to a line between Agedabia and El Haseia. Thus, on the morning of 16 December, Hay led his men off, not towards the advancing Indian brigade, but into the path of an Axis army pulling back in orderly fashion.

Cyril Richardson described in his log what happened when, at 0800 hours, they spotted some trucks in the distance.

> Everyone was quite sure that we had run into our own force. There were no shots fired at us as we approached. The first three trucks were roughly two or three hundred yards from these supposed Indians. The other two were about three hundred yards behind us. Everyone was feeling sleepy and hungry and [we] were not as careful as we should have been. The officer [Hay] drove forward and disappeared over a rise in the ground. Everyone was walking around their trucks trying to keep warm.

Hay had taken his sergeant, Jim Nolan, with him in the pick-up, while the patrol's other sergeant, Harry Roebuck, was in one of the two trucks a few hundred yards to the rear of the lead vehicles. He, like Richardson, assumed his officer would soon be back after a brief parley with the Indians. Before long the pick-up appeared, coming over the lip of the wadi into which it had disappeared a few minutes earlier. Roebuck sensed immediately that something was not quite right. Why was the skipper driving it in a 'peculiar way', grinding the gearbox as if he was a novice? At the same moment, Roebuck saw figures appear on the skyline.

Richardson recalled that 'the fun started' when machine guns opened up from about four places. He and the two other members of his truck dived behind one of the rear wheels. Other vehicles roared over the wadi and began firing at the vehicles below.

Roebuck screamed at his men to withdraw as the still morning air was whip-cracked by bullets. It was easy enough for the two vehicles at the rear of the patrol to make good their escape despite the incoming fire, but the three trucks close to the wadi were trapped.

'It was useless attempting to climb into the back of the truck for the lead was flying in all directions,' said Richardson. 'The three of us made ourselves as small as possible behind the rear wheel and spent a very uncomfortable two or three minutes while the supposed Indians peppered our truck. A section of them then came out to collect us, or I suppose they thought to bury us.'

Miraculously, none of the LRDG men had been killed in the onslaught, and as the Germans approached the Britons emerged from behind the trucks, hands raised in surrender. 'They came up shouting in their guttural language,' remembered Richardson, and one soldier in particular approached holding a 'nasty looking' heavy machine gun. The soldier was clearly on edge and the moment he saw Richardson rise from behind the wheel he fired a burst from the hip. Fortunately for Richardson 'his aim was not so good', the weapon being too heavy for the German, and the bullets tore into the ground, although one round hit Guardsman Chapman in the ankle.

The German's comrades berated the machine gunner and applied a dressing to Chapman's shattered ankle. Meanwhile Richardson and the other LRDG men were taken into the wadi where they found Hay and Nolan under armed guard. The officer was inconsolable over his mistake. He and eleven of his men were now prisoners and the Germans had four LRDG vehicles in their possession. 'We were sat around for about an hour in which time the Jerries searched our trucks, mostly for food, and to change the tyres which had been punctured by the bullets and to patch up the trucks good enough to run them again,' Richardson wrote later.

The prisoners were taken in their own trucks to Agedabia, where they were handed over to the Italians and held overnight before being 'bundled into the back of a 30 cwt lorry with nine men as escort including the two who were in the front cabin'. They were heading north-west to Benghazi, guarded by Italians who didn't speak English. Within a few minutes of leaving Agedabia the prisoners had their escape plan worked out. They were confident of success, all they had to do was wait for the signal from Captain Hay before leaping into action and overpowering the guards.

The prisoners stopped muttering and sat back in silence, feigning boredom, misery, hopelessness, any emotion to lull their guards into a false sense of security. The truck continued north-west. One or two of the soldiers stole a sideways look at Hay but he avoided their glances. The guardsmen shot each other confused looks, their eyes asking the same question: what was Hay playing at? And then suddenly the moment had passed. They were nearing the outskirts of Benghazi and any attempt at escape would be futile so close to a large enemy garrison. 'Whether he got the wind up or [was] afraid of the responsibility of any of us getting hurt or shot in the attempt to overpower the guard I do not know,' recorded Richardson in his log.*

* Cyril Richardson was sent to an Italian POW camp, from which he escaped when Italy surrendered in September 1943. He died of pneumonia in a Swiss internment camp a month later.

CHAPTER THIRTEEN

'He didn't think much of our shabby appearance'

The capture of Captain Hay and eleven members of 'G1' Patrol was not the only misfortune to hit the Long Range Desert Group in December 1941. Three days before Christmas two members of 'S2' (Rhodesian) Patrol (The 'S' stood for Salisbury, capital of what was then Rhodesia), Corporal Laurence Ashby and Robert Riggs, were killed by a marauding RAF fighter as they returned from escorting an SAS sabotage party led by Lieutenant Bill Fraser to Agedabia airfield.

Nonetheless the attack on the airfield had been an outstanding success, Fraser and his SAS raiders destroying thirty-seven Axis aircraft before slipping away undetected to their rendezvous with the LRDG. Their exploits were matched by a small SAS party under the command of Paddy Mayne, a pre-war Ireland rugby international, who had destroyed nearly fifty aircraft during two raids on Tamet airfield earlier in the month.

It had been Lieutenant-Colonel Prendergast's suggestion that the SAS might be more effective as a guerrilla raiding force if they relied on the LRDG, not parachutes, for their infiltration. Thus on 28 November, when Prendergast received an order from General Neil Ritchie instructing the LRDG to launch a series of raids against Axis airfields to coincide with a secondary Eighth Army offensive, he signalled GHQ from Siwa: 'As LRDG not trained for demolitions, suggest pct [parachutists] used for blowing "dromes".'

On 8 December 'S1' Patrol, comprising nineteen men and commanded by Captain Charles 'Gus' Holliman, had left Jalo to take two SAS raiding parties to the airfields at Tamet and Sirte, 350 miles to the north-west. Holliman's navigator was actually an Englishman, Mike Sadler, who had been trained by Lofty Carr a few weeks previously in Cairo. Carr recalled that he taught Sadler 'the rudiments of astro-navigation and how to use a theodolite', and that Sadler proved a quick learner.

Born in London in 1920, Sadler had emigrated to Rhodesia in 1937 and on the outbreak of war enlisted in an anti-tank battery. Sadler had a similar character to Carr's, intelligent and impetuous, and liable to irritation when confronted by small-minded officers. An argument over his boots with his officer prompted Sadler to seek an escape from his battery and a chance encounter with some members of the Rhodesian patrol in a Cairo bar provided him with that opportunity. 'I learned navigation quickly because I was interested in it and when you are interested in something you learn,' explained Sadler. 'And I suppose I had a natural feel for it.'

Navigating the SAS the 350 miles from Jalo oasis to the airfields at Tamet and Sirte was Sadler's first test in the LRDG. 'One of the essential things was not to let doubt creep into your mind,' he reflected. 'You had to be confident because it was awfully easy, especially at night, to start to feel you were going wrong and you should be further to left or right. It was rather easy to give way to that feeling if you weren't confident. It was a challenge, navigating, but I liked the challenge. I was young and you don't really think about pressure at twenty-one.'

The raiding party made good progress in the first two days but they then hit a wide expanse of rocky broken ground, covering only twenty miles in three painstaking hours on the morning of 11 December. Soon, however, the going underfoot became the least of their problems. 'Suddenly we heard the drone of a Ghibli [the Caproni Ca.309, a reconnaissance aircraft],' recalled Cecil 'Jacko' Jackson, one of the Rhodesian LRDG soldiers. 'Not having room to manoeuvre in the rough terrain, Holliman ordered us all to fire on his command. The plane was low and when all five Lewis guns opened up, he veered off and his bombs missed.'

The Ghibli broke off the fight but the British knew the pilot would have already been on the radio. It was only a matter of minutes before fighter aircraft appeared in the distance. 'We doubled back to a patch of scrub we had passed earlier,' said Jackson, who, along with his comrades made frantic efforts to camouflage their vehicles with netting. 'We had just hidden ourselves when three aircraft came over us and strafed the scrub.'

It was obvious to the Italians where the enemy was hiding, but they were firing blind all the same, tattooing the ground with machine gun fire without being able to see their targets. It was a terrifying experience for the LRDG and SAS men cowering among the patchy cover, a feeling of utter helplessness. All they could do was remain motionless, fighting the natural impulse to run from the fire. 'I was lying face down near some scrub and heard and felt something thudding into the ground around me,' remembered Jackson. He didn't flinch. Only when the drone of the aircraft grew so faint as to be barely audible did he and his comrades get to their feet. Jackson looked down, blanching at 'bullet holes [that] had made a neat curve round the imprint of my head and shoulders in the sand'.

Remarkably, the strafing had caused no damage to either men or vehicles and, once Sadler had taken a fix, the patrol moved off. The going soon improved and at 4.30 p.m. Sadler 'called a halt and told Holliman we were forty miles from Sirte'. The officer decided to press on while the light was still good. When darkness did fall the raiders were twenty miles from their target and Sadler had to lead the patrol by magnetic compass and without lights. 'Two hours later at 9.00 p.m. Sadler halted and told Gus [Holliman] we had four miles to go to the coast road,' recalled Jackson. A few minutes later Jackson's vehicle became bogged down in the sand. The rest of the patrol waited. Holliman inspected the trapped truck and began issuing instructions. Suddenly they heard voices out in front, foreign words drifting through the darkness. Then there

The gravel desert, as seen in this photograph, was called in Arabic *serir*, and was good to travel across because the wind had removed the sand, a process known as 'deflation'.

An LRDG patrol prepares to depart for the desert. Note the variety of headdress and the twin Vickers on the second truck and the Lewis gun on the third vehicle.

Smoke billows from Murzuk fort following the LRDG attack in January 1941.

Members of G Patrol pose with some Senussi at Kharga in February 1941. Captain Michael Crichton-Stuart is fifth from left front row *(with cap)* and Lt Martin Gibbs sixth from left front row *(with cap)*.

Members of Y Patrol at Kufra in 1941. Lofty Carr is the big man in the back row wearing the cap comforter and not taking much interest in the camera.

The LRDG based themselves at Siwa for many months, living cheek by jowl with the villagers who lived in houses constructed from mud and the trunks of palm trees.

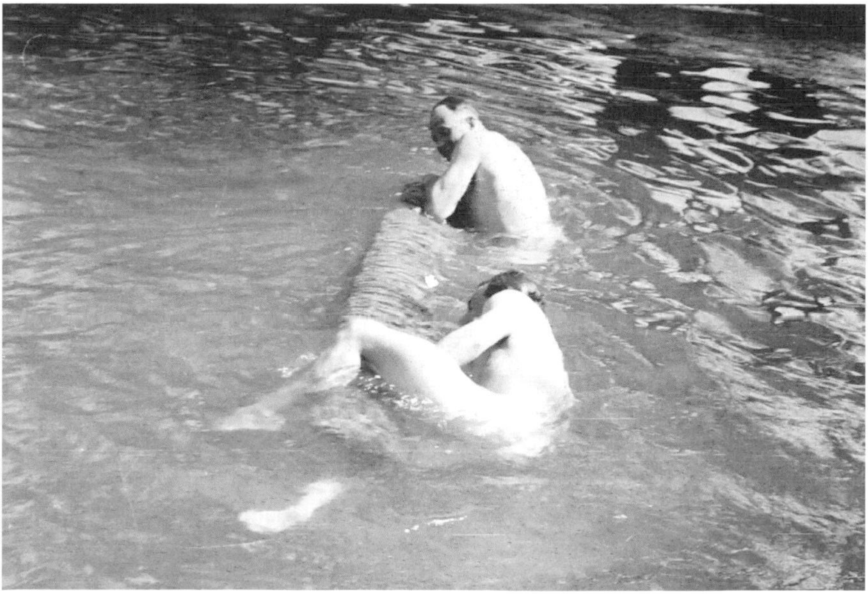

John Olivey *(top)* and Bill Kennedy Shaw cool off with some fun and games in Siwa's Sheik's Pool.

An LRDG patrol behind enemy lines in 1941. Tyre tracks persisted for years in the desert and, as Bagnold noted, 'a European with years of experience can extract a wealth of information from the marks of motor traffic.'

Lofty Carr carries out some maintenance on the Lewis gun, alongside 'Ali' Barber, an LRDG signaller and Mickey Coombs, one of the unit's heartbreakers.

Some of the men of John Olivey's S2 Patrol in December 1941, the same month in which they launched the one and only attack in conjunction with the LRDG's short-lived artillery section.

Benny Watson, Ginger Low, Ron Low and Tiny Simpson of S2 Patrol pose with the spoils of war following their capture of a remote Italian fort at El Gtafia in December 1941.

With the help of the LRDG, the SAS destroyed dozens of enemy aircraft in December 1941. Here some of Paddy Mayne's *(far left)* pose with their escort after a raid on Tamet airfield.

Cecil Jackson, Ron Low, Mike Sadler and John Kroeger. Sadler later joined the SAS and ended the war a decorated officer.

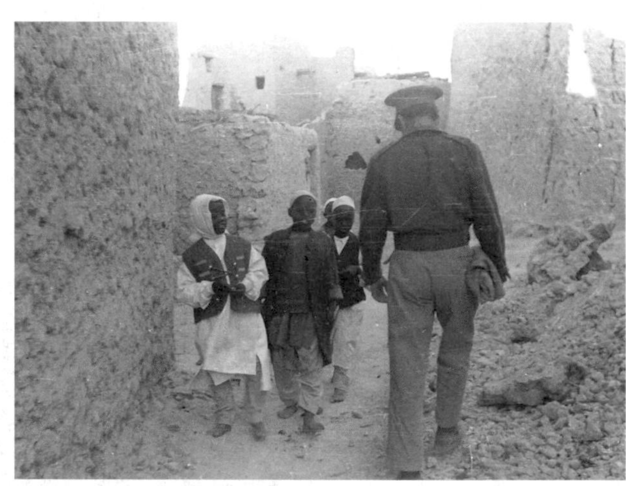

The LRDG intelligence officer, Bill Kennedy Shaw, greets some of the local children in Siwa, in early 1942.

Guy Prendergast unloads one of the two Wacos he purloined for the LRDG. Bill Kennedy Shaw has his back to the camera while sergeant Trevor Barker, the other pilot, leans against the wing.

David Lloyd Owen *(standing far left)* and Eric Wilson, VC, chat to members of Y Patrol. Sergeant Jock Carningham stands *(far right)* and Tich Cave is in the centre of the soldiers seated.

(l–r) Lt T. W. 'Plugs' Ashdown, in charge of LRDG vehicle maintenance, Lt Tim Heywood, LRDG Signals Officer and Captain Dick Lawson, LRDG Medical Officer, seek shade at Ghetmir, 15 miles north-east of Jalo, in 1942.

(l–r) Derek Rawnsley, SAS intelligence officer, Alastair Timpson of G Patrol, Plugs Ashdown and Captain Anthony Hunter, at A Sqn HQ in Siwa, otherwise known as the Farouk Hotel.

David Stirling *(in cap, fourth from right)* leans against his Blitz Buggy in May 1942 at Bir Hacheim surrounded by a mixed patrol of SAS and LRDG after the raid on Benghazi harbour.

Some of the Rhodesian Patrol relax with a cold beer after returning from a mission deep behind enemy lines.

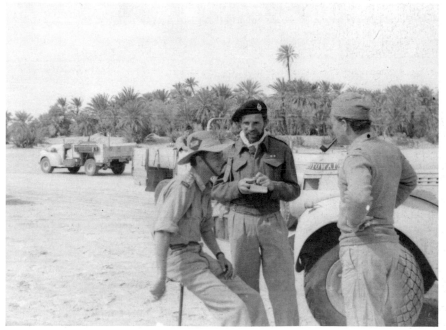

Three of the most respected officers of the LRDG unwind with a smoke: *(l–r)* David Lloyd Owen, Jake Easonsmith and Gus Holliman. Only Lloyd Owen survived the war.

This photograph was staged for the press with one LRDG soldier wearing the Arab headdress that to British minds evoked memories of Lawrence of Arabia.

Lofty Carr fixes a position with his theodolite. Along with John Stocker and Dick Croucher, Carr was one of the three First Navigators in the LRDG.

Albert Bartliff, R. N. Scott and Lofty Carr (with the catapult he crafted). 'Scotty' was an Anglo-Indian fitter and Bartliff a bully who left the LRDG after picking one fight too many with Scott.

Digging out a vehicle was an occupational hazard and the desert terrain caused numerous mechanical problems, hence the respect with which fitters were held.

The indefatigable Captain John Olivey *(seated second from right)* with some of the members of his Rhodesian Patrol.

Bill Kennedy Shaw *(left)* and Shorty Barrett, the LRDG Quartermaster, who after the war became an archdeacon in his native New Zealand.

Captain Nick Wilder and troopers Dobson, Burke and Parker of T Patrol await evacuation after the raid on Barce.

Some of the men wounded in the disastrous attacks on Barce and Benghazi await transportation from Kufra to Cairo in September 1942.

Dick Croucher *(far right)* with a group of the LRDG at Kufra Oasis in 1942. On the far left is New Zealander Hector Mallett, who died of wounds received on the ill-fated landing on Levita in 1943.

As can be seen in this photo of three unidentified members of the LRDG, the men wore what they wanted on operations, choosing their own headgear and wearing animal skins for warmth.

Rudolf Schneider digs his American jeep out of the sand. The teenage soldier was sent to Rommel's Kampfstaffel unit because of his knowledge of British and American vehicles.

These desert tribesmen are smiling at a German camera in late 1942 but further to the east the Senussi nomads provided valuable information to the British.

The LRDG sent their messages in commercial procedure so as to confuse Afrika Korps' radio vehicles, such as this one in Rudolf Schneider's Kampstaffel.

(above left) Charles Dornbush of T2 Patrol poses glumly for Rudolf Schneider after his capture on 22 December 1942. Dornbush survived the war and returned to New Zealand after captivity.

(above right) The mountain warfare school at Cedars in Lebanon hosted the LRDG in the early summer of 1943 and provided a good training ground for subsequent operations in the Balkans.

(left) Fresh-faced he may have been, but James Patch proved himself a courageous and resourceful soldier in the desert and later when he escaped from captivity and joined the Chetniks.

Ralph Bagnold, scientist, author and soldier. An unlikely figure for a founder of a special forces unit, this shy man proved that in war brains triumph over brawn.

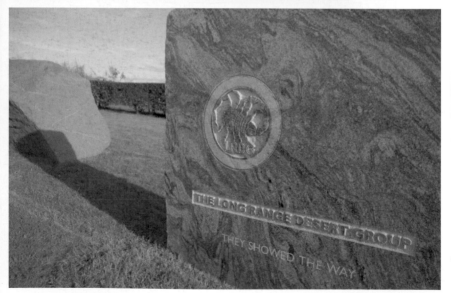

In 2014 a memorial to the LRDG, paid for by the SAS Regimental Association, was unveiled in Scotland close to the statue of David Stirling. The inscription honoured the debt owed by the SAS to the LRDG.

was the sound of a vehicle starting. 'The coast road!' exclaimed Sadler. 'We must be almost on it. Damn these maps!'

David Stirling decided to alter his plan in light of the brush with the Italian aircraft. They would wait a further twenty-four hours and then he and Sergeant Jimmy Brough would attack Sirte airfield while Paddy Mayne and the rest of the SAS would make for Tamet.

Holliman accepted the modification and detailed Jackson and Sadler to transport Mayne in two trucks to within striking distance of Tamet. 'Sadler got us into a position near Tamet airfield before daylight where we had some much needed sleep,' recalled Jackson. 'As soon as light faded that evening, I moved the party up to a rise from which we could see the airfield about three miles away'.

Mayne and his men shouldered their haversacks and vanished into the darkness while Sadler and Jackson waited at the rendezvous in wadi Tamet. At around 11.15 p.m. the silence was shattered by a thunderous roar three miles distant. 'We saw the explosions and got quite excited, the adrenaline pumping through us,' recalled Sadler. 'The SAS were similarly excited when they arrived back at the RV. We buzzed them home and on the way they talked us through the raid, discussing what could be improved next time.'

Though Stirling had no success on Sirte – the Italians alerted by the fireworks on nearby Tamet – he and his men were in high spirits as they returned to Jalo, a base shared in December 1941 with 'E' Force, a flying column under the command of Brigadier Denys Reid, which had captured the oasis the previous month. Reid was a brilliant soldier, brave, determined and indefatigable. Yet he had been born in the Victorian era and still believed a British soldier, no matter the circumstance, should be immaculate. 'Reid inspected us at Jalo,' remembered Sadler. 'We all had beards and he was a smart regular soldier. He didn't think much of our shabby appearances and our failure to shave.'

* * *

Emboldened by their success in December 1941, Captain David Stirling submitted a request to Eighth Army HQ for the loan of a 'specially modified Wellington' from the RAF. The Brigadier General Staff (BGS) of the Eighth Army, Alexander Galloway, sent a secret memo to Lieutenant-Colonel Prendergast asking his advice on the matter. It seemed Stirling had not learned his lesson from the catastrophe of November's parachute operation and Galloway told Prendergast that General Ritchie was of the opinion that 'at present more valuable results are obtained by using the SAS Detachment with [LRDG] patrols and he is not in favour of the parachutists being employed as such.' Prendergast agreed that it was a bad idea. Equally inadvisable, he had soon discovered, was his idea that the LRDG might inflict greater casualties on the enemy if they attached an artillery unit to their patrols. The honour of blooding the innovation in battle fell to Second-Lieutenant Paul Eitzen and his small artillery section, including Bill Morrison and Jim Patch. They left on their first operation in the middle of December, travelling in 'S2' Patrol, commanded by John Olivey, with the remote fort of El Gtafia as their first target.

Olivey was an interesting character. At thirty-six he was older than most patrol commanders, his thinning hair and furrowed forehead belying his physical and mental strength. Born in England, Olivey had read medicine at Cambridge 'without success' before emigrating to Rhodesia in the late 1920s. Olivey was one of those men able to absorb life's heaviest blows without a murmur of complaint. He failed as a tobacco grower so took up ranching. He married but his wife died young. When war came, his energy and good humour undimmed by personal tragedy, Olivey enlisted in the Sherwood Foresters, rising to the rank of corporal before his energy, initiative and intelligence were rewarded with a commission.

'We hid the gun behind the hill and I ran a telephone cable up to the top of the hill with Blitz Eitzen,' recalled Patch. From the top of the hill the crew of the 4.5-inch howitzer had a clear view of the fort. It resembled something out of *Beau Geste*, an isolated outpost in a hollow with a battlemented wall all around. From his position at the hill's summit Eitzen relayed orders to the gun crew below who fired fourteen rounds at the fort. Then Olivey and the Rhodesians moved in. They were expecting at least some resistance but instead encountered only four native soldiers, none of whom was prepared to die for the Italian flag. 'They were bewildered, total peasant types,' remembered Patch. 'I think they were rather glad to be out of the way.' There was very little inside the fort worth having, so the LRDG destroyed anything that might be of use to the enemy in the future, and set out for base with their prisoners. But that was when the problems began. The howitzer was carried on the back of a 10-ton lorry and the weight meant that the vehicle frequently got stuck in the sand. Eventually Olivey's patience ran dry and he ordered the gun to be disabled beyond repair and then abandoned.

Prendergast disbanded the artillery section when the patrol returned to Siwa; it was too cumbersome for the LRDG. Jim Patch and Bill Morrison were transferred to 'Y2' Patrol and came under the wing of David Lloyd Owen. He had quickly adapted to life in the LRDG, shedding the skin of the regular army officer to reveal underneath a man with a gift for guerrilla warfare. Like Easonsmith and Olivey, Lloyd Owen was brave, tenacious and charismatic, but above all he had the common touch. He surmounted class barriers the way he did sand dunes – swiftly and effectively. And his men loved him as a result. In contrast, some of his fellow officers found the new Lloyd Owen rather off-putting. One, Carol Mather, who had a short stint in the SAS in 1942, recalled that when he encountered Lloyd Owen he 'was brown as any Arab and sat now in only a pair of shorts with a black beard fringing his young face'.

While Lloyd Owen welcomed Patch and Morrison into his patrol, 'Y1' Patrol had been ordered deep into enemy territory on a hazardous mission under the command of Captain Frank Simms. Their task was to conduct a reconnaissance of Marada, approximately sixty-five miles south of El Agheila. There was a major radar direction finding (RDF) station at Marada and its detection of Allied shipping in the Mediterranean had made it a nuisance that had to be eliminated. The task of the LRDG was to pinpoint the RDF station – which in fact was situated inside a fort built in a hollow – so the RAF could launch an air strike. 'It was hundreds of miles behind enemy lines over difficult terrain, rough, cut up by wadis, interspersed by soft, powdery rock,' recalled Lofty Carr, whose job was to navigate the three-vehicle patrol towards Marada. 'I aimed my bearing at a false target to mislead aircraft which might spot our tracks as to our true destination. When we came to rocky ground where we left little or no tracks I changed direction towards the target.'

When Carr had navigated the patrol to within five miles of the fort, he and Simms went forward on foot at night for a closer reconnaissance. Carr had with him his theodolite. 'There was a risk because I had to use a torch to see the hairline on the theodolite and Frank had to read the exact time by the chronometer as I took readings on half a dozen stars.'

Once Carr had his readings he and Simms returned to the rest of the patrol 'where I worked out the position of the RDF station'. Meanwhile Simms decided to carry out another recce of the fort, taking with him Harry Chard, one of 'Y' Patrol's most competent operators, who had recently recovered from a bout of dysentery. Chard was instructed to travel light, just a revolver, his water bottle and a small pack of hard biscuits.

The pair disappeared into the darkness. But without Carr as his guide, Simms struggled to make much headway across the bullying terrain. Eventually the pair decided to camp for the night and wait for first light. 'We had to huddle together to keep warm,' remembered Chard. They were up with the dawn sun, washing down their biscuits with a swig of water, before striking out in the direction of Marada. 'The sand dunes finished about one hundred yards before the fort so we were able to get quite close,' said Chard.

They observed the fort for a few minutes but then to their dismay they heard the approach of two German trucks. Simms and Chard ducked out of sight and watched as the vehicles bumped over the sand towards the dunes. 'One truck stopped at the base of our dune and the driver got out and climbed up the dune,' said Chard.

Unbeknownst to the British soldiers, the trucks belonged to an infantry unit recently arrived in the area to protect the flank of the Afrika Korps. Rommel had withdrawn his men from Jedabia the previous week and they were now fighting a rearguard action on the Marada to El Agheila line.

An officer, Lieutenant Kost, and his driver, Franz Seidel, dismounted their vehicle and climbed the hill to observe the surrounding countryside. The two LRDG men knew they were in trouble. Their footprints trailed behind them, pretty patterns of betrayal. Glancing up, Chard saw a head peer over the top of the dune. 'Captain Simms shouted at him in Italian, hoping to fool him.' When that didn't work Simms screamed at Chard to shoot the German. Chard aimed his revolver at the Italian and fired. Click. He squeezed the trigger again. Another forlorn click. A curse, and then a command from Simms to run for it. The pair took to their heels, racing towards a salt marsh. Above them Lieutenant Kost shouted at Seidel to throw him his rifle. Taking careful aim, the German officer shot Simms in the back of the leg. 'I ran back to help him but he gasped to me to try to get back to our patrol,' recalled Chard. 'I jumped up and ran zig-zagging but the bullets were flying thick and fast so I dived to the ground.'

Back at the three trucks Carr and the rest of 'Y1' Patrol listened to the gunfire. 'With no officer I automatically took over as the navigator,' said Carr. 'There was no question of trying to rescue them. Our instructions in such situations were to get the hell away. The Germans would know that Simms and Chard hadn't walked there so we had to make ourselves scarce. The first thing was to head south because the Germans were afraid of following us too far into the desert. So we did that and obviously maintained radio silence as we were so close to a major radio station.'

Carr led his patrol south for a while and then found a suitable hiding place to see out the daylight hours away from the prying eyes of enemy pilots. 'I knew that not far to the south-west lay a large area of *serir*, which was flat and hard like a billiard table,' said Carr. 'So we drove on to that in the dark and that night covered nearly 300 miles.'

Chard and Simms were well treated by their captors. There was a desultory interrogation but the Germans didn't expect anything other than the standard name, rank and number. The two men ended their first day as prisoners dining in the officers' mess. It was a good meal, recalled Chard, the last that either would enjoy for a long while as the next day they were separated and transported into captivity.

The capture of Simms, coming so soon after the loss of Captain Hay, was another blow to the LRDG that they could ill afford. Then a few days later there was yet more bad news.

Lloyd Owen inherited Simms' task of reconnoitring the coast ahead of a planned thrust by XIII Corps. The Corps Commander briefed him on what he wanted in the way of intelligence and was of the belief that 'we really had them on the run'. 'Y1' Patrol set out for Marada at almost the precise moment the Germans went on the offensive. By 24 January the Afrika Korps had occupied Msus, and the LRDG withdrew from Jalo, first to Ghetmir, twenty miles east, and then as the German advance continued, all the way back to Siwa. One of those caught unawares by the speed of the German thrust was Captain Richard Carr (no relation to Lofty Carr), the adjutant of the LRDG. He, and seven other men from the HQ section were on their way to Msus to collect a quantity of petrol when they fell into enemy hands.

After the fluidity of the winter months, the desert war had become a stalemate by late February 1942. Auchinleck was consolidating his defensive positions at Gazala and Rommel was augmenting his thinly stretched supply lines while planning his next move. The British would not be in a position to launch a fresh offensive for several more months but Auchinleck ordered the LRDG to carry out a series of reconnaissance patrols deep into enemy lines, gathering intelligence on fuel dumps and weight of traffic on the roads out of Benghazi. He was delighted with the results, and on 7 April his Chief of General Staff, Lieutenant General Thomas Corbett, passed on a message to Prendergast: 'The commander-in-chief directs me to say how impressed he is with the work of the LRDG in the carrying out of their deep reconnaissance along the Tripoli–Benghazi road, and elsewhere. The information which they are producing is of the utmost value to us at the present time.'

Prendergast decided to have no more than two patrols at a time on operations. The others would alternate between Siwa and Cairo, where the vehicles would be refitted and the men rested. There were many distractions in Cairo in the spring of 1942. Once the pyramids had been climbed, and the camels ridden, there were shows at the Cairo opera house, roulette wheels at the casino and an open-air cinema at Heliopolis, to the north-east of the city. If it was a meal the men were after, the place to go was Groppi's. Not only was the food good, but on top of the restaurant was a roof garden where afternoon tea dances were held.

If soldiers were after something a little less sophisticated they went for a beer in one of the many bars in the city: Sweet Melodies (popular with the SAS), the Tavern Francais or the Long Bar, where there was a fight most nights.

The men of 'Y' Patrol could often be found in a bar run by a local woman called Wahiba, the girlfriend of Bert Woolley. He was the unofficial doorman of the bar and enjoyed nothing more than flattening unruly Australians. Officers and men never went out together in Cairo, although Lloyd Owen was known to treat his patrol to a night on the town. The social distinction occasionally caused trouble. 'One time me, Tich Cave and Mickey Coombs were out when we heard dance music from a building,' recalled Lofty Carr. 'We went inside and discovered it was an officers only affair.' Cave didn't care. He started to dance and within seconds the three soldiers were ordered to leave. One of the officers who had expelled them made the mistake of manhandling Cave, so he hit him, sending the man tumbling down the steps. 'By the time we reached the bottom of the stairs this officer was just staggering to his feet,' remembered Carr. 'So we hit him over the head with a flower pot.'

The Guards Patrol also landed in trouble now and again, on one occasion instigating a mass brawl in Groppi's with a patrol of military policemen sent to arrest them. All reports of unruly behaviour were sent to Prendergast who dutifully adhered to the same procedure. 'We would be marched in to see Prendergast,' recalled Carr. 'The charge would be read out and without looking up, he would say "severely admonished" and carry on with his work. That would be the end of that.'

By this point in the conflict it was already a challenge for the LRDG to walk far in Cairo without being congratulated for all they had achieved in the war against Rommel. Their scorpion cap badge gave the men a certain cachet and many were the offers of a free drink from a well-wisher.

On one leave, however, recalled Carr, they were instructed by Prendergast not to wear their LRDG insignia. 'It was a trap for deserters,' he explained. 'There were hundreds of them in Cairo – 'Loose Wallahs', we called them – and a lot of them claimed to be in the LRDG. So on this occasion the Red Caps [military police] arrested anyone wearing an LRDG cap badge because they knew them to be an imposter.'

Most of the LRDG began to get bored after a few days' leave. Everyone enjoyed scrubbing the dirt from their pores, their hair, their crevices, and the first few cold beers were heavenly. But then they started to feel the call of the desert once more. 'When we went on leave we couldn't wait to get back to the desert,' said Lofty Carr. 'We loved it. It was so pure.'

Throughout the spring of 1942 General Auchinleck came under increasing pressure from Winston Churchill to break the stalemate in the Western Desert. He and Rommel were biding their time, like two chess grand masters waiting for one to make the first aggressive move and it infuriated the British prime minister. He believed Malta was in danger of falling into German hands: something that, as he emphasized in a wire he sent to Auchinleck at the end of April, would be 'a disaster of the first magnitude for the British Empire'. Auchinleck retorted that he must have more time to build up his reserves but when Churchill was told a large convoy would sail for Malta during a moonless period in June he issued Auchinleck with an ultimatum: either launch an offensive against the Axis forces before the middle of June or be relieved of your command.

During this time the LRDG had continued its surveillance of enemy traffic – road watches – and also transported several SAS raiding parties deep into enemy territory. The operations had proved largely unsuccessful, although they lacked for nothing in audacity, and by May Prendergast was increasingly fed up with what was being asked of his unit.

In February he had written to Eighth Army HQ complaining at what he saw as SAS intrusion on the operational area of the LRDG. 'I consider that it would be most unwise for Capt. Stirling's party to operate anywhere along the road for the present,' he wrote. He also said that he understood the SAS wished to procure some of the old LRDG vehicles so they could start operating independently of them. Not wise, he counselled. 'The old LRDG Fords which Capt. Stirling is proposing to take are in very bad order,' he wrote. 'I consider that Capt. Stirling is taking a big risk in using these vehicles for such a long journey in their present condition.'

Stirling didn't take the vehicles and the SAS continued to rely on the LRDG as their 'Libyan Taxi Service'. He also looked to them for guidance in helping his embryonic SAS develop. 'We passed on our knowledge to the SAS and they were very grateful to receive it,' recalled Jim Patch. 'David Stirling was a frequent visitor to us and he would chat and absorb things. He took advice, man to man, he didn't just stick with the officers, he went round to the men, too.'

There was an additional reason why the SAS didn't become self-sufficient early in 1942 – navigation. The SAS had recruited forty more men following November's ill-fated parachute drop, and while the recruits had initiative, endurance and courage, none was a trained navigator. So Stirling approached Lofty Carr, by this time the LRDG's most experienced navigator.* By the end of 1941

* Dick Croucher was commissioned in 1941 and transferred to the General Staff at GHQ, Cairo, before returning to the LRDG as adjutant in 1943. The other first navigator, John Stocker of 'G' Patrol, suffered terribly from desert sores and was forced to undergo a skin graft and a long stay in hospital.

Carr was the unit's first navigator, attached to no single patrol but instructed to go on missions as and when required. Shortly before leaving the LRDG to return to the Sherwood Rangers Yeomanry, Pat McCraith had asked Carr if he would like a commission.

'What would it entail?' enquired Carr.

'Not much,' replied McCraith. 'You'd do exactly the same job as you are now.'

'So what's the point?'

'Well,' said McCraith, 'if you get your legs blown off you'll get a better pension as an officer.'

Carr laughed and told McCraith he'd prefer to stay in the ranks. It better suited his temperament. It was much the same answer Carr gave Stirling in early 1942.

'I'd done a number of jobs navigating for Stirling and he wanted me to go with him,' said Carr. He declined the offer and Stirling took the rebuff with his customary good grace. He asked Carr if he could recommend any other navigators. Carr suggested Mike Sadler.

Prendergast had no objection to losing one of his second navigators, as they were known, if it would reduce the demands on the LRDG. In May 1942 he wrote in the unit diary that in 'recent weeks LRDG has found itself more and more in the position of "universal aunts" to anyone who has business in the desert behind enemy lines'. He listed those the LRDG had been obliged to chaperone: the SAS, commandos (European and Arab), stranded aviators, lost travellers, secret agents, and concluded his diary entry thus: 'These demands have usually been met, but not without straining the unit's own resources and personnel.'

One of those to whom the LRDG played 'universal aunt' was Vladimir Peniakoff, of Russian origin, but born in Belgium and schooled at Cambridge. Peniakoff was too much of a mouthful for the British so they nicknamed him 'Popski'. He was brave but in the words of Lofty Carr 'a bullshitter'. 'He had tried to join us but Prendergast wouldn't have him,' he said. So Popski formed his own unit, 'Popski's Private Army' (PPA), and much to Prendergast's irritation the LRDG had another hand to hold in the summer of

1942, escorting members of the PPA on espionage missions deep behind German lines.

David Lloyd Owen was detailed to escort Popski on one such operation and was 'horrified by the rubbish' with which the Russian loaded up his trucks. It amounted to six tons of miscellaneous stores, a stark contrast to the spartan efficiency of the LRDG, who never carried any superfluous items. They set off from Siwa on 27 May, just a few hours after Rommel launched the offensive that became known as the Battle of Gazala.

CHAPTER FOURTEEN

'Rommel didn't fear anything'

Throughout the spring of 1942 Rommel had urged Berlin to give him the tools to finish the job in North Africa. His counter-thrust against the Eighth Army in December 1941 had convinced the 'Desert Fox' that he had the beating of the British – if only he was given enough men and equipment. But, as Rommel wrote in his memoirs, 'our demands for additional formations were refused on the grounds that with the huge demand for transport which the Eastern Front [Russia] was making on Germany's limited productive capacity, the creation of further motorized units for Africa was out of the question.' It was, in Rommel's opinion, 'a sadly short-sighted and misguided view,' and one that could have damaging ramifications in the Desert War.

In March 1942 the Afrika Korps received 18,000 tons of supplies, 42,000 tons fewer than he estimated his army required for victory in North Africa. He also received a few thousand additional men to augment his three German divisions 'whose fighting strength was often ludicrously small'. One of those reinforcements was a nineteen-year-old from Stauchitz, a small town in Saxony, thirteen miles west of Dresden in eastern Germany.

Rudolf Schneider had been drafted into the Wehrmacht in April 1941, the month he turned eighteen. Within a few months he was in North Africa, recruited into Rommel's elite Kampfstaffel, his 400-strong reconnaissance and bodyguard unit. 'I was selected for the Kampstaffel because I knew a lot about British and American vehicles,' explained Schneider. 'Before I was called up into the army I was studying agriculture at Witzenhausen [The German Institute for Tropical and Subtropical Agriculture] and I planned to go and farm in South-West Africa [present day Namibia]. As part of my education I had learned how to drive English and American tractors and trucks.' In the summer of 1942, 85 per cent of the Afrika Korps transport consisted of vehicles manufactured in Britain and America.

Schneider also had a reasonable grasp of English so he was posted to the Kampstaffel, the unit that in the German desert force most resembled the LRDG. It was commanded by Rudolph Kiel, the owner of a large farm in East Prussia whom Schneider had first met in 1938. 'We used English field guns, armoured cars, and the Matilda and Stewart tanks, all captured on the battlefield,' remembered Schneider, a small, sociable and shrewd man. 'But we used German rifles and machine guns, and German uniform, it was strictly forbidden by Rommel to wear British uniform even though we liked it because it was lighter than our own. The Afrika Korps uniform was made of a heavy cotton and with all the sweat it could be uncomfortable.'

But for the uniforms, little separated Schneider from the British soldiers he had been sent to North Africa to fight. He too had a sweetheart back home. Her name was Alfreda and he had her photograph in his tunic pocket. 'Every evening as I lay on the ground in the desert I would look up at the stars and talk to her and ask her to look after me,' recalled Schneider. 'She was my angel.'

He bartered for eggs with the Arabs and sometimes received cakes 'baked with the milk of a woman'. The Arabs also gave them information on the British in return for sugar.

The Afrika Korps suffered from the same illnesses as the British – malaria and dysentery the most common – and they groused about their rations just as their enemy did. The Germans even shared the British opinion of the Italian army. 'The Italian soldier was quite a good soldier but they were badly treated,' said Schneider. 'The Italians officers had something special to eat and the soldiers had bad food. The Italian officers had brothels but not the soldiers. There was a better standard of living for the Italian officer, whereas in the Afrika Korps officers and men shared the same food and the same hardships.'

There was, however, one crucial difference between the Kampstaffel and the Long Range Desert Group. Whereas the British saw the desert as a friend, albeit one that should always be treated with respect, the Germans viewed it as their enemy. 'We knew the LRDG were situated around Siwa but we were told to keep our distance,' remembered Schneider. 'We didn't like to go too far into the desert because if we were wounded no one would come and help us. Occasionally we saw LRDG patrols but we had instructions not to go after them.'

There were also, of course, sound military reasons why Rommel never saw fit to raise a close equivalent to the LRDG; notably constant fuel constraints and the fact that the British military installations were less remote and better guarded. Ultimately, however, it was because of the difference in mentality. 'It is true that we didn't have the initiative of the British,' reflected Schneider. 'We were trained to fight and think as a team, not as individuals.'

Rommel was not a general who sought the opinions of his peers, an attitude that earned him the dislike of several German officers, some of whom would never forget what they perceived as his aloofness. Schneider said Rommel was never arrogant, just supremely confident in his own ability. 'Rommel didn't fear anything. We all respected Rommel,' he said. 'We were also intimidated by him. He was not one for small talk. He was a soldier. He asked a question and he wanted a short answer. The only time he spoke to me was when I was driving him and he asked if I had a girlfriend. I said I did. "Just the one, I hope," he said.'

There were no SS units in the Afrika Corps, nor any members of the Gestapo interrogating British prisoners. In so much as any conflict can be considered 'clean', the war in North Africa was fought for the most part with integrity. Rommel despised the Nazis, as he did anyone who transgressed his strict moral code. 'There was one German soldier who raped a local woman in Buerat [Tripolitania],' recalled Schneider. 'So Rommel ordered him to be shot, and the men who shot him came out of our unit.'

The LRDG's attitude to the rules of war was ambivalent. In November 1941 when 'Y2' Patrol overran a small Italian fort at El Ezzeiat they captured seventeen soldiers, a haul that presented David Lloyd Owen with a dilemma: namely, what to do with so many prisoners deep inside enemy territory. He signalled Guy Prendergast, telling him of the raid and saying he would 'await your instructions'. Back came the tetchy response from Prendergast, angry at Lloyd Owen for attacking the fort when he had been ordered to harass enemy transport in the Gazala-Derna-Tmimi area. 'Dispose of your prisoners and do what you were told.'

Lloyd Owen considered shooting the prisoners a violation of the Geneva Convention and his 'own moral principles'. He presented the dilemma to his men and discovered 'there was a definite school of thought which wanted blood.' But then what were the options? Kill them in cold blood or let them go and have them reveal the patrol's whereabouts and strength. A compromise was eventually reached. Lloyd Owen first furnished the prisoners with a small but sufficient quantity of food and water and then transported them to a point eighty miles from the nearest enemy position. In that way they would stand a reasonable chance of survival while the LRDG would be able to complete its patrol.

On other occasions the LRDG flouted the conventions of war. Armourers loaded Vickers machine guns with bullets called 'bluebottles', non-conventional rounds that exploded on impact (also known as dum-dums), in violation of the Hague Convention that outlawed expanding bullets. In another instance an LRDG soldier on a road watch killed two Arabs who approached him and threatened to reveal their location to the enemy if they were not given sugar, tea and money. But as one LRDG soldier put it: 'I'm against war but I'm also against the Geneva Convention. If you get into a war, don't pussyfoot around pretending about conventions that nobody sticks to. Because when you're a young man, scared to death, with a gun in your hand, you're not going to worry about the Geneva Convention.'

* * *

There was one man on the Axis side of the desert who believed he could accomplish what Bagnold, Clayton, Kennedy Shaw and Prendergast had achieved. Count Lászlo Almásy was a Hungarian aristocrat, a veteran of the Great War, an inter-war desert explorer, and a proud member of the Zerzura Club. Bagnold had publicly praised Almásy's aerial exploration of the Libyan Desert in the 1930s but also suspected him of passing information to the Italians.

In May 1942 Almásy was back in the desert, commanding a small German commando unit comprising eight men in six vehicles. They set out from Jalo – now in Axis hands – and headed south, through Kufra, and then east to Kharga. Almásy soon discovered his companions were not made for desert exploration. 'He has no initiative,' the Count wrote in his log of one soldier. 'I have to keep asking and ordering everything – the men still cannot understand anyway, that despite experiences in the sea of sand, a long-range expedition through this realm of death is nothing else than a flight from the desert itself.'

Four days later Almásy complained that he always had to do everything myself and on 23 May he was bemoaning his 'worried, tense group'. Nonetheless he had gathered some useful intelligence on his operation, but when he reported to Rommel that he believed he had discovered a route to the Nile via Kufra he was shocked by his commander's reaction. 'Count Almásy, I hope to arrive there soon with my whole army by a shorter route.'*

That route involved Rommel leading his troops in a right hook, sweeping past the French garrisoned in Bir Hacheim, and attacking the British behind the Gazala line. While this audacious outflanking manoeuvre was performed, the Italian X and XXI

* Bagnold and Almásy met in 1951 when the count described this conversation with Rommel. Bagnold subsequently passed on the anecdote to a friend, writing: 'If true it throws a curious light on Rommel's attitude even at that relatively early date. Poor Almásy. With his knowledge of the interior and of how to travel in it he must have longed to do what my people were doing. But Rommel was no Wavell and he was kept on a tight rein.'

Corps launched a frontal assault on the Gazala Line to deceive the British. 'Rommel led us on this occasion, he navigated the unit,' recalled Schneider. 'We didn't know where we were going. He just ordered us to follow him.'

The fighting was ferocious. For three days the Axis and Allied armour fought while the First Free French Brigade held out at Bir Hacheim. Rommel's supply line was stretched to breaking point so he pulled the Afrika Korps back and formed a defensive position called 'The Cauldron'. The British drove on, confident victory was within their grasp, and so it seemed with the Afrika Korps having lost nearly 200 of its 320 tanks in four days of fighting.

But the 21st Panzer Division countered and the German anti-tank guns inflicted a heavy toll on the British armour. Slowly the battle began to turn the way of Rommel. On 10 June Bir Hacheim fell and three days later the British armour was decimated in what became known as 'Black Saturday'.

The Eighth Army began to retreat, pulling back from the Gazala Line and withdrawing all the way to El Alamein. On 21 June Tobruk finally fell, along with the surrender of 50,000 British and Commonwealth troops. Rudolf Schneider remembered the fall of Tobruk as a 'wonderful' moment; not because he and his Kampstaffel comrades believed it heralded the beginning of the end of the war in North Africa, but because they got their hands on the British rations. 'We had lived for months on black bread and these awful Italian rations. Suddenly we found fresh fruit and vegetables, even strawberry jam.'

CHAPTER FIFTEEN

'You have to get inside his mind'

With their customary black humour the British dubbed their headlong retreat east the 'Gazala Gallop'. For the Long Range Desert Group it meant the evacuation of Siwa, their base since the spring of 1941. The rear party left the oasis on 28 June and established a new base at Fayoum, a town sixty-two miles south-west of Cairo. 'It was hot and the sand blew and we had little cover, but on the whole it was a suitable spot,' wrote Bill Kennedy Shaw. 'And strategically Fayoum was a convenient place, for now having lost the good base at Siwa we had to find another back door to the country behind Axis lines.'

The back door was through the 'Qattara Depression', an astonishing natural feature 150 miles long, half as broad, and 450 feet below the Mediterranean at its deepest point. It was a pin-prick on the earth's surface but a crueller, more desolate spot would be hard to imagine, particularly in July under the midday sun. 'In the basin the heat is stifling,' recorded Kennedy Shaw. 'No hill gives shade, no tree breaks the monotony of the salt marshes. Drive your truck two yards from the beaten track and it will be sunk to its axles in the quicksands.'

'The Germans thought it impossible to enter the Qattara Depression,' recalled Rudolf Schneider. So, too, the Italians who, having moved into Siwa a few days after the LRDG's withdrawal, remained in the oasis, too timid to risk venturing east across the Depression.

Auchinleck, shortly before he was removed as Eighth Army commander and replaced by Lieutenant General William Gott (who was killed in a plane crash on his way to take up his appointment and succeeded by Bernard Montgomery), ordered the LRDG ahead of a new Allied offensive 'to do everything possible to upset the enemy's communications behind the Alamein line, and to destroy aircraft on his forward landing grounds'.

From the start of July LRDG patrols began using the Qattara Depression as the back door into the enemy's house. Crossing, admitted Lofty Carr, was hazardous in the extreme. 'Its salt marshes could turn to slush at night with the danger of our five trucks being lost in the quicksands. So we had to risk being seen by the Luftwaffe and cross by day.'

Carr recalled that the LRDG was confident in its ability to outwit the enemy on the ground. 'We thought the other side was inferior to us and in terms of brain power they probably were,' he said. 'One of Bagnold's sayings was "your target is always the mind of the enemy commander," and he didn't just mean the generals, he meant in your own particular engagement. What you think about is you are up against an enemy and there's a boss there, you have to get inside his mind, try to read his thoughts.'

Carr described the Afrika Korps as 'conventional' and believed they were hostages to their tradition of efficiency. 'The Germans, apart from not liking the desert, were predictable in any situation,' explained Carr. 'They would go along the road with a two-minute interval [between vehicles] in their convoys. We worked this out and threw bombs into them, adjusting the time pencils accordingly, and they'd all go off along the road at the same time. The Germans were systematic in everything but they didn't seem to realize the weakness.'

But while the Axis ground troops held little fear for the LRDG, their aircraft troubled their every waking moment out on patrol. 'I was terrified of low-flying aircraft,' admitted Carr. It was not the Messerschmitts or the Junkers JU 87 – Stukas – that disturbed the LRDG as much as the Italian Fiat CR.42, a single-seater biplane that was vastly inferior to the Messerschmitt in performance and firepower. That was why it frightened the British. 'They were a damned sight more dangerous than the others because they were so slow,' said Carr. 'When a plane dived to strafe us, the driver would drive, the rear gunner would do his stuff and I as the navigator would look at that plane and I would give instructions to the driver, like "right" or "left", and we would do very quick turns. Messerschmitts couldn't turn that quickly but the CR.42 could practically stand on the tip of one wing and follow you round.'

On one occasion Carr's truck was strafed by a CR.42 for several long minutes as he and his comrades lay spread-eagled in the clay among the tamarisk shrub. 'I was more terrified then than at any other point in the war,' reflected Carr. 'Afterwards I saw I'd hugged the ground so hard I'd left the outline of my body in the clay.' On another patrol the CR.42 came in so low, and so slowly, that Carr got a clear sight of the pilot hunched in the cockpit. 'For a moment we were face to face and I suppose the best way to describe it is having a feeling of evil,' said Carr. 'Here was this bloke, he didn't know me, and I didn't know him, and we were both trying to blow the living daylights out of each other.'

On 12 July a Guards patrol ('G2') under the command of Lieutenant Robin Gurdon was attacked by Italian Macchi C.202 fighter aircraft near Minqar Si'da as it transported an SAS party back from a raid on Fuka Landing Ground No. 17. The death of Gurdon, a popular and above all highly effective officer, was a severe blow to the LRDG, but it signalled the end of the unit's 'Taxi Service'.

In the first six months of 1942 the SAS, thanks in no small measure to the LRDG, had destroyed 143 enemy aircraft. As David Stirling noted: 'By the end of June L Detachment had raided all the more important German and Italian aerodromes within 300 miles of the forward area at least once or twice. Methods of defence were beginning to improve and although the advantage still lay with L Detachment, the time had come to alter our own methods.'

He might also have been aware – directly or otherwise – that Lieutenant-Colonel Prendergast's patience was wearing thin with the SAS. According to Captain Alastair Timpson, Prendergast objected to tying up the loose ends left undone by the SAS on their operations. 'One cannot blame Prendergast for being a little sour about the episodes when he had to cope with what went wrong in the administration of Stirling's glamorous sorties,' said Timpson.

Prendergast wasn't alone among the LRDG in feeling pangs of occasional resentment towards the SAS, in much the same way a big brother might take umbrage at the arrival of a younger, attention-grabbing sibling. 'They were a gung-ho lot,' said Arthur Arger. 'They were very good at what they did but they couldn't stop out for the length of time we did. If we were going to do something for the length of time we did, if we were going to do something like the SAS, we would go further afield and do it, and then go further afield still and do it. But the SAS could only do one thing and come back . . . they were short term, we were long term.'

It was a view shared by Lieutenant-Colonel John Hackett, a staff officer supervising light raiding forces in North Africa in 1942 (who would later command the 4th Parachute Brigade at Arnhem): 'One of the chief problems was to keep these little armies out of each other's way,' he recalled after the war. 'There was the LRDG practising its intricately careful, cautious, skilful reconnaissance . . . but the SAS would come out to blow up some aeroplanes and they were very careless about it. Lovely men, but very careless and they would leave a lot of stuff around, and they would stir the thing up no end and out would come the Axis forces to see what had stirred it up, and they would find the LRDG.'

Nonetheless there was little animosity between the two units, at least not in the first months of the SAS's existence. 'We were very pally with them,' recalled Carr. But in 1942 when the SAS began to expand (MEHQ promoted Stirling to lieutenant colonel on 28 September 1942 and authorized the expansion of the unit to a full regiment comprising four squadrons) he noticed a slight drop in standard of recruit. 'Prendergast was aghast at the way the SAS expanded so quickly,' reflected Carr. 'I remember him saying, "you only take the cream off a pint of milk once." That might have been the case with the SAS. One time at Siwa a bunch of SAS blokes arrived, they were pretty green, and they parked right by us. Then they dumped all their ammunition out in the sun, and we said – realizing they were green – you can't leave your ammo out there in the sun, it will blow up. Well, they were gung-ho, tough guys, they weren't having us telling them what to do so they told us to get stuffed. We did the sensible thing and moved.'

David Stirling returned to Cairo shortly after the death of Robin Gurdon and procured a consignment of American-built Willy's jeeps. With Mike Sadler as his navigator, Stirling now had the independence he craved, and on the night of 26–27 July eighteen SAS jeeps drove on to the landing strip at Sidi Haneish, an airfield approximately thirty miles east-south-east of Mersa Matruh, and destroyed or damaged thirty Axis aircraft for the loss of just one man. It was a brilliant example of guerrilla warfare, yet in the opinion of David Lloyd Owen it was the acme of the SAS in North Africa.

'From the moment [Stirling] began to get his own transport, and became independent of the LRDG, he began to lose his effectiveness because he necessarily had to concern himself with the mechanics of administration,' wrote Lloyd Owen. 'David Stirling was a magnificent fighting leader, but the tedious business of worrying where the food, the ammunition, the communications, the fuel and water were to come from was something with which he did not want concern himself. Up until then the LRDG had done all that for him.' This was a view shared by Peter Upcher, the quartermaster officer at Kufra in 1942, who described Stirling as 'an outstanding commander, brilliant, charming in every way', but he did have a flaw: 'The one thing about the SAS, they weren't very good at Q [Quartermaster]. They weren't interested in Q and expected it to be produced for them, or else . . . [but] the LRDG were absolutely magnificent. They appreciated the whole of the responsibilities as regards supply and they realized how long it was to build up all these things. Guy Prendergast used to tell me exactly what was required and I knew exactly what was required with regard to the LRDG.'

The Long Range Desert Group were fortunate to have three administrators of the highest calibre in Ralph Bagnold, Bill

Kennedy Shaw and Guy Prendergast, all of whom were considerably older than Stirling and therefore no longer prey to youthful impetuosity. 'Some said he was a bit dour but we all liked Prendergast, reflected Carr, who saw a lot of his commanding officer when he was appointed first navigator. 'He was a father figure, certainly to me. My parents sent me a cardboard "key of the door" for my twenty-first birthday and Prendergast risked his life flying to deliver it to me hundreds of miles behind the lines. And he definitely had a sense of humour, a sort of laconic one. I remember early on he told us we should learn how to pee lying down. Why? we asked. "Because if any fool stands up to pee he'll get bloody shot."'

Lloyd Owen held Prendergast in similar esteem, recalling that under the dispassionate exterior there was 'a very kind and generous heart', which few were ever permitted to glimpse. What the LRDG did see, however, was a commanding officer who 'never sent out a patrol unless he personally knew that the tasks were within its capabilities; he never sent one out unless he knew that it had a reasonable chance of attaining its aim [and] he always ensured that it was given the best possible equipment, communications, weapons, or intelligence, and he worked tirelessly towards that end.'

Even Prendergast, however, was powerless to prevent the LRDG becoming caught up in an ambitious and unwieldy operation in September 1942. Lloyd Owen had just arrived in Cairo from an enjoyable few days at the Cecil Hotel in Alexandria when he was called into Prendergast's office and informed he was 'going to have a big job.' The next day Lloyd Owen, Prendergast and most of the other LRDG officers gathered in GHQ in the office of John Hackett to learn of the 'big job'.

CHAPTER SIXTEEN

'The whole raid was a nonsense'

The price for losing Tobruk and the gallop east from the Gazala line was paid by General Auchinleck. On 15 August he was replaced as commander-in-chief by General Harold Alexander, two days after Bernard Montgomery's appointment as commander of the Eighth Army. The pair took up their posts full of optimism, Montgomery confident he could win the desert war with a huge offensive in the late autumn.

Before that, however, something had to be done about the supply convoys arriving in the ports of Tobruk and Benghazi. In August just 42,000 tons of supplies were shipped across the Mediterranean to the Italian and German forces in North Africa. It was, wrote Rommel, grossly inadequate (32 per cent of what his Afrika Korps required), but together with the arms, equipment and fuel captured in June it sufficed.

Benghazi had been the target of two previous small-scale SAS raids, neither of which succeeded, so Montgomery instructed David Stirling to make a third attempt to destroy the port's shipping and oil storage tanks, an operation codenamed Bigamy. This time, however, instead of a small raiding party of a few soldiers, Stirling would be in command of a force of 200 men as well as two light tanks. An LRDG patrol led by Ken Lazarus ('S2' Patrol) would guide the raiding force to Benghazi from Kufra, and while the SAS attacked the port, they and John Olivey's 'S1' Patrol, would assault the airfield at Benina.

Meanwhile at Barce (now called El Marj), approximately sixty miles north-west of Benghazi, an LRDG force comprising 'T1' and 'G1' Patrols under the overall command of Jake Easonsmith – now the unit's second in command – would attack the airfield in what was codenamed Operation Caravan.

The third raid was codenamed Nicety, and intended to complement the SAS attack on Benghazi. 'Y2' patrol, led by Captain Anthony Hunter, would guide a detachment of the Sudan Defence Force (SDF) to the Italian-held oasis and seize it, so that the SAS could use it as a base from which to launch a series of hit-and-run raids on the enemy's lines of communication throughout the early autumn.

The fourth raid was the most audacious. Codenamed Operation Agreement, it involved naval cooperation and the use of a small unit of Palestinian Jews recruited from Middle East Commando into the Special Interrogation Group (SIG), alongside Commandos, Gunners and Engineers, on an attack on Tobruk. Once they had penetrated the port from the land, the raiders – led by Colonel John Haselden – would destroy the coastal guns, fuel-storage tanks and the port installations which had the capacity to handle 600 tons of Axis supplies a day.

David Lloyd Owen's 'Y1' Patrol was tasked with leading Haselden and his commando force to Tobruk from the desert while two Royal Navy destroyers landed soldiers from the Northumberland Fusiliers and Argyll and Sutherland Highlanders in the harbour once the coastal guns had been eliminated.

David Stirling was horrified by the whole operation, which 'violated every principle' on which the SAS had been founded. His men were not assault troops, they had been trained to operate in small sub-units. In addition, Stirling worried that 'the number of troops involved [in the four raids] and the fixed day for the operation made them security vulnerable'.

Stirling was right to worry. D-Day for the four simultaneous raids was the night of 13–14 September, time to plan for the operations but also time for enemy agents to learn of their details. 'The whole raid was a nonsense,' recalled Mike Sadler, who was to navigate the SAS to their target. 'In the lead-up to Benghazi rumours had been buzzing around Cairo that something was up.'

David Lloyd Owen recalled that there was 'gossip at parties and in the bars of Cairo' about the raids, although security clearance was still limited to those few officers who had assembled in John Hackett's office.

The LRDG left Fayoum on 24 August for the 1,000-mile journey south-east to Kufra, arriving a week later. Soon they were joined by the other units involved in the raid: SAS, commandos and the SIG, all of them as ignorant as their LRDG comrades as to why they had assembled at Kufra. Lloyd Owen grew so concerned with the rumours – many of them fantastical and far from the truth – that he told John Haselden 'the sooner we could scotch the rumours by telling the men the truth the better it would be for all concerned'. Haselden agreed. The next day the officers in charge of the four raiding parties revealed details of their respective assaults to their men.

Lofty Carr had the responsibility of navigating 'Y2' Patrol and the Sudan Defence Force to Jalo for the attack on the Italians. 'Captain Hunter told me about it but I already knew,' recalled Carr. 'I'd heard all the details down in the village from the Arabs. They were all telling me "*Jalo*, *Jalo*, *Bokra*, *Bokra* [tomorrow]" and making throat-cutting movements with their hands.'

Peter Upcher, Kufra's quartermaster officer, was disturbed by what he regarded as the lax attitude towards security, particularly from the SAS. 'The Germans knew exactly what was happening and when we were going,' he recalled. 'And there were times when I felt the SAS weren't quite as good from the point of view of taking care as regards to the information they got as the LRDG and others.'

Of the four raids, only the attack by 'T1' and 'G1' patrols on Barce met with success. Easonsmith's force destroyed twenty-four aircraft, damaged a further twelve, and shot up everything and anything they encountered. Elsewhere it was unmitigated disaster.

The SAS were ambushed on the approach to Benghazi and forced to withdraw in the face of heavy enemy fire towards the shelter of a faraway escarpment. Dawn broke soon after and those vehicles still out in the open were picked off by enemy aircraft.

Jim Patch described the raid on Tobruk as a 'terrible slaughter'. A member of Lloyd Owen's Yeomanry patrol, Patch recalled that they escorted Lieutenant-Colonel John Haselden and his eighty-strong force of commandos and SIG to within striking distance of Tobruk on the night of 13 September: 'And they drove quite boldly into Tobruk just as dark was falling . . . but Tobruk was ready for them and they ran into terrible opposition and hardly got out.' Haselden was killed, so too most of the men with him and the two Royal Navy destroyers were lost.

Patch and the rest of 'Y1' Patrol waited on the eastern perimeter of Tobruk with orders to stop any German reinforcements entering the port. 'We installed ourselves near the road in a bit of a depression to keep out of sight,' remembered Patch. 'There were searchlights scouring the land for anything they could pick up but we were too low for them to pick us up.'

They shot up a German staff car that appeared on the road to Tobruk but by first light it was obvious the raid had failed. Lloyd Owen told his men: 'We don't want to be found here in daylight, we'd better get out.'

Operation Nicety was the attack on Jalo by 'Z' Force, a detachment of the SDF under the command of *El Miralai* (Colonel) Brown Bey, and escorted to the target by 'Y2' Patrol with Lofty Carr responsible for navigation. His first task was to prove to the Sudanese troops that the desert was neutral. 'I suppose I was surprised when I first realized they were scared of the desert but they had been brought up to fear it,' explained Carr. 'In the end Tich Cave and I rigged up a demonstration at Kufra to help them overcome their fear.'

Cave, armed with some petrol and a box of matches walked out into the desert on a compass bearing given to him by his friend. A short while later Carr marched the SDF troops into the desert and zig-zagged them around. 'When I knew I was near to Tich

Cave, their officers told them they had to give a big shout and the moment they gave a big shout, Tich put a match to the petrol,' said Carr. The effect was just as Carr had envisaged. The SDF didn't understand navigation but they now believed it was a form of magic.

In reality, of course, it was a science that Carr had mastered long before the autumn of 1942, the year the War Office agreed that all qualified navigators would be paid a shilling a day as a reward for their expertise.

Some navigators rode in the lead vehicle, sitting alongside the driver in the windscreen-less truck. Carr preferred to travel in the rear truck having first given the bearing to a second navigator in the front vehicle. 'That made my dead reckoning easier,' said Carr, referring to the method of calculating one's position on the basis of compass readings, speed and distance from a previous navigational fix. 'I could just lie in the back truck instead of having to give hand signals from the front.'

As the patrol made its way across the desert, Carr would record the course, making a note of bearings and mileage, so that when the commander called a halt he could show him their exact position. The most demanding part of the navigator's job came at the end of the day, when the patrol stopped for the night. 'When we pulled up at the end of a day's driving, the navigator would plot the dead reckoning as he waited for darkness to arrive,' said Carr. 'Then he would he take a snap shot of the stars with the theodolite to confirm the position.'

While the navigator performed this task, drivers checked tyre pressures, lubricating oil, petrol and water. They would also investigate any wear and tear to the vehicle – a damaged half shaft, a track rod that had been bent and so forth. This would all be written down and presented to the navigator. 'Then we reported to the officer on the state of the supplies,' said Carr. 'The most important was water because if there was a shortage then we would have to close down the patrol and return, and this sometimes happened. As a navigator I could only advise the officer; it was he who had to make the decision.'

The officer of 'Y2' Patrol when they set out from Kufra on the afternoon of 11 September for the attack on Jalo was Anthony Hunter, an experienced soldier who had joined the LRDG the previous year. Carr liked Hunter, who on previous patrols had entertained him with mischievous accounts of his schooldays, the punchline to most stories being a sound thrashing from his housemaster. For his part, Hunter was amused by his navigator's odd-looking beard. 'I couldn't grow a proper beard,' recalled Carr. 'It was thick on the outsides but nothing down the middle. Hunter described it as a "bugger's grip".'

Hunter's orders were to:

(a) To guide Z Force to Jalo
(b) To guide Z Force columns into Jalo for a night attack
(c) Such recce tasks as the OCZ Force will require.

The Yeomanry Patrol comprised Hunter, Carr and eighteen other ranks, travelling in five 30-cwt vehicles with three weeks of rations and water. The biggest threat as the force travelled north was enemy aircraft, but none were seen as they neared the target. 'The final stage to Jalo was begun at 1400 hours 15/9/42,' wrote Hunter in his report. 'The column halted for a star shot fifteen miles west of Jalo and when 4½ miles to the village on a bearing of 95 degs., debussed.'

Hunter and *El Miralai* Brown Bey split the raiding force into three columns with the right column ordered to attack the new fort, the centre one the Praesidium and the left column the old fort. After encountering a minefield, Hunter issued instructions to the left-hand column to find a way to the fort. Then he and Carr led the remaining two columns to the right of the minefield. A short while later they were challenged by the nervous Italian sentry, blasted to death a few seconds later by Carr's Vickers K machine-gun. Now all hell broke loose and the SDF troops fled, leaving Carr and Hunter 'high and dry'.

Hunter had his eardrums blown out and Carr, blasting away with his Vickers, attempted to fight his way round to the left where the left column was engaging the defenders inside the old fort. Hunter scrambled back to safety, writing in his subsequent report: 'Only some of them got inside [the fort] and the opposition from an enemy waiting for them with small arms fire and hand grenades was too strong, and they had to withdraw. At first light the attacking troops retired to the remainder of Z force, now on the western edge of the oasis. L/Cpl Carr was missing from this operation.'

When dawn broke on 16 September, Carr was hiding in a well on the outskirts of Jalo. Climbing out of the well, he crept unseen through the mud houses of the village until he found a hen house. Carr knew he had to take a risk and seek the help of a local. There was no way he could escape on his own. Not long after stealing into the hen house Carr saw the owner emerge from his own home. Catching his attention, the British soldier explained with his basic Arabic and some hand gestures that he wanted a camel. The villager nodded enthusiastically and disappeared, promising to return. 'Unfortunately the further west you went in the desert the less reliable the Arabs were because there had been more inter-marriage between them and the Italians,' recalled Carr. 'So this Arab returned not with a camel but the Germans.'

On seeing the approach of the enemy, Carr bolted from the hen house and took flight through the village. The Germans gave chase, their shouts audible to Carr as he weaved his way through the mud huts searching desperately for somewhere to hide. He spotted a large pile of harvested corn stalks. It was better than nothing, a slim chance of avoiding detection. But these Germans were no fools. Carr, hidden under the stalks, heard the soft tread of footsteps, and the low murmur of voices. Then a bayonet sliced through the corn. Once, twice . . .

'All right!' shouted Carr, sticking an arm up through the corn. The Germans began barking instructions. Come out, slowly, hands up. Carr did as ordered, brushing off stalks as he emerged from under the corn and got to his feet. The Germans looked up in nervous surprise, backing off a pace or two, rifles pointed at the gut of their prisoner. They had captured a giant. Carr now understood why the attack on Jalo hadn't been the formality they'd expected; the oasis had been reinforced by the Afrika Korps, rushed to Jalo after the raids twenty-four hours earlier on Benghazi and Tobruk.

'I was handed over to the Italians and the Italians had got so scared of us, the LRDG, that they treated us as if we were supermen,' said Carr, who was taken under armed guard in a convoy of three vehicles to a landing strip and then bundled aboard an Italian aircraft. 'Inside there I had a bloke either side of me with a revolver, and another opposite with a machine gun. I asked them if they intended to shoot the bloody aeroplane down. We landed somewhere, I think Benghazi, and I was interviewed by a very courteous German intelligence officer. I told him my name, rank and number, and that I didn't know what was going on.'

When it was put to him that he was a member of the Long Range Desert Group, Carr feigned incredulity. 'I replied that I was just the clerk of the Staffordshire Yeomanry, who had got lost in the desert and didn't know anything.' The German officer listened patiently to Carr's story and then affably informed his prisoner that they knew he was Lance-Corporal Stuart Michael Carr, First Navigator of the Long Range Desert Group.

Hunter and 'Y2' patrol reached Kufra on the evening of 22 September, their return and subsequent account of the botched attack on Jalo adding to the dark cloud that hung over the oasis.

The next day Hunter sat down to write his report, concluding that the raid failed for two reasons:

1. The enemy obviously knew of the operation and were waiting for it.
2. Owing to the darkness of the night the guides could not recognize the exact location of their objectives until they were close up to them.

With the report finished, Hunter joined Lloyd Owen and the other officers recuperating in the oasis. 'We bathed, lay out in the sun and rested,' recalled Lloyd Owen. 'We met friends who had been engaged on the other raids and we exchanged experiences and yarns.'

The cost to the LRDG had been heavy: six men wounded, ten men captured and the loss of fourteen vehicles. At least there had been no deaths and Lloyd Owen considered that the unit was 'bloodied but unbowed'.

Early the next morning, 25 September, the peace was shattered by a series of sharp whistles. Aircraft! A few moments later a flight of eight Heinkel bombers swooped over Kufra. 'They bombed the Italian fort up on the hill first,' recalled Jim Patch, 'but of course that was the last place we would think of staying. We were camped in the trees, all over the rest of the oasis.'

However the fort was just the start of the bombing raid. Next the Heinkels came in low over the palm trees. 'I was standing looking up into the small area of sky that I could see through the trees when suddenly I saw a great shiny silvery Heinkel come bearing down on us,' wrote Lloyd Owen. 'Its four cannons were spitting flame and lead as it roared towards us.'

Close to Lloyd Owen was Gordon Harrison, pumping bullets skywards from the Browning machine gun mounted on his truck. 'We got the vehicles in fairly open positions for a good range of fire,' he said. 'Suddenly Lloyd Owen let out a cry and I looked round and he was lying there.'

Lloyd Owen had been hit in the back and left arm. The first of his men to reach him were Tich Cave and Mickey Coombs, who dragged their skipper into cover as cannon shells continued to tear up the ground around them. 'Rotten fucking shots, aren't they?' gasped Lloyd Owen through his pain. Later, as Lloyd Owen waited to be evacuated by air to Cairo, Cave and Coombs continued to care for their officer, ensuring he had a steady supply of cigarettes and rum. He learned later that five of the eight Heinkels had failed to get back to their base because of the damage caused by the ground fire from Kufra.

It was a small comfort, however, to the LRDG. The entire operation, the four raids, had achieved little other than imbuing the enemy with confidence. 'The British suffered considerable losses in killed and prisoners,' noted Rommel, who flew to Tobruk to congratulate his men on repelling the raiders. He was particularly pleased to discover the SAS and LRDG were involved in the raids, soldiers who have 'caused considerable havoc and seriously disquieted the Italians'.

CHAPTER SEVENTEEN

'Please give my thanks to all concerned'

Field Marshal Rommel had good reason to celebrate the failure of the raids on Tobruk, Benghazi and Jalo. A fortnight earlier his Afrika Korps had attacked the Alamein line, hoping to smash through the British defences and capture Alexandria sixty miles to the east. The offensive was broken on the ridge at Alam el Halfa and the Allies now had the advantage in supplies and also intelligence.

The British had cracked the German Enigma codes through the Ultra team at Bletchley Park and in North Africa the information gained proved invaluable. 'I remember very vividly the day when I was introduced to uncle Henry, for uncle Henry was the pet name by which Ultra went in the Middle East,' recalled Lieutenant-Colonel Enoch Powell, a member of the Joint Intelligence Committee in Cairo. '[It] . . . told us the most significant and important things, in particular facts that enabled the German supply position in North Africa to be calculated more accurately than was known to Rommel himself. The cargoes, places of arrival, capacity of ships, ammunition state, the transportation difficulties, these became part of a picture.'

The picture was not complete, however, and so Montgomery turned to the LRDG to fill in the rest of the intelligence canvas. Enoch Powell already had experience of what he described as their 'mastery of desert travel'. In the summer of 1942 he had been sent by his superiors to survey the Qattara Depression and 'to ascertain whether it was possible for the German armour to execute a flanking movement'. Travelling in a three-ton lorry, Powell and his LRDG escort carried out a series of tests on the Depression's surface and he returned to Cairo confident that German armour would flounder in the basin should they try to outflank the British. The trip also impressed on Powell the skill of the LRDG, what he called this 'very remarkable unit'.

In early October the LRDG received its orders to coincide with the Eighth Army's forthcoming offensive: it was a reversion to Bagnold's original idea, a small reconnaissance force exploiting the mastery that had so excited Enoch Powell.

To Prendergast's satisfaction they would no longer operate in tandem with the SAS. Lieutenant-Colonel John Hackett, in charge of supervising light raiding forces in North Africa, recalled that to prevent the SAS encroaching on the LRDG's territory in the autumn of 1942 he 'drew a line down the map like a medieval pope separating out the Italians from the Portuguese in the Atlantic. And I said west of this line LRDG only, east of this [line] SAS only, and that kept them more or less out of each other's hair.'

The line designated by Hackett was the twentieth meridian of longitude east, a line that ran north to south through Jedabia, and that necessitated a move in October for the LRDG from their HQ at Fayoum back to Kufra.

For the next two months the LRDG, comprising twenty-five officers and 278 other ranks, was the eyes and ears for the Eighth Army as the great battle of El Alamein that had begun on 23 October gathered an inexorable momentum.

Yeomanry Patrol, now under the command of Captain E.F. Spicer, was in position overlooking the Tripoli Road in the neighbourhood of 'Marble Arch'* seven days after Montgomery launched his massive offensive 700 miles east.

From 1900 hours on 30 October until relieved by the New

* The 120-foot high Arae Philaenorum was built by the Italians in the 1930s, a lasting monument to their North African Empire, or so Mussolini had hoped when it was inaugurated in a lavish ceremony in 1937. The British didn't think much of it and dubbed it 'Marble Arch'.

Zealand R2 Patrol at 1900 hours on 8 November, the Yeomanry patrol watched the road, recording every vehicle that passed in either direction. 'We would camp a couple of miles from the road and each night two men would go up to the road to hide in among the bushes and sit there for 24 hours and make a note of everything that went past,' recalled Jim Patch. The pair took it in shifts, one peering through the binoculars, the other jotting down in a notebook his companion's mutterings. After a while they swapped roles. The men had water and dry rations, and answering the call of nature had to be done lying down, a test of the men's dexterity.

The LRDG didn't just note the weight of traffic on the road, they broke their surveillance down into motorcycles, staff cars, 15 cwt trucks, 30 cwt trucks, oil tankers. They even described – if they could see it through their binoculars – what the trucks were carrying: barrels, rations, barbed wire, tents and poles. On one occasion, there was an 'Italian girl inside'.

One of 'Y1' Patrol, Ron Cryer, recalled that though they knew their surveillance was of great value to GHQ, 'it was intensely boring because when you weren't actually down on a two-man road watch you were back by the trucks, and all you could do was lay under them all day. You couldn't walk about because you might attract attention from the road.' The men slept or read or played cards. Sometimes they had a competition to see who could kill the most flies. When a pair returned from a road watch their intelligence was radioed back to HQ, and then they might enliven their comrades' boredom with a tale or two from the past twenty-four hours. The excitement would soon, pass, however, replaced by the ennui that accompanied each road watch.

In the ten days of the 'Y1' Patrol road watch, the average number of vehicles in both directions was just under 100 a day. Yet within three days of the New Zealanders relieving their British colleagues, they were reporting to Kufra that enemy transport was streaming westward at a rate of 3,500 vehicles a day.

On 19 November 'G2' Patrol was ordered to a new observation area, forty miles west of Marble Arch, where they remained for the next eight days. The patrol commander, Lieutenant Ken Sweeting, noted that 30 per cent of the Axis vehicles had been captured from the British in previous offensives; he also said that there were more Afrika Korps heading west, away from the enemy, than travelling east to reinforce the frontline. And, added Sweeting, the soldiers going west were 'in much better form that those going east, judging by the shouts they gave each other when they passed!'

Pleasing though the results of the Alamein offensive were to the LRDG, the sheer weight of traffic on the Tripoli road made their existence far more precarious than when the road watch began at the end of October.

Alexander Stewart, a member of the 'G2' patrol, recalled that on one occasion he and a comrade were scrutinizing the traffic from their camouflaged position among some scrubs when 'a German convoy came along the road and stopped'. Recalled Stewart: 'The German soldiers pulled in off the road, and about 100 yards from us they got out of the trucks and walked as if they were coming straight towards us.'

The two LRDG men froze, hardly daring to breathe as the Germans came ever closer to their hiding place among the shrubs. Then, just when it seemed inevitable the Germans would see the pair, they unbuttoned their trousers and dropped to their haunches. Once done, the Germans sauntered back to their lorries and continued withdrawing west towards Tripoli.

One of the Germans retreating across Libya was Rudolf Schneider. 'After the attack came [at Alamein] we just began withdrawing west,' he said. 'We couldn't believe it. But the power of Montgomery's troops was too much. We didn't know what power the British had, and we were surprised by that.'

But it was no undisciplined flight from the enemy. Schneider and his comrades in the Kampstaffel withdrew with calm precision, disappointed but far from demoralized. They were certainly prepared to engage the enemy if the opportunity arose, as it did in late December when they encountered a New Zealand LRDG patrol – 'T2', commanded by Lieutenant Ron Tinker.

The New Zealanders had arrived to relieve the Rhodesian 'S1' Patrol in the Gheddahia to Tauorga area of the Tripoli Road on

19 December. Establishing a rear base of three vehicles at Gheddahia, Tinker and eight men set out in two vehicles towards Seddada the following day. But Tinker had underestimated the extent of the German withdrawal and on 22 December the patrol was attacked by the Kampstaffel. Tinker and two men managed to escape but six others were captured, among them private Charles Dornbush, a twenty-five-year-old truck driver from Mangaweka on New Zealand's North island. Twelve months earlier Dornbush had been awarded the Military Medal for beating off a Stuka attack with accurate fire from his machine gun.

Rudolf Schneider recalled that he and his comrades were delighted to have caught some of the legendary LRDG, and to mark the auspicious occasion he produced his camera and took a photograph of Dornbush.*

GHQ in Cairo viewed the LRDG's contribution to the advance west across Libya as invaluable, a report in December from the director of military intelligence in Cairo, stating: 'Not only is the standard of accuracy and observation exceptionally high but the Patrols are familiar with the most recent illustration of enemy vehicles and weapons . . . Without their reports we should frequently have been in doubt as to the enemy's intentions, when knowledge of them was all important.'

The role of the LRDG started to change at the end of 1942, the unit adapting to the fluidity of the Allies' advance. Tony Brown and his NZ Patrol had guided the New Zealand Division and the 4th Armoured Brigade round Rommel's defensive line at El Agheila in late December, the Kiwis outfoxing the Desert Fox so that the Field Marshal was compelled to pull back all the way to the Mareth Line, approximately 170 miles west of Tripoli.

Bernard Montgomery informed Lieutenant-Colonel Prendergast that the Eighth Army would launch a 'holding frontal attack on the Mareth position, while his main effort would be swung round

---

* Schneider was taken prisoner along with thousands of other Afrika Korps in May 1943. Shipped first to Texas, he later spent three years as a prisoner in the north-west of England, returning home to then East Germany in October 1948. He married Alfreda, his girlfriend, and still lives in the village of his birth.

to the south to outflank it'. The task of the LRDG was to reconnoitre the country over which this 'left hook' into Tunisia would be delivered.

The first LRDG patrol to penetrate into Tunisia was Nick Wilder's 'T1' Patrol of New Zealanders. They found the going so rough that on the night of 15–16 January they continued their reconnaissance on foot but Wilder soon appreciated the hopelessness of the terrain for what Montgomery had in mind. Three days later, however, on 19 January, the Kiwis discovered a route onto the plain 'where there is a break in the hills east of Ghermessa, and about 25 miles S.W. of Foum Tatahouine, which is wide'. This break was named in the LRDG's honour, and 'Wilder's Gap' proved of great value when Montgomery launched his attack on the Mareth Line. Again the LRDG had a role to play, and again it fell to the New Zealanders to fulfil the task demanded of them by Montgomery. As Bill Kennedy Shaw noted, 'it was only fitting that the Group's last task in Africa should be carried out by the New Zealanders, who had begun its work two and a half years earlier and a thousand miles to the east.'

A section of Ron Tinker's 'T2' Patrol guided the New Zealand Division on its left hook round the flank of the Mareth Line, a task that began on 2 March when Tinker and three other ranks set off from Hon. On 23 March their task had been accomplished and the patrol returned to the HQ of the NZ Division, while to the north the Eighth Army pushed on up into Tunisia, their victory in North Africa all but complete.

There was no further need for the Long Range Desert Group in the desert. In the first week of April they started to withdraw east, heading all the way back across Cyrenaica to Alexandria.

Bernard Montgomery took a moment to convey his thanks to the unit's commander in a letter dated April 2:

My dear Prendergast

. . . I would like you to know how much I appreciate the excellent work done by your patrols and by the SAS in reconnoitring the country up to the Gabes Gap. Without your careful and reliable

reports the launching of the 'left hook' by the NZ Division would have been a leap in the dark; with the information they produced, the operation could be planned with some certainty and as you know, went off without a hitch.

Please give my thanks to all concerned and best wishes from Eighth Army for the new tasks you are undertaking.

B.L. Montgomery

Once in Alexandria the men of the LRDG went into camp on the beach, swimming, sunbathing, and shaving. Addressing his men, Lieutenant Colonel Prendergast pointed to the unit medical officer, Captain Dick Lawson, whose extravagant whiskers camouflaged his somewhat chubby jowls. With the merest hint of a smile Prendergast declared: 'Those with a beard like the doctor's, or worse, must shave them off and the rest can trim and keep theirs.' He gave the men until 0800 hours the next day to reacquaint themselves with a razor.

Prendergast also gave them their pay, a small fortune for most who had been 'Up the Blue' (army slang for deep in the desert) for months. The priority, recalled one LRDG soldier, was to purchase 'bush-jackets, tailored shorts and desert boots'. One or two men even bought officers' pips so they could spend the rest of their pay in enjoying the amenities exclusive to 'officers' only' establishments. It was not long before most of the men were merrily penniless again, though Alexandria was as welcoming to the LRDG as Cairo the previous year. The unit's fame knew no bounds; there had been further articles in the newspapers back home, and the May 1943 edition of *Parade*, the weekly publication for the Armed Forces in the Middle East, featured a glowing account of the LRDG in action, under the headline 'Against Impossible Odds'. Adorned by a large photograph of three bearded members of 'Y' Patrol taken by the noted photographer Cecil Beaton, the article began: 'Now that the whole of Libya and most of Tunisia is ours I can reveal something of the tremendous British organisation which for the past three years has existed behind enemy lines in North Africa.'

Gossip abounded as to the future. A posting to Greece was mooted, a rumour that grew in substance when volunteers were required to learn the language. 'With a number of others I attended Greek classes, which were given by a very attractive young Greek woman called Maria,' recalled Jim Patch. 'But then in the middle of May we were moved up to the Lebanon to the Middle East ski school.'

CHAPTER EIGHTEEN

'Intelligence, initiative and discipline'

B squadron was the first to arrive at the Ski School, on 20 May, followed a month later by A Squadron. The school had been a hotel in peacetime, a ski resort at an altitude of 6,000 feet a few miles above the village of Becharré and named after the small grove of the original Cedars of Lebanon nearby. Originally the idea of the Australian Imperial Force, the ski school opened for business in December 1941 and such was its success it soon expanded to house the Mountaineering Wing of the Middle East Mountain Warfare School based close to Tripoli. One of the dozens of instructors who taught at the school was Captain Griffith Pugh. Arriving at Cedars in January 1943 he wrote in his diary that when on his first morning he 'looked out of my window a marvellous view greeted my eyes. Wonderful snow peaks all round rising 8000 ft above the hotel. It was perfect alpine scenery.'

Not only was Cedars an idyllic spot, the facility itself was an unimagined luxury after two and a half years living rough in the desert. But the men were not there to frolic. Captain Dick Lawson, 'Doc' to the LRDG, had explicit instructions from Prendergast. 'What I had to do on the medical side was to find out the best way to change completely motorized patrols into small groups of mountaineers carrying everything they needed from start to the finish of their objective.'

There was only one practical way to achieve such an aim: weed out the weak. 'Training began with three-hour walks without packs and later with empty packs working up to 40 lbs and two-day trips by the end of the month,' recalled Lawson, a highly respected medical officer who had been awarded the Military Cross for his courageous care of the wounded following the LRDG raid on Barce airfield in September 1942. Men soon began to fall by the wayside, succumbing to old injuries from the desert or the bitter cold of the mountain air.

As the men adapted to their new environment, so Lawson felt confident in recommending an increase in the intensity of their training, which started each morning at 0545 hours and ended with a 'cocoa or tea' at 2000 hours. Each week they marched with heavier packs, and for longer distances, until soon they were covering '80–100 miles with 60 to 80 lbs' across mountainous terrain against the clock. The men experimented with clothes, equipment and weapons. They found that they preferred the American Winchester .300 carbine, 'light and easily carried' over the heavier Lee-Enfield .303 rifle. There was less unanimity when it came to footwear, however, some soldiers wearing the Arctic Knee boot, others the American combat boot and a few choosing the South African brown leather boot.

They marched with mules but found them too conspicuous in the mountains; they went on patrol with an officer and eleven men but decided this was 'too cumbersome and was cut to seven'. But what sort of men were in these patrols?

Lieutenant-Colonel Prendergast required soldiers who 'had ideas and sympathies in common': who were friends as well as comrades as so much of their time would be shared in close proximity to one another. With several old hands returned to their former unit during the mountain training, the LRDG once more had to recruit. Prendergast drafted a list of requirements in any potential member of his unit:

(a) Tact, initiative, and a keen understanding of his fellow men.
(b) Intelligence above the average, and a sound military background.
(c) Courage and endurance.

(d) Perfect physical condition.
(e) A readiness to undertake any task that might be required of him.
(f) Some technical or language qualification.
(g) Youthfulness. Few men over the age of thirty [will be] accepted.

That was the other ranks. For officers, Prendergast expected all of the above as well as a 'knowledge of men'. 'For days on end he [the potential officer] would have to live with his men, endure their hardships, share their disappointments, and rejoice in their success,' stated Prendergast. 'Not only did he need to know more about their job than they knew themselves, but he also had to be more expert than they in handling weapons and equipment.'

The final characteristic sought by Prendergast applied to both officers and men, and was arguably the most important trait in any potential LRDG recruit: 'A man who had the reputation of being "tough" was by no means a first choice,' said Prendergast. 'Too often the "tough"' man is the man who lacks intelligence, initiative and discipline; often enough he lacks courage as well.'

Prendergast, who was still in Egypt, left much of the selection of personnel to Jake Easonsmith and David Lloyd Owen, back with the unit having recovered from his wounds. One of the 'few' men over thirty accepted into the LRDG in the summer of 1943 was Ashley Greenwood. For the 31-year-old pre-war solicitor they made an exception, but then Greenwood was an exceptional man. Tall and sinewy with a long neck, big ears and warm eyes, he was a scholar (he had a double first in classics from Cambridge) and an adventurer (he had been elected to the prestigious Alpine Club in 1936); he was also desperate to see some action. There had been none with the Royal Artillery, nor with the Commandos, and Greenwood feared that at his age he was destined to spend the war instructing men ten years his junior.

In 1943 the war was at a critical stage, yet Greenwood was in the Middle East attending a conference on Mountain Training. That he was there at all was on account of a freak accident to another instructor at the School of Mountain Warfare at Glenfeshie Lodge in the Scottish Highlands. He had broken a leg shortly before he was scheduled to leave for Beirut so Greenwood took his place and, en route to the conference, had a brief stopover in Cairo. Prendergast got wind of Greenwood's presence and asked if he had an hour to spare. 'With his usual thoroughness and foresight he questioned me in detail about the specialist equipment for operations in the European mountains,' recalled Greenwood.

When the Beirut conference was over Greenwood heard that the LRDG were on the hunt for experienced instructors. He applied, was accepted without hesitation, and arrived at Cedars in July with orders to train the New Zealand Squadron. From the start Greenwood was 'entranced': 'I had never known New Zealanders before and their whole attitude was different,' he remembered. 'They decided everything by conference and their relationship between officers and men was much easier, they just mixed.'

Ashley Greenwood, with his polished accent and slender frame was not at first glance the embodiment of 'tough'. Nor was Jim Patch, who had neither a powerful physique nor a confident swagger. In the desert Patch enjoyed the company of Lofty Carr because they shared a similar thirst for knowledge and, in the opinion of the former, the towering navigator possessed 'a splendid independence of spirit and contempt for back-room theorists'.

After Carr's capture Patch had taken on some of 'Y' Patrol's navigational duties and by the time the LRDG moved up into the mountains he was one of the unit's veterans. At Cedars Patch he palled up with Ron Hill, another man who at first glance was far from a frightening physical specimen. A librarian in Manchester, Hill had suffered from tuberculosis as a child and considered it prudent to conceal the fact when he was enlisted into the Lancashire Fusiliers. From there he was posted to the Royal Gloucester Hussars as a wireless operator: their interest in communications was one of several subjects that brought Hill and Patch together. 'By and large we used to think in the same way,' reflected Patch. 'He was a librarian and he thought in rather a more academic way than most of the other chaps in the patrol, and we could talk.'

Hill recalled that in the summer of 1943 the training to which the LRDG was subjected 'tested our endurance to the limit'. He continued: 'Sometimes we were skiing in the morning on the high peaks, where there was still some snow, and in the afternoon at sea level or sub-sea level, learning the joys of submarining and folboating [the folboat was a folding canoe] with the Special Boat Service at the Levant Schooner Flotilla base.'*

The worst, however, was still to come. Prendergast had arrived at Cedars to assess the progress of the men. He did a skiing course himself under Captain Greenwood, and enjoyed it, as he did seeing his men practise seaborne assaults off the Lebanon coast. But he was troubled by the limited scope of the LRDG, despite all their intensive training. They needed to increase their operational range, and the only way to do that was to become trained parachutists.

David Lloyd Owen recalled that when the men were informed of the decision – one which he sweetened by mentioning the extra two shillings a day a trained paratrooper earned – they were given the option to decline. Only six men did. The rest began to go off in small groups under Jake Easonsmith to Ramat David, the British Army parachute school in Palestine. First there was the obligatory medical, which involved nothing more than a test for colour blindness 'We were all lined up in front of [Doc] Lawson,' remembered Jim Patch. 'The only means he had to test us was the coloured cover of a magazine. He would point to different colours and we had to say which they were. I was as colour blind as could be.' Lawson thought for a moment and then advised Patch that when it came to leap out of the aircraft he should 'just follow the man out in front'.

Patch and his section of trainee paratroopers underwent their preliminary training and at the end of one morning's instruction were informed they would make their first jump the following day. 'We were given the afternoon off and went down to Haifa for

* It was the Special Boat Squadron, which was formed in March 1943 from members of D Squadron, 1 SAS, following the capture in January 1943 of Lieutenant-Colonel David Stirling. Hereafter it shall be referred to as the SBS.

a meal,' recalled Patch. 'When we got back to Ramat David in the evening there was a panic on, and we were told we were going to invade the Dodecanese islands.'

Ashley Greenwood was still at Cedars when instructions arrived ordering the LRDG to Haifa to board a ship to the Dodecanese. 'They asked if I would like to go, I said "Yes" and got permission from Guy Prendergast,' remembered Greenwood. 'But then a signal came saying I was to go back and instruct. Prendergast asked if I wanted to go [back] and I said "No". So he signalled back that I was "operationally vital" and I stayed with the LRDG for the rest of the war.'

CHAPTER NINETEEN

'Like hell, I am!'

Throughout the summer of 1943 the subject of where they might next be headed had never been far from the minds of the LRDG. It was a topic discussed as they marched through the mountains, as they returned from the firing range and as they endured parachute training. Jim Patch and a handful of other men had continued to learn Greek (others took German lessons) while Ron Hill refreshed his 'rather forgotten skills as a wireless operator'. News reached them of the Allied landings in July in Sicily and Sardinia, and soon the rumour took hold in Cedars that they were to participate in the invasion of Rhodes.

Rhodes certainly loomed large in the thinking of Winston Churchill and his generals; it had done ever since Benito Mussolini was overthrown as Italian leader in July 1943 and replaced by General Pietro Badoglio. By mid-August the Germans had withdrawn from Sicily across the Straits of Messina onto the Italian mainland, chased in the first week of September by the Allies. As the battle for Italy began, so Churchill turned one eye to the south-east, towards the Aegean Sea, the stretch of the Mediterranean from Greece in the west to Asia Minor in the east.

In the context of the war as a whole the Aegean appeared at first glance an insignificant backwater, but it contained three groups of islands that were of strategic importance. To the north the Sporades, the Cyclades in the west and in the east the Dodecanese. It was the latter that were considered key to the Aegean with

Rhodes, Cos and Leros among the most important islands. The airfields of Rhodes were of crucial importance in determining who controlled the Aegean and its islands, but at the end of August the British chiefs of staff recognized that they didn't possess the resources to overpower the 7,000-strong German division on Rhodes; instead they proposed an invasion of the smaller islands of the Dodecanese.

When Badoglio signed an Armistice with the Allies on 3 September (the announcement of which was not made public until 8 September), the LRDG were finally given a role. Along with the SBS they were ordered to the Dodecanese, ready to seize all the islands in the Aegean from the Italians before the Germans could intervene.

The lead elements of the LRDG began departing from the Middle East a week later, sailing from Haifa aboard a Greek sloop. David Lloyd Owen held deep reservations as to the haste at which they were being dispatched. 'The lack of reliable information was disgraceful,' he recalled, though he and the men welcomed the prospect of putting into practice all they had learned in the Lebanon.

In the evening of 13 September Lloyd Owen and some 100 men arrived at the port of Castelrosso, the principal settlement in Castelorizzo, the most easterly of the Dodecanese islands, lying just off the Vathi Peninsula on the Turkish mainland. 'We were received rapturously by the inhabitants and we spent a night there,' recalled Jim Patch. Their stay was brief. The following afternoon Lloyd Owen received a signal from Cairo instructing him to take his men north to Leros, approximately 170 miles north-west. GHQ had received intelligence that a German emissary had arrived to discuss with the Italian garrison the terms of a surrender. Lloyd Owen must seize the island, 'for it had a wonderful natural harbour and a good, sheltered seaplane base'.

Lloyd Owen sent Captain Alan Redfern ahead in a seaplane while he organized sea transport for the rest of his men. Redfern, a Rhodesian, was an officer Lloyd Owen could rely on, even if he had joined the LRDG only the previous April. As a young man he had shot and killed a lion that was mauling his father before transporting him 200 miles to the nearest hospital.

While Redfern flew to Leros, Lloyd Owen commandeered an Italian motor launch and crammed as many men as possible into the vessel, ordering the reluctant skipper to take them past German-occupied Rhodes to Leros. Ron Hill was one of those chosen by Lloyd Owen. 'It was a cold, wet ride and most people were horribly seasick,' he recalled.

Redfern and an Italian admiral were waiting for the motor launch when it arrived at Leros, the latter less than impressed with the strength of the British invasion party. The admiral soon realized the LRDG was just the advance guard and within days three Royal Navy destroyers and a brigade arrived in Leros harbour.

The LRDG were now instructed to revert to what they had done so effectively in the desert, sending out reconnaissance patrols to spy on the enemy: no longer watching the roads of Cyrenaica but the shipping lanes around islands such as Pserimos, Calinos, Kithnos and Syros. One of the most successful recces was by the New Zealand 'T1' Patrol skippered by Captain Charles Saxton. On the afternoon of 6 October they reported 'a convoy of 6 LC [landing craft], one tanker and one minesweeper', intelligence that resulted the next morning in the destruction of the convoy by the RAF in the waters close to the island of Stampalia, west of Rhodes.

Of the 1,000 soldiers and seamen in the convoy, fewer than 100 survived. They swam to Stampalia and reeled ashore into the arms of the LRDG patrol stationed on the island. A Royal Navy vessel, HMS *Hedgehog*, was sent to Stampalia to collect some of the survivors for questioning, but on its return to Leros, the ship developed engine trouble and put in to the island of Levitha.

When radio contact was lost with the *Hedgehog*, the British assumed the fifty or so German prisoners had overpowered the eight crew members as well as the ten men stationed on the island and were holding them hostage.

The LRDG was ordered to Levitha to quell the uprising, the task falling to Captain John Olivey in what was codenamed Olforce. 'I had attached to my patrol another half patrol making up my number to 25 and also 25 NZ [New Zealand] troops under Jack Sutherland,' recalled Olivey. The 'half patrol' attached to Olivey's Rhodesian section was made up of men from 'Y' Patrol, including Jim Patch and Ron Hill.

Olforce spent the morning practising rowing and paddling folboats ashore, each boat capable of holding eight men and their equipment. They then drew rations for three days, an additional Bren gun and 2-inch mortar and a powerful wireless transmitter. At noon on 23 October Olivey received his final instructions: the fifty-strong raiding force would travel to Levitha in two motor launches and land on opposite ends of the island, one section of twenty-five men landing on the south-west under Olivey and the other under Lieutenant Sutherland on the north-east coast. Olivey was informed that there were fifty enemy on the island, all survivors of the convoy attack a fortnight earlier, and he envisaged little difficulty in the two patrols sweeping inland and rendezvousing on the high ground in Levitha's centre.

Jim Patch was in Olivey's party, Ron Hill in Sutherland's and he recalled that the operation began ominously. 'Embarking into the tossing and pitching folboats, down the scramble mats from the ML [motor launch], in pitch darkness, was almost suicidal,' wrote Hill. One New Zealander slipped and plunged into the sea, his mates hauling him into the folboat before he was washed away. Despite the weather, said Hill, 'somehow we staggered ashore through the surf and heavy swell, dragged the folboats into hiding among the rocks, scaled the cliffs and our invasion was on.'

Olivey and his force of Rhodesians and Yeomanry had got ashore without too much difficulty on the south-west side of Levitha. 'I sent one patrol on in front to the right and one to the left,' said Olivey, 'and kept one to carry the wireless gear and equipment.'

The men climbed a short steep hill, their objective the ruins of an ancient Greek fort. 'We moved slowly up to this hill with the moon setting just behind it,' recalled Olivey. 'It was an excellent time to approach and I pushed on. The fort had a wire fence around it with a machine gun pointing out our way.'

Oliver gestured silently for his men to halt, then he and three soldiers advanced cautiously towards the gun emplacement. It was unmanned. Nonetheless Olivey was troubled. 'All the way up I had thought I saw people moving in the shadows,' he said. He and his men searched the fort but found no enemy. Their compatriots on the north-east end of the island clearly had, for suddenly they heard a prolonged exchange of gunfire. Olivey was unworried; he had confidence that Sutherland and his twenty-five-strong New Zealand Patrol would swiftly conquer the fifty or so lightly armed German soldiers and sailors.

But what Olivey didn't know was that the convoy survivors, having overpowered the crew members of HMS *Hedgehog*, had then radioed German HQ in Cos requesting assistance. In response, the Germans had despatched a large force of crack mountain troops recently arrived in the Aegean to help in the campaign to retake the islands.

After an hour's rest among the ruins of the fort, Olivey detailed Corporal Thomas Bradfield to lead a patrol up the hill to the north on which there was a meteorological station. The patrol didn't get very far before they came under fire. Bradfield was wounded in the arm and they withdrew from the hill to the fort, from where Olivey and his men 'settled down to exchanging rifle and machine gun fire'.

As morning approached, Olivey could hear the sounds of renewed fighting in the north-east. Then came sounds closer to his position: incoming mortar fire. 'The Germans' mortars were ranging on this slit trench I was in, and I thought "right, the next one is going to hit me,"' remembered Jim Patch. 'Which it did, it landed right on the parapet of the trench but didn't explode. It showered me with stones and things, so I got out a bit sharpish.'

In between ducking mortar fire, Olivey thought he glimpsed enemy troops moving down the hill towards their left. He ordered two patrols to move forward and check any attempt at encirclement. Jim Patch was in one of the patrols, along with Arthur Arger, one of Bagnold's original 'Blue-eyed Boys'. 'John expected us to attack the Germans where they were hiding out, but we didn't get very far,' said Patch. 'As we were crossing open ground some

German planes [Stukas] zoomed over our heads. They didn't fire but they were clearly ready to stop any activity we might want to engage in.' Patch and his patrol took cover and began exchanging fire with the Germans further up the hill.

The second patrol had more luck, returning with three German prisoners they had picked up close to where they had come ashore the previous night. 'We bundled them into the fort and tried to question them,' said Olivey. He got little of use out of them. The three Germans were too junior in rank, and too scared by their predicament. Their nerves frayed still further when their own aircraft launched an attack, 'machine-gunning the walls and dropping bombs in the area'. Olivey and the rest of the LRDG derived a cold amusement from observing the 'three sat under the table shivering and bemoaning their fate that they should be inside the fort, which they were certain would be flattened'.

As the day wore on the Germans began to move in behind the stranded LRDG patrols. Lieutenant Kay and his men were captured and the officer was marched by two Germans down the hill towards the fort.

Shortly after 1600 hours, Olivey heard a shout from Lieutenant Kay. Clambering out of the slit trench, Olivey went forward and 'found Francis standing between two Germans with steel helmets on. I quickly pulled my revolver – I had left my rifle in the trench – and at the same moment Francis K[ay] noticed me and shouted "I'm in the bag, so are you, and the whole show is over."'

Olivey screamed 'Like hell, I am!' fired twice at the Germans and then dashed back to the trench, ducking as bullets cracked over his head. There was one other soldier in the trench, a Rhodesian called Karrikie Rupping, and he and Olivey withdrew down the hill, scrambling down a 15-foot drop as the Germans stormed through the fort. The pair dived into a thick spray of maquis shrub and listened as the enemy bombed and machine-gunned the slit trench.

Patch and his patrol had seen none of this but when the Germans brought more firepower to bear on their positions they decided to pull back to the fort. 'We tried to get back but by then Jerry had overrun the place,' said Patch. 'As we were crossing the open ground, we came round some sort of bend, and we were confronted by a German machine gun . . . we didn't try and get up to anything desperate, to do so would have been suicidal. So we gave up.'

Olivey and Rupping remained hidden for the hour and a half until sundown and then slithered out of the shrub for a dusk reconnaissance. 'We now saw our own troops filing down the path,' he recalled. 'There seemed to be no guard over them though Germans were still looking for our men on the hills to the left and sometimes throwing grenades or firing into the bushes.' Meanwhile Olivey could still hear gunfire in the north-east but soon it began to slacken 'and at dark, completely stopped'.

Ron Hill and the New Zealand patrol had spent the day beating off all enemy attacks, and capturing as many as thirty-five Germans, but as the afternoon wore on they began running out of ammunition and were compelled to use the weapons of dead Germans recovered from no-man's-land. The LRDG's casualty list was rising and, recalled Hill, 'the only hope was to last out until dark and endeavour to make our way back to the folboats and the rendezvous with the motor launch.'

At 1700 hours Captain Sutherland arranged with the Germans a ceasefire so the wounded could be evacuated. Hill helped carry two New Zealanders to the inlet where they were handed over to a German medic. 'The German told us that about twelve of Captain Olivey's force had been captured and more Stukas were on their way from Rhodes,' recalled Hill who, on his way back to Sutherland, saw enemy troops advancing along the eastern edge of Levitha. It was dusk by the time Hill reached the LRDG's position. 'The mortaring had now stopped but the enemy was close enough to subject the area to fire from rifle grenades,' said Hill. He and his comrades now appreciated that their situation was hopeless. Two men had been despatched earlier to reconnoitre the beach ahead of a night-time withdrawal but neither had returned. A little after 1800 hours Sutherland sent out a German prisoner with a white flag. 'While this was going on I threw what arms I could including the captured machine gun and mortar over the cliffs into the sea,' said Hill. 'I turned and found myself looking down the barrel of a German machine gun. I froze. My terror at that moment can only be described by the old clichés – my blood ran cold, my knees turned to water, the hairs on the back of my head bristled.' The soldier at the other end of the machine gun belonged to the Gebirgsjäger, the elite mountain troops who had as their cap insignia the white edelweiss. 'He motioned me away from the cliff edge to join the others who, with their hands above their heads, were being searched by their captors. I let out a long, long breath of relief and thanked the powers that be for the Geneva Convention. The German prisoners we had taken earlier in the day then took over and we were taken to the German HQ where we met most of Capt. Olivey's party.'

But not Olivey himself. He and Rupping had evaded the German sweep of the island and at nightfall the pair began creeping down the hill towards the beach where they had hidden the folboats. They arrived at 2000 hours. 'We launched one of our boats, not without difficulty, as it is a four man load at least, and rowed out in the bay a little way, ' remembered Olivey, 'putting into the west side where it was dark and hauled our boat onto the rocks and proceeded to wait for the expected ML.'

Olivey and Rupping waited in the dark, both of them cold, hungry and tired. Olivey had a few dried peaches in his pocket, a small treat at the end of a demoralizing day. At one point Olivey fell asleep and then woke with a start at the sound of what he believed to be an engine. But it was only Rupping snoring. Then at 2300 hours he did most definitely hear the motor launch. 'We quickly launched our boat and paddled for all we were fit for the boat,' said Olivey. 'I was frightened that receiving no signal from us they would move out again.'

As they rowed they suddenly saw 'a fire burning on the shore and at the same time, a voice called us from the opposite shore'. It was Captain Dick Lawson, 'Doc', who had escaped from Sutherland's position with his medical orderly and a wounded New Zealander. There were also two other soldiers who had dodged the Germans and made it to the RV.

And that was it. No one else appeared at the RV and Jake Easonsmith on board the ML saw no signal from shore when he cruised close to the north-east of the island in the hope of picking up a stray New Zealander or two from Sutherland's patrol. 'So we had lost forty-three of the best chaps for nothing, as far as I could see,' reflected Olivey.

Back at LRDG HQ on Leros, Olivey made out his report, not to Guy Prendergast but to Jake Easonsmith, the unit's new commander. There were other changes. David Lloyd Owen was the new second in command and Alan Redfern had been promoted to major and appointed commander of B Squadron. Olivey was delighted to learn of Easonsmith's appointment, confident he 'would make an excellent CO . . . and everyone anxious to serve him'.

Nonetheless Lloyd Owen was dismayed at the upheaval at such an uncertain time. Prendergast had been appointed second-in-command of 'Raiding Forces', the coordinating headquarters of all the disparate special forces units operating in the Aegean. Now, the LRDG, the SBS, the Levant Schooner Flotilla and the Greek Sacred Squadron would come under the command of Colonel Douglas Turnbull with Prendergast his second in command. 'Prendergast was never consulted about any of this,' reflected Lloyd Owen, 'and suddenly found himself called away from the LRDG, which he had commanded so well for two and a half years. It was a tragic blow to us, and we all missed him dreadfully. It was such a waste of talent.'

It was not that Lloyd Owen doubted Easonsmith's capabilities, far from it. His concern was more that in Turnbull the LRDG were now under the overall command of a man who did not fully appreciate their talents and who, in any case, was answerable to GHQ in Cairo and they were starting to lose control of the Aegean campaign.

CHAPTER TWENTY

'We buried him in a cottage garden'

While the Long Range Desert Group and other special forces units had been engaged in bitter fighting in the Aegean, Prime Minister Churchill had been locked in a peevish argument with President Franklin Roosevelt. The American president was being begged by the British leader to help in the fight to defend the Aegean from the Germans. 'I have never wished to send an army into the Balkans,' stressed Churchill in a cable sent on 7 October to the White House. 'But only by agents, supplies and commandos to stimulate the intense guerrilla movement prevailing there.'

But the Americans did not trust Churchill, believing him eager to embark on a Balkan adventure as he had in the First World War with such disastrous consequences at Gallipoli when the attempted Allied invasion of western Turkey foundered in the Dardanelles Straits. Instead they wished to concentrate solely on maintaining pressure on Italy ahead of the planned invasion of France the following year. Roosevelt replied to Churchill's cable with one of his own, stating: 'It is my opinion that no division of forces or equipment should prejudice "Overlord" [the codename for the invasion of France] as planned. The American Chiefs of Staff agree.'

Churchill tried again on 8 October, reiterating to Roosevelt the importance of the Balkans theatre particularly with the Soviet forces beginning to threaten the region. But it was to no avail; the Americans saw no strategic importance in the Aegean and as a consequence the British were on their own in the Dodecanese

By the time of the Levitha disaster the British had abandoned any pretence that their strategy in the Aegean was anything but defensive; instead of trying to seize the islands from the Germans the focus switched to reinforcing the existing garrison on Leros.

The SBS arrived on the island in the first week of 4 October, disembarking at the deep-water port of Lakki (known to the Italians as Porto Lago) on the south-west coast of the island. Their commanding officer, David Sutherland, wrote: 'Leros is eight miles long and four wide with two narrow mile-long beaches in the middle . . . There are three barren, hilly features, each about 1,000 feet high. In the south-west corner is the all-weather harbour Porto Lago Bay.'

Sutherland considered that the island resembled in shape 'a large cowpat trodden on by two feet!'. Owing to its rocky and undulating terrain Leros had no airfield, but what the Italians had installed in their thirty-one years of occupation was a series of formidable coastal batteries overlooking the island's six bays.

Throughout October the SBS and the LRDG sat helpless in their defensive positions as German aircraft launched daily attacks on the island. 'We were on a gun position and had a fair view of the beach,' recalled Private James Swanson, a desert veteran. 'The Stukas used to come over day after day after day and come screaming down on that place . . . [with] the Stukas, it was more or less the sound of the wailing siren as they're coming straight down that demoralized folk more than the actual damage.'

At the start of November Leros was divided into three defensive zones – north, south and central – with the 4th Royal East Kent (The Buffs), 2nd Royal Irish Fusiliers and 1st King's Own Royal Regiment responsible for the sectors.

This force was augmented by Sappers, Ordnance Corps and the SBS and LRDG, as well as the existing Italian garrison. In overall command of the island's defence was Brigadier Robert Tilney, whose fortress HQ 'consisted of a single twisting tunnel blasted right through the peak of Meraviglia', in the centre of Leros.

Tilney had arrived on Leros breathing fire and brimstone, declaring to the men under his command that: 'No enemy shall set foot in this island unless to be a prisoner of war.' Tilney's plan was to ensure the Germans could not establish a beachhead but in doing so he deployed his men along too wide a front. Tilney held his two special forces units in reserve as a rapid reaction force in the unlikely event the Germans would risk dropping airborne troops onto the island's craggy surface.

After a lull in air raids, the Luftwaffe resumed their bombing runs on Leros in the first week of November with the Italian gun batteries receiving the brunt of the attacks. One such 6-inch battery was reinforced by John Olivey, recently returned from Levitha and now once again in the thick of the action. His position was on Point 320, 'an almost sheer rock mound rising 1,000 ft above the sea [also known as Mount Clidi]. It commanded a complete view to the north with the exception of the N.W. corner'. To the north, approximately two miles away, were two large bays and dotted beyond them were a smattering of small islands. To the east, the coast swung round 'passing a cave with steep sides and a sandy beach on the southern end and disappeared from our view by a high hill'. It was a concern to Olivey that this hill obscured about a mile of coastline and therefore made it impossible to bring his gun to bear on the bay about one and a half miles away. To alleviate this problem, Olivey ordered his men to dig a trench overlooking the bay and position some Bren Guns and a heavy Italian machine gun within range of the beach. A trench linked this machine gun emplacement to the coastal gun on Point 320.

With the defensive position completed, all Olivey and his men could do was sit and wait, and take cover when the small black specks appeared in the sky to their south-east. 'Alan [Redfern] used to come and spend odd evenings with me and we would talk about the possibility of invasion,' recalled Olivey. The pair had a bond that stretched beyond their immediate predicament; both were married men, both aged thirty-six, and though Olivey was an Englishman by birth, he considered himself as much a Rhodesian as the Salisbury-born Redfern.

Redfern was in charge of a combined force of Yeomanry and New Zealand troops – thirty in total – who were billeted about one a half miles south-west of Olivey, at Point 112, just north of Gurna Bay in the middle of the island. During one of their chats, Olivey told Redfern he 'was almost certain that no invasion would take place'.

On 5 November David Lloyd Owen was instructed by Easonsmith to return by Italian submarine to Haifa, and thence to Cairo where he was to recruit more men; Easonsmith had heard a rumour the New Zealand government were so furious with the fiasco on Levitha they had ordered the immediate release of all New Zealand troops from the LRDG. Lloyd Owen sensed there was an ulterior reason, however, for Easonsmith ordering his departure. He 'knew that disaster lay ahead', reflected Lloyd Owen, and he was being ordered off Leros so that at least there would be someone to ensure the continuation of the LRDG.

George Jellicoe, the SBS commander, adopted a similar policy and on 11 November ordered his second in command, David Sutherland, to sail to Turkey and contact Lieutenant Commander Croxton of the Royal Navy in order to 'make arrangements for the Leros evacuation should it be necessary'.

Sutherland's patrol sailed from Leros at 2300 hours in a wooden caique, cruising south-east at a leisurely four knots. As they passed the island of Kalimnos, Sutherland spotted through the blackness the outline of other vessels heading in the opposite direction. It was the first wave of a German seaborne assault group that had sailed from Kos Town a little before midnight. Their destination was Leros.

The first wave of the German invasion fleet – 800 troops in total – appeared off the north-east of Leros at dawn on 12 November. Captain John Olivey on Point 320 had a grandstand view as the vessels approached. 'The enemy's objectives were obvious, the cove below us,' he wrote, 'and the dead ground behind the hill to our N.E.'

All the Italian guns on the high ground in the north of Leros began firing at the ships below, the shells sailing off the hillside with a tremendous rush. A landing craft (LC) was hit just as it was about to disappear behind the headland, erupting in a ball of flame, but other vessels were reaching their destination. One LC dropped its ramp and out poured dozens of German soldiers. In the trench overlooking the bay Bren guns began firing. 'They returned machine gun fire and we could hear the bullets whining overhead,' said Olivey. 'They managed to put [up] quite an effective fire, however, and must have landed about four guns and a few rifles.' More LCs had disembarked their troops in the dead ground out of sight of Olivey and, with the beachhead established, the Germans began to probe inland, up towards the hill on which Olivey's section was positioned. A mortar was brought to bear on the LRDG and Olivey directed his men's fire at some German soldiers carrying boxes of mortar bombs up the hill to the east. A detachment of British infantry arrived and Olivey asked their commander to send one platoon down the hill to the left and another to the right with one held in reserve on Point 320.

The infantrymen set off down the hill but the platoon on the right became disorientated and the platoon on the left came under mortar fire that 'rather upset them and I found the whole lot streaming back to the hill in the rear'. Olivey 'pleaded' with their commander to hold their ground but his exhortations had no effect.

In desperation Olivey signalled Jake Easonsmith at Brigadier Tilney's fortress HQ 'imploring him to do something to get the infantry to stay on the hill with us'. A signal came back assuring Olivey that they intended to hold the hill 'at all costs' and soon the infantry began digging in alongside the LRDG. Throughout the morning there was sporadic sniper fire from down the hillside but it was clear the German invaders did not have the numbers to break out of their beachhead.

Olivey exchanged jokes with Easonsmith over the radio, something that 'put great heart into me', and shortly after noon all firing ceased and Olivey was able to pause to regain his breath. As he lazily scanned the horizon he spotted something away on the skyline to the west. 'I could see a low dark cloud very close to the sea and stretching about a mile wide,' he recorded. 'I looked again and the cloud was moving rapidly closer . . . the cloud came closer and closer and as it approached, it seemed to close in on the centre and got higher in the centre. The thought at once rushed into my brain – parachute troops.'

Inside the fleet of Junkers 52 transport planes was a battalion of paratroopers from the elite Brandenburg Division. Olivey stared at the 'truly wonderful sight' as the forty aircraft approached in perfect formation at a height of 300 feet above the island's narrow waist between Alinda and Gurna Bays. 'Everything was silent, every man on his gun, every gun pointing in their direction,' recalled Olivey. 'I shouted "paratroops" and ordered every gun to fire just below the aircraft.'

For what seemed an age, there was no reaction, but then, just seconds after Olivey's command, the first paratrooper left the aircraft. 'As the first man jumped, everything on the island seemed to open up at once,' said Olivey. 'Bullets flew overhead from our troops below. Everyone seemed to be firing. I'm not sure the officers didn't fire their revolvers. I had a Bren which got rid of three mags in almost no time.'

Olivey counted at least three aircraft that crashed into the sea and it was impossible to note how many men drifted away from land and to a watery grave in the Aegean. Olivey and his men continued to blast away at the paratroopers but even as he shot them dead he could not help admiring their valour. 'One must give the Germans top marks for that performance,' he reflected, 'which was a wonder I never expect to see again, from such a perfect position.'

Of the 470 paratroopers who emplaned for Leros, 200 were killed on the drop, either shot as they dangled uselessly from their canopies or drowned in the Aegean, and a further 100 sustained injuries as they fell on to the treacherous slopes of Leros. Nonetheless nearly 200 airborne troops were down in the middle of the island, with orders to cut Leros in two.

The bulk of the Germans landed close to the position occupied by Major Alan Redfern and his LRDG force. 'They dropped right across the narrowest part [of Leros] on the west of island, quite within easy range of our weaponry and it was impossible to miss firing into the clouds of paratroops coming down,' recalled Ron Cryer, a Bren gunner. Redfern instructed the Yeomanry half of his patrol to advance north towards Point 64 (Germano) so Cryer ran forward with his Bren 'and then suddenly found myself all on my own. I stayed where I was in a small ditch and spotted a couple of Paratroops crawling along a wall in an olive grove about 600 yards in front of me. I opened fire and hit them, and they went down and stayed down.'

Redfern appeared, 'and asked me if I could see anything. I told him I could see men in the olive grove. He said "good" and left me and went back round to other side of the hill'. Redfern returned to his command post, collected the New Zealand half of his patrol and began leading them towards the northeast side of the hill. Not long after he was shot dead by a German paratrooper.

By nightfall the Germans held the ridgeline on Leros's narrow waist, in effect severing the British defences in two so that the troops in the north were cut off from the troops to the south.

Throughout the next twenty-four hours the battle for the ridgeline, and control of the island's heart, was fought between invader and occupier. The Germans dropped airborne reinforcements but again they suffered heavy casualties and failed to provide the impetus needed to oust the British.

At 0200 hours on 14 November the British launched a counter-attack against the ridgeline occupied by the paratroopers. It failed, and the SBS and the LRDG were then ordered to prevent the Germans pushing north from the ridge.

Heavy fighting marked the following day, the fourth of the invasion, and the Wehrmacht war diary was pessimistic as to the chances of success, noting: 'The fighting is confused and information scarce, and changes in control by the enemy results in a confused crisis.'

Ultimately it was German air superiority that proved the decisive factor with Stukas, seaplanes and fighters pummelling British positions. A flight of Stukas had attacked a reconnaissance patrol led by Jake Easonsmith as they returned to the LRDG HQ at first light on 16 November. One of the eight soldiers, twenty-three-year-old signalman Cliff Whitehead from South Africa, was killed. He was buried later that morning, during a lull in the fighting, or so the LRDG thought. As Whitehead's comrades prepared to lay him to rest in a hastily-dug grave, a lone Stuka suddenly appeared, the group of men flush in the pilot's sights. There was nowhere to hide for the LRDG, recalled one member of the patrol, Signalman Toity du Toit, as the Stuka swooped. But 'at the last minute [it] pulled away without strafing or bombing, circled overhead several times, waggled its wings and disappeared.'

Before daylight on 16 November, Brigadier Tilney felt that his fortress headquarters at Meraviglia might be imperilled by the small number of German troops who had infiltrated the nearby village of Leros. Jake Easonsmith was again instructed to reconnoitre the village and determine the enemy's strength. Easonmith decided to lead the recce himself, taking with him just one man, a Rhodesian sergeant called Syd Jenkinson, 'Jenky' to his pals. The pair set off towards the village, walking along a road the sides of which sloped down to rocky terraces. There was a burst of fire. Jenkinson 'dived off the road onto a lower terrace and sheltered there'. He was aware in the darkness of Easonsmith following him down off the road. Jenkinson scrambled behind some cover but his officer remained where he was. Above him on the road he heard the approach of the Germans, the crunch of their boots on the stones and barked instructions at whoever hid below. Jenkinson 'saw them reach Jake who was lying motionless on the ground'. One of the Germans used his boot to heave Easonsmith from his front onto his back. He stared down at the handsome face and Jenkinson 'heard one of them pronounce the word "*tot*" [dead]'.

The death of Easonsmith was just one of a number of calamities to befall the British on Leros that day, the cumulative effect of which was to prompt Brigadier Tilney to formally surrender at 1730 hours.

When George Jellicoe, CO of the SBS was unable to establish communication with brigade headquarters he drove in a jeep to the fortress HQ, only to discover Tilney discussing surrender terms in the presence of several other senior British and German officers.

Concealing his disgust, Jellicoe listened to proceedings and then made for the exit. The Germans blocked his path. 'Where did he think he was going?' they demanded. With the same languid charm his men knew so well, Jellicoe explained that if the Germans wished his unit to surrender they must hear the news from their commanding officer in person. The Germans stepped aside and Jellicoe raced back to the squadron. His men greeted the surrender, what Jellicoe dubbed 'the Anglo-German Peace Conference', with a mix of 'surprise and horror'. Neither they nor their CO had the slightest wish to spend the rest of the war a prisoner.

Nor did Captain Ashley Greenwood, who asked Jellicoe's permission to round up as many LRDG men as possible before rendezvousing at the harbour. Permission granted, Greenwood roared off in a jeep to some of the gun batteries he knew to be occupied by members of the LRDG. Greenwood collected eleven men in all, one of whom was Ron Cryer, and they arrived at the harbour just as Jellicoe was preparing to cast off in a caique. 'We clambered on board and made our way out,' recalled Cryer. 'A couple of miles away from shore, it started to get light, so we decided to pull into a small island which had plenty of scrub on it . . . we all got ashore and hid in the bushes and there were German aircraft flying round all the time but they didn't spot any of us in the bushes. When it got dark that night we all got into boat and it took us most of the night to get into harbour at Bodrum.'

Behind them on Leros was a scene of utter devastation. In the five-day battle for the island the British had lost an estimated 1,000 men with another 4,800 wounded or taken prisoner. The Germans lost 1,109 soldiers killed or wounded on Leros, 41 per cent of the raiding force. One of the few British soldiers still on the island who had evaded capture was John Olivey. The last contact he'd had with British HQ was a message on the sixteenth instructing him 'to hold Point 320 for as long as we could to enable as many of our troops as possible to leave'. It had always been

Olivey's intention. On the morning of 17 November, the day after the formal British surrender, Olivey guessed the game was up. He could hear the sound of German singing from the village below his position, and the proliferation of enemy seaplanes in the bay – all of them landing unmolested – was further proof that the Germans now controlled Leros. Olivey ordered his soldiers to 'withdraw as quickly and quietly as possible and make for the broken and rocky country to the north'. His told his men he'd follow. First he had to sabotage the coastal guns before they fell into enemy hands. But the Germans arrived sooner than Olivey had anticipated, 'driving sheep before them' as they marched up the hill towards Point 320. 'I disguised myself as a body and the German soldiers passed by down the road, concluding that the position was deserted.'

Jumping to his feet, Olivey scrambled down the hill and hid until dark. He emerged at dusk, creeping to the nearest gun emplacement and laying a charge inside its magazine. Then he realized he'd forgotten the matches. Cursing, he returned to his command post on Point 320 to retrieve his matches. He got a nasty surprise when he entered. There were two Germans inside. In the twilight they mistook Olivey for their officer. 'I was forced to shoot them both but the noise attracted others and I had to make a hasty withdrawal,' he said. Dozens of Germans emerged from foxholes and slit trenches to hunt down the man who had shot dead their comrades. 'By moving quickly down the hill and disguising my whereabouts by throwing stones and immediately hiding I was able to make the searchers pass by.' Olivey crawled between a couple of large rocks. In the excruciating minutes that followed he counted three patrols searching the nearby countryside. None found him.

At dawn, having heard no sign of enemy activity for several hours, Olivey wriggled out from the rocks and continued north, intending to rendezvous with the rest of his patrol. But the going was tough, the drama of the previous few hours had left him tired, hungry and thirsty. He saw in the distance an Italian barracks. Surely it wouldn't hurt just to stop for a couple of minutes and see if he could forage some food from the abandoned building?

In his normal condition Olivey would never have countenanced such a risk. But he wasn't himself on this morning. To his delight he discovered bread, bacon fat and water. He wolfed them down. 'A bed with sheets proved too great a temptation and I climbed in,' recalled Olivey. He 'woke to find two German officers and some men at the foot of my bed'.

Of the 123 men from the Long Range Desert Group on Leros, 70 managed to escape but the rest were captured, a grievous figure when added to the 40 taken prisoner on Levitha. Among those captured on Leros was the unit's medical officer, Dick Lawson, whose luck had finally expired after his narrow escape from Levitha the previous month. Herded into a POW holding camp at Lakki, on the south-west of the island, word reached Lawson of the death of Jake Easonsmith. Like everyone in the unit he was devastated by the loss. Easonsmith had been the yardstick by which the LRDG measured themselves, not just in terms of physical courage but in moral integrity also. 'His most remarkable achievement,' reflected Vladimir Peniakoff, AKA 'Popski', 'was to create a standard of behaviour which came to be followed as a matter of course by hundreds of men who came under his influence.'

Lawson received permission from the Germans to bury his commanding officer. 'The party I took consisted of [Lance-Corporal Bill] Whitehead, Curle, Jenkinson [who had evaded capture], Hill, Booker, McKay and a German guard,' he recalled years later. 'We found him on the coast road and buried him in a cottage garden with a vineyard. Whitehead made a cross and wrote on it, and the owners of the garden promised to care for it.'

CHAPTER TWENTY-ONE

'All was right with the world'

Ron Hill found captivity a 'humiliating experience'. The word used by Jim Patch was 'shame'. 'Being a prisoner is not particularly honourable or praiseworthy,' said Patch. 'Ron was just as infuriated at the fact of being a prisoner as I was. We got chatting and decided to get together and make a run for it, and within a day of being captured we were talking of getting away, seeking every opportunity.'

Their captors, the mountain troops, treated the LRDG correctly, though Patch recalled 'they were full of the "*Heil Hitler*" thing, which we found very amusing. I don't think they had any idea what we were laughing at.'

The prisoners were interrogated in a rather perfunctory manner, an attitude mirrored in the way they were searched. All the LRDG had a silk map of the Balkans sewn into their beret, a thumbnail-size compass concealed in the neck of their battledress and a little hacksaw hidden inside the fly of their battledress trousers. None was discovered, not even Hill's map, though the interrogating officer asked to examine his beret. He was curious that it seemed to be padded. Hill replied that all tank corps berets were padded. The German gave a small laugh of triumph. He had winkled from his prisoner his regiment.

From the Aegean, the prisoners were flown by seaplane to Piraeus and marched north through the city to a POW camp, where they remained for a week. On 2 November they were taken through Athens to the railway station and entrained for the long trip north to Germany. 'While loading the trucks Jim and I had a good look round and thought we would break out if a guard didn't ride in the wagon with us,' said Hill.

There were around forty prisoners to each wagon and two men in Hill's and Patch's suffered from dysentery, creating a stench so overpowering it dispelled any lingering doubts the pair had over the wisdom of an escape attempt. On the morning of 3 November they had reached Thermopylae and there they remained for the rest of the day, sheltering from the possibility of being attacked by marauding RAF fighters. The train began jolting north at dusk but after two hours it stopped, and the guards stormed through the train, shouting and cursing and kicking the prisoners. It transpired that two of the LRDG – Eric Bamford and Harry Chatfield – had escaped during the stop at Thermopylae by kicking out the boards of the cattle truck. 'The German *Feldwebel* [sergeant] was very cross about this,' recalled Patch. 'He paraded us the next morning and made us understand that if anybody else tried to get away they would be shot out of hand. But when we saw these broken boards we just fell about laughing and that made him crosser than ever.'

On 4 November the train reached Salonika and the next day they crossed the border from Greece into Yugoslavia. All the while Patch and Hill had been sawing through the planks and the barbed wire that was bound round the outside of the cattle trucks. 'Eventually we had sawed round three sides so that the whole tangle of barbed wire would lift up like a window,' said Patch. They agreed they would go the next day and tossed a coin to see which of them would leave first. Patch won and had the choice: he was happy to lead off.

'As we approached the tunnel Jim was lifted up and passed, feet first, through the ventilation slot,' said Hill. 'His small pack was handed out to him as he clung to the side of the horsebox, then as the tunnel entrance loomed he let go and jumped clear. In the meanwhile I had been fed out, and with my small pack and blanket tried to remember my parachute drill . . . I hung on the sill and swallowed hard – the wheels of the train were disturbingly close – then pushed against the side of the train and rolled away across the ballast into the ditch.'

Patch executed a perfect parachute roll and lay for a few seconds by the side of the track until the train had chugged out of sight, its red light at the rear vanishing into the blackness. It was raining hard and suddenly he was overcome by a feeling of immense isolation, of loneliness, hundreds of miles inside enemy territory. He'd been in a similar situation before but now, in Macedonia, he had no idea if he could trust the locals as he had trusted the Senussi. He got up and walked back along the track until he found Hill crouched behind a telegraph pole, clutching the leg he had injured on landing. Nothing serious, he assured his friend. Not long before their leap from the train they had passed a city they believed to be Skopje, the capital of Macedonia, but in fact the 'city' was the town of Veles. They were still some way south of Skopje but that was irrelevant to their objective, which was to march on a bearing south of west, right across Albania, until they hit the Adriatic coast. From there 'we would steal a boat somehow and get across to Italy'.

It all sounded easy but within hours of striking out from the railway line the pair were in trouble. 'It was pouring with rain and pretty chilly and we just had our battledresses and a little Italian blanket that had been issued to us,' remembered Patch. As well as the injury to Hill's leg, the two tins of food inside his haversack had been crushed during his jump from the train.

Deciding it would be safer to travel only at night, the pair hid up in a small gorge at dawn on 7 November and spent the day huddled together under their blankets. The next day they encountered heavy woodland so they decided to risk walking in daylight and by 9 November the pair were tired, hungry and dangerously close to succumbing to exposure as they began climbing up into mountains. 'I was walking in front on the compass bearing and I looked behind me and Ron wasn't there,' remembered Patch. 'So I went back and found him sitting on a rock . . . he said "Sorry, I can't go any further."' Patch examined his friend's leg and saw that the wound was beginning to fester. 'I looked round for somewhere to stay for the night and found a little crevice in a rock which was dry but there was only room for one. So I put him in there and found another spot for myself which wasn't quite so sheltered. We were very tired and I went straight to sleep. In the morning as it was getting light . . . I found to my astonishment that I couldn't move.'

It took Patch several minutes to regain the use of his extremities but at least once he returned to his friend he saw Hill had benefited from a sheltered night's rest. Nonetheless, with their food gone and Hill's leg infected they agreed they could no longer rely just on each other: they would have to risk approaching the natives for help.

On 11 November they emerged from a gorge and saw in the valley below the village of Belitza. It was easy to reach the village, just a question of following the stream from the gorge into the settlement's centre. As they approached the outskirts the two soldiers saw several people filling up containers from a spring. Patch and Hill waited in line and filled their water bottles, smiling at the villagers who 'seemed completely struck dumb by our appearance'. Their water bottles full to the brim, the pair walked on towards the village square but suddenly saw an old man coming towards them, shooing them away with his arms and hissing '*Bulgar, Bulgar*'. Hill glanced up over the man's head and saw a soldier shaking out a blanket on the balcony of a house. Knowing that Macedonia was occupied by pro-German Bulgarian troops, Hill and Patch beat a hasty retreat, crossing the river Treska and heading north in an attempt to throw any would-be pursuers off their trail.*

By nightfall they were exhausted so when they spotted an isolated cottage in the woods, and the warm glow of a fire within, they agreed to take another risk. 'It was just about as primitive a hut as you could find,' recalled Patch. 'There was a thatched roof, there was a brick wall – mud bricks – about three feet high

* In 1973 Patch and Hill returned to Belitza and learned that the old man who had warned them of the Bulgarians' presence had been executed as a consequence.

all way round, and the rest was wattle. It was divided into two, the humans lived on one side of the divide, and animals [oxen] on the other. There was a fire burning in the middle of the earth floor, and a cooking pot suspended by a chain from one of the roof timbers.'

Patch tried out some of the Greek he had learned earlier in the year on the frightened old couple, reinforcing his words with gestures for food. They were given some sour milk and rye bread and then shown a corner of the cottage on which to sleep. 'All very rough and ready but it was heaven,' recalled Hill. 'We were fed, we were warm and tomorrow was another day.'

Ron Hill's celestial slumber was shattered by the barrel of a rifle prodding him awake. Opening his eyes he stared up into the face of several rough-looking men, their rifles pointed at his head. '*Documenti, documenti*,' said their leader, holding out his hand. 'So we showed him our pay books and he looked through them and we tried to persuade them that we were escaped POWs,' said Patch. None of the men looked satisfied. Use your Greek, Hill urged his friend, but that got them nowhere either. Then one of the men produced a Serbian dinar note and thrust it towards the soldiers. On it were printed the words 'Thomas de la Rue, Printed in England'. Patch and Hill pointed to the words and then to themselves, exclaiming 'English, English!'

The armed men visibly relaxed, and through sign language and the odd word both parties understood, it was communicated to Patch and Hill that they were in the presence of partisans. They left the cottage and marched through the night, the partisans explaining that they were in Bulgarian territory. For the next day and a half they were escorted across rivers, through forests and up hillsides until, on 13 November, they reached the partisan HQ. It was a cave, halfway up a mountainside, screened by a portcullis of branches and with a roaring log fire inside. 'A council of war was in progress and our arrival evoked little notice so we found an unoccupied corner and sat quietly with our guides to watch,' recalled Hill.

Hill and Patch soon understood it was a court martial, the defendant a 'huge black-bearded soldier, ashen pale, flanked by two armed men'. This giant of a man was dressed in a lavish embroidered waistcoat with the double-headed eagle badge of the Royal Yugoslav Army sewn into his cap. For several minutes the defendant argued his case while his accusers stated theirs. Then the man in charge of the court martial drew proceedings to a close with a sharp word. The two armed men marched the huge bearded man out of the cave and seconds later there was the sound of a shot. The pair returned to the cave without the defendant.

Introductions were then made between Patch and Hill and their hosts, who it transpired were not partisans but Chetniks belonging to the Vardarska Command of the Royal Yugoslav Army, loyal to King Peter and his government in exile in Britain, and hostile to the communist partisans, the Bulgarians and the Germans. They were loosely controlled by General Draža Mihailović, whose regional command was at Niš, about 100 miles north in Serbia.

The pair were told that the giant had been executed for failing to hand over all the gold sovereigns cached a few weeks earlier by Major George Morgan. 'Who is Morgan?' asked the two soldiers. In response to the question, recalled Patch, 'a radio set was produced, a very posh affair in a suitcase and with an acid accumulator. And a little battery charger with a handle, and then we were told the story of Major Morgan.'

Though the Chetniks were not in possession of all the facts – they had no idea Morgan belonged to the Special Operations Executive (SOE), the organization formed in 1940 to help conduct espionage and sabotage operations in German-occupied Europe – they were able to provide Hill and Patch with the bare bones of the story. Together with his radio operator, a corporal called Bukan, and a Yugoslav officer called Aleksandar Tasich, Morgan had parachuted into Macedonia in April 1943, dropping blind without a reception committee close to Veles. A few weeks after their insertion they had been captured by Bulgarians at the village of Tazhevo, fifteen miles west of Veles, and nothing had been heard of them since.

The story over, the Chetniks looked expectantly at the radio, and then at the two men before them, as if to say 'You are British, operate it, get in touch with somebody.' The Chetnik leader, Captain Siković, pushed some of the gold sovereigns taken from the executed man towards the pair 'and said he would give them to us if we could make the radio work'. It didn't take the two soldiers long to discover that the coil in the transformer had burnt out, so they rewound it and were able to show the Chetniks that the set functioned. That was the good news. The bad news, as Hill explained, was that 'the people at the other end had long since abandoned the transmission schedules' and no response was forthcoming from either Niš or Cairo, when Hill and Patch attempted to contact GHQ.

The day after their arrival at the cave, Hill and Patch were introduced to the Chetniks' regional commander, Colonel Dušan Marković, who spoke enough English to make himself understood. He explained the situation on the ground, in particular the considerable animosity that existed between the Chetniks and the partisans. The latter were led by Josip Broz, better known as Marshal Tito, whose strong leadership since the German invasion had turned the Yugoslav Communist Party into an organized and effective resistance force. Though Marković was well turned out, the twenty or so men living in the cave were dressed in an assortment of rough clothes. 'One chap was so ragged that all his clothes consisted of nothing but patches, all sewn together,' recalled Patch, while Hill was horrified to see a young woman among the Chetniks without any boots. Bloody footprints trailed behind her.

It was apparent to Patch and Hill that the Chetniks intended to use their presence in the mountains to their advantage. After all, two British soldiers operating with the Chetniks would give them some status, and might even prise from London some much needed arms and equipment. For the moment they were using old rifles from the First World War, along with one or two German submachine guns taken from dead Bulgarians. The Chetniks began referring to Patch and Hill as the 'British

Military Mission', as if they had been sent officially from London to replace Major Morgan. The pair made it clear to Marković they were anxious to contact the British to pass on the intelligence they had been mentally gathering ever since their capture, but he was cagey about the possibility of smuggling them out of Yugoslavia.

By the middle of December the Yugoslav winter had well and truly arrived. Food was scarce and both Patch and Hill fell ill, the former with lumbago, the latter with a bout of recurrent malaria. For a few days they had nothing to eat but chestnuts, and by now word had reached the Bulgarians of the 'British Military Mission' up in the mountains. There were 'sweeps' conducted, dozens of enemy soldiers suddenly arriving in the area, cordoning off escape routes and sending small teams up into the mountains via different routes. The Chetniks were wise to such operations, however, and were in the habit of using goat herdsmen – usually young boys – to drive their animals into the path of the Bulgarians so that they had plenty of time to escape.

Few of the 'sweeps' were successful. The Chetniks knew too much was at stake to risk being caught so they had several escape routes and frequently moved hideouts. Patch remembered being told about one Chetnik caught by the Bulgarians: his fingernails were torn out during his interrogation and then he was buried alive. But it was a savage war on both sides. 'We caught the odd Bulgarian from time to time but they didn't live long either,' remembered Patch. 'There was one occasion when it was learned that a man in a certain village was collaborating with the Bulgarians so our chaps got up a little party to go and visit him . . . they accepted his hospitality, had a meal from him, and when they'd finished their meal they took him outside, took him to a bridge over the river where they shot him. Then they dismembered his body and . . . the parts were then spread around the four corners of the bridge with the head placed on the trunk in the centre.'

When the men returned to the hideout Patch asked one of their number what had happened. Grinning, the partisan produced a dirty rag from his pocket. 'He unfolded it and there were two obscene looking pieces of gristle in there and he said "Look, these are his eyes."' Patch and Hill 'protested against the barbarity but were told it was an old Turkish custom to prevent the spirit re-entering the body (by placing it over running water) and, by dismembering, ensuring the victim was denied access to the *houris* in paradise.'

Even without the stress of possible capture it was a hard way of life for Patch and Hill, two men from big British cities, who had spent two years fighting in the searing heat of North Africa. They passed the winter in mending their equipment, darning their clothes and playing nursemaid to the Chetniks 'who were quite incapable of looking after themselves if anything went wrong . . . we became their doctors, handy men and advisors on all sorts of subjects'.

Their lowest ebb was at the end of December. On Christmas Day itself the pair had toasted each other with a small tin of syrup they had saved for the occasion. Then they turned on the radio to hear the King's Speech. 'Tried <u>hard</u> not to think of home,' Hill wrote in his diary.

A few days later the battery charger for the radio died and it felt like the death of a friend. Now they didn't even have the wireless for company. They did have each other, however, and it was their kinship that kept them strong when they felt their spirits dip. Often they would sit and talk, recalled Patch, 'discussing a wide range of subjects, including politics. It never got to any serious disagreement. We were both I suppose mild characters, certainly not used to all this violence. And that was the reason . . . we were both middle of the road men. Neither of us had very strong views, to the left or the right. And we were willing to accept points of views and we never had any serious disagreements.' They also possessed that most invaluable of British qualities – an eye for the absurd, an ability to find humour even in the blackest of circumstances. When Patch was afflicted by a bout of crippling lumbago in the middle of January 1944, the only way he could sleep was if he was tied to a tree. Hill tried to look sympathetic but his giggles won through and he told Patch he was giving Rowton Houses a good name.*

On February 7 the Chetniks welcomed a senior officer called Milanović, who had arrived at their hideout with another Yugoslav army officer, and a British-trained wireless operator from MO4, a Middle East branch of SOE. He had recently parachuted into the area to work for the British Military Mission in Serbia under a Major John Sehmer, a liaison officer whose task was to organize the various resistance groups in the region.†

Milanović wished to see for himself the two British soldiers who had stumbled into the mountains two months earlier. Satisfied that Patch and Hill were genuine, Milanović told his wireless operator to send a message to Major Sehmer. 'The wireless link with Major Sehmer was a godsend as we were able for the first time to send a message, via him, to Cairo, to say we were safe and well,' said Hill.

There was no reply from Sehmer for nearly a week. Then on 14 February he sent a message telling Patch and Hill to 'hold on'. The pair assured Sehmer they would do just that, and then they sent him their intelligence report about Greece. Their hopes raised by the link they had established with a British officer, the two LRDG men spent several frustrating days waiting for news from Serbia. Surely, they told one another, some means of getting them out of Yugoslavia would be found.

But February dragged into March and no news came from Major Sehmer while the Chetniks showed no inclination to help them leave the country. Far from it. They were proud to have the pair with them. A captured Bulgarian was brought to their camp and abused verbally for fighting against his own people, a people that used the same alphabet, spoke nearly the same language, shared the same Greek Orthodox religion. 'Jim and I were also paraded

---

* Rowton Houses were a chain of hostels at the turn of the century used as accommodation for working men. For one shilling a man would be allocated a cubicle and the use of a communal bathroom.

† Sehmer, an Englishman born to a Yugoslav mother, was a 41-year-old engineer, who had joined SOE in January 1943. He spent more than eighteen months operating in the Balkans before being caught in Slovakia in December 1944. He was executed at Mauthausen Concentration Camp.

before him as the British Military Mission,' said Hill. 'But this cut no ice with him for he said, scornfully, he wouldn't have anything to do with such a lot of bandits.' He was shot and his clothes shared among the Chetniks.

Soon the radio broke and the Chetniks prevaricated over securing the replacement parts. Hill and Patch began to despair of ever leaving their mountain hideout, Hill recording their angst in his diary.

> March 20: Much recrimination especially as regards W/T sets
> March 23: Will not allow us to go to Albania . . . but Marković has promised to send for sets so that Jim and I can mend them.
> March 28: Further quarrel with Marković. Told him we were determined to go off on our own as soon as the weather permits.
> April 5: Have again asked to go to Serbia

But again there was no reply from Major Sehmer who, unbeknown to Patch and Hill, had received orders from London to focus his energies on improving ties with Tito's partisans rather than General Draža Mihailović's Chetniks.

Eventually Hill and Patch became resigned to their fate, realizing that they would just have to exercise patience. At least spring had arrived so they could sit outside in the warmth and try to forget their troubles. One evening the pair were sitting among some wild thyme in a dense forest when a nightingale burst into song nearby. 'Its clear, pure music soared and trilled in musical ecstasy,' recalled Hill. 'Soon other nightingales took up the singing and filled the valley with magic. We crouched among the bushes and let the music pour over us. We forgot the war, the danger we were in and the tribulations of the winter. God was in his Heaven. All was right with the world.'

On the morning of 30 March Hill and Patch saw another welcome sight in the sky: fifty Liberator bombers returning from a raid on some enemy-held city. 'Might the war soon be over?' they asked one another.

CHAPTER TWENTY-TWO

'The bravest man I've ever met'

The signal that Ron Hill and Jim Patch sent to Cairo on 7 February was in time passed on to the LRDG HQ. In the three and a half months since the pair's capture on Levitha, the unit had undergone great upheaval. Not only had the LRDG suffered the death of their commanding officer, Jake Easonsmith, they had also lost A Squadron in its entirety, withdrawn at the insistence of the New Zealand Government, whose fury at events on Levitha was palpable in a series of telegrams sent to the British government in November. '[We] are greatly disturbed over events in the Dodecanese Islands,' began one such cable, concluding: 'His Majesty's government in New Zealand wish to observe that they were never consulted as to the use of their troops in this connexion nor, they are advised, was their Commanding Officer [General Freyberg] in the Middle East advised until the men had actually landed.'

The New Zealand position irritated Anthony Eden, Secretary of State for War, who considered it naive and displaying a core misunderstanding of the exigencies of war. Furthermore, he wrote in a letter to the Rt Hon. Lord Cranborne, Secretary of State for Dominion Affairs, he had consulted with General Alexander, commander-in-chief, Middle East, who assured him 'that General Freyberg was kept in the picture and agreed to the use of the New Zealand squadron in the Aegean operation before the squadron was sent to Castelloriso [*sic*]. It is clear from this that General

Freyberg's agreement was obtained before the squadron was actually involved in any fighting'. In addition General Alexander had been led to believe that 'Freyberg informed the New Zealand government at the time that he had given his approval.'

Nevertheless, the upshot was that on 29 December 1943 A Squadron, the Kiwi squadron, was withdrawn from the Long Range Desert Group.

David Lloyd Owen, who had replaced Easonsmith as commanding officer (and been promoted to a half colonel) therefore reorganized the squadron, handing command of the Rhodesian A squadron to Major Ken Lazarus, and appointing Major Moir Stormonth Darling commander of the British B squadron. Each squadron comprised eight patrols of one officer and ten men with a signaller, medical orderly and trained navigator included.*

Lloyd Owen himself had taken the death of Easonsmith badly, as he had the loss of 'many of our oldest hands'. There were still one or two faces from early days in the desert, men such as Tich Cave and Gordon Harrison, but the LRDG was short of experience.

So, too, was Lloyd Owen as a commanding officer, so he paid a visit to Egypt, to see the 'one man whose advice I felt I must first seek'. Ralph Bagnold was by now a brigadier and the deputy chief signal officer in Cairo. The two discussed the future of the LRDG candidly.

There was the problem of filling the ranks of the LRDG after the loss of so many men in the Aegean, and then of training them to operational standards. Lloyd Owen's greatest concern, however, was whether the LRDG any longer had a role to play. Had it just been a desert force, as the name implied, and was it unrealistic to expect the unit to employ their unique talents so painstakingly learned in North Africa to other theatres? Lloyd Owen recalled that Bagnold listened intently as he poured out his fears and then, in that shy, understated way of his, said: 'I think you should try and keep the unit in being.'

---

* A squadron comprised the following patrols: S1, S2, T1, T2, R1, R2, Z1, Z2; and B Squadron Y1, Y2, M1, M2, W1, W2, X1, X2.

Lloyd Owen left Cairo inspired by the confidence shown in him by Bagnold. He received much encouragement also from Guy Prendergast, even though he was obliged to fly to England in January. When he returned on 7 February he had with him 'much valuable data about new equipment and ideas'.

By early February 1944 Lloyd Owen had moved the LRDG to Syria, where they underwent mountain training. On the twenty-eighth of the month Lloyd Owen's presence was requested in Italy 'to discuss future operations with Field-Marshal Alexander's Headquarters'. Lloyd Owen arrived at the HQ at Caserta and spent the next week discussing the possibility of LRDG operations in Italy. He had his misgivings about whether the terrain was compatible with his men's training but after talking to senior officers and reconnoitring first-hand some of the countryside over which the Eighth Army were fighting their way north, Lloyd Owen wrote to Prendergast to tell him: 'Everyone was inclined to tell me that the mountains were dangerous and difficult to move over but I hope that fact will be an ally to our Patrols, who are trained for it. On the whole I think the country is ideal for our kind of work'.

Prendergast's direct involvement with the LRDG was about to end. In the spring of 1944 he was posted back to the UK where he joined the staff of the Special Air Service Brigade as they began preparations for the invasion of France.

More than ever Lloyd Owen was now on his own as he led the LRDG to Italy. After a year in the Levant he left the Eastern Mediterranean without a backward glance, writing in the war diary: 'This phase has not been a happy one but the brighter prospect of the future makes up for the many failures of the past. LRDG were incorporated in Raiding Forces at a time when it may have been a feasible proposition, but it later became evident that the various units in the formation could never work together under one control which had never experienced any of the operational or administrative complications which always arise.'

The LRDG moved into their quarters in Rodi, on the Gargano Peninsula, or as the soldiers liked to call it, the top of the spur on the Italian boot. 'It was a lovely situation but very isolated,' recalled Lloyd Owen. But that was why he decided on Rodi in the first place; it was off the beaten track, a place where they could train hard and where they would not 'be disturbed by inquisitive people'.

Unfortunately for Lloyd Owen the move to Italy failed to usher in a new phase of dynamism for the LRDG. He shuttled back and forth between Rodi and AAI (Allied Armies in Italy) HQ at Caserta, mooting plans of his own and listening to those of others. 'Some ideas were totally impracticable and others were good,' reflected Lloyd Owen. Eventually, on 7 May it was agreed that Ken Lazarus's A Squadron, the Rhodesians, would be loaned to Force 266, the Allied organization comprising members of the SOE and OSS (Office of Strategic Services, the SOE's US equivalent), who were responsible for coordinating resistance in Yugoslavia with Tito's partisans. Meanwhile on 18 May the Allies finally seized Monte Cassino after a hard-fought and brutal struggle. The Germans withdrew from the Gustav Line, the defensive position that crossed the Italian peninsula from the Garigliano in the west through Cassino and then to the Sangro in the east. On 23 May the US VI Corps broke out of the Anzio beachhead and suddenly the Americans, as well as the Eighth Army, began advancing rapidly north after months of bitter and bloody stalemate. The speed with which the Allies pushed north threw Lloyd Owen's plans into disarray. He and Major Stormonth Darling, CO of B Squadron, had been drawing up a proposal for a jeep operation but the 'rapid advance of the Army towards Rome had overrun the areas where we were to operate'. So it was agreed instead to insert four patrols by parachute on the nights of 11 and 12 June 'to get information about enemy traffic on certain roads north of Rome'.

The first two patrols to insert were those of Lieutenants John Bramley and Simon Fleming. Fleming was an Irishman, from County Down, who had come to the LRDG from the Royal Artillery at the end of 1943. Lloyd Owen appreciated his 'glorious sense of humour' and his 'carefree attitude to life', two traits he also possessed, and he regretted that a conference at Eighth Army

HQ prevented his seeing off the two patrols in person when they departed from Foggia.

The drop zone (DZ) for Fleming and his eight men in 'M2' Patrol was Montepulciano, approximately thirty-five miles west of Perugia in Italy, and their task once down was to gather intelligence on German troop movements during the Allied advance. 'I went last on the drop as the sergeant,' recalled James Swanson, a desert veteran and the most experienced LRDG operator in the patrol. 'We jumped with the minimum, just a Tommy Gun and a spare magazine. The rest of the kit was in containers.'

Swanson landed in a tree and by the time he had cut himself down the rest of the patrol had assembled in a cornfield about 400 yards square, minus Lieutenant Fleming. He was nowhere to be found but one of the men reported hearing four shots from close to where he believed the officer had landed. The priority, however, was to retrieve their equipment. 'We found the wireless hamper quite close and I ordered Locke and Keeley to start unpacking,' said Swanson. 'Savage was left with the parachutes about 20 yards away. Murray and Parry-Jones went off again to see if they could locate Lt Fleming.' Swanson took Eric 'Kip' Kiley and began a search for the missing officer in another area of the cornfield. They bumped into Murray and Parry-Jones, who hadn't found Fleming but had discovered another of their containers.

Swanson now had a decision to make. Before the drop Fleming had told him the men should stay where they landed and he, as No. 1 jumper, would 'roll up' the stick, backtracking on a bearing to collect No. 2, No. 3 and so on. 'Unable to say whether he was able to keep to the original plan . . . I decided that as we had very little darkness left we had better unpack the kit and hope that Lt Fleming would turn up,' said Swanson. The men started to unpack the kit. Suddenly twenty yards ahead they heard movement through the cornfield. 'We crouched down and listened,' said Swanson. 'Someone called out "Hey Johnny, over here."' Swanson wondered for an instant if it was not someone playing a joke. He was sure they had said 'Johnny', not 'Tommy'. He went to issue instructions to his men and suddenly 'there was a hail of bullets flying around our ears.' The men dived into the corn and Swanson yelled instructions, telling them to split up and head for the pre-arranged emergency rendezvous.

Swanson found himself hugging the ground alongside Kip Kiley and Robert Parry-Jones as the Germans hosed the cornfield with bullets. The blind firing stopped. Then the LRDG heard the barks of dogs. One of the animals tore through the corn and was shot by Bob Savage. The Germans turned their fire on Savage, shooting him dead. In the confusion Swanson and Kiley leapt to their feet and started to run. Parry-Jones was too slow getting to his feet, and the Germans were on to him before he could join his comrades.

But his capture presented a distraction that enabled Swanson and Kiley to escape out of the cornfield and into the trees. 'We hid up in a wood all that day,' recalled Swanson. 'We moved off just as it was beginning to get dark and the first rise we went over there were some Germans sitting round. They must have heard us because there was firing straight away. I doubled back but [Kiley] went the other way, over the rise.'

Kiley sprinted over the crest and looked frantically around him. 'I could hear the Germans following up my trail with the aid of their dogs,' he remembered. 'In the best Hollywood tradition I took to the river to cover my tracks.' Splashing through the river, Kiley shook off his pursuers and carried on through the woods until daylight. For the next three days he continued south towards Castiglione until, too exhausted to go on, he found what he thought was a safe place to hide in the woods and fell asleep. A young farmer came across Kiley a few hours later, took him back to his farm, fed him, watered him, and sent him on his way in some civilian clothes. The farmer contacted a local partisan group, who arrived and explained to Kiley that the Allies were just south in Radicofani but for the moment it was dangerous to attempt to slip through German lines. On 22 June the German unit in the vicinity began withdrawing towards Ucello, leaving half a dozen soldiers behind with orders to fire occasional shots to give the enemy the impression the line was still occupied. Kiley, in the company of three partisans, 'liquidated an isolated Hun'. Hours later he contacted a company of French native troops and 'passed on all information relating to enemy positions and movements to French IO (Intelligence Office).'

Swanson had also managed to outstrip his pursuers but then he found himself confronted by an unexpected menace. 'I was walking along a rough track and there up ahead were two partisans,' he remembered. 'We were dressed in windcheater top, not standard battledress, and . . . I was fair haired and blue eyed.' The partisans couldn't believe their luck, a German had strayed right into their camp. Swanson was taken to the partisan leader but he sensed his story was not believed. 'He asked for proof of identification but I had none on me . . . I stayed with them that night but they still weren't convinced I was English.'

Eventually Swanson persuaded the Italians he was a British soldier and they guided him through the German lines to the same French native regiment that Kiley had encountered.*

Captain Ashley Greenwood's patrol, M1, left Foggia at 0130 hours on 14 June. It would soon be his thirty-second birthday and he promised his men that once the mission was over 'we'll wander back and have a drink in Rome'. Greenwood had been awarded a Military Cross for his actions on Leros, where he had volunteered to return to the island to help evacuate several dozen stragglers.

Greenwood, like so many of the LRDG officers, didn't conform physically to the stereotype of the special forces officer but he was, in the words of Gordon Harrison, 'probably the bravest man I've ever met in my life'. Harrison was Greenwood's patrol sergeant, one of the few remaining Yeomanry originals recruited by Pat McCraith in January 1941. Harrison's experience was in stark

* Murray and Keely also evaded capture, and it was later discovered that Lieutenant Simon Fleming's parachute had failed to open because of a faulty static line and he had been killed on landing. In the 1969 LRDG Association newsletter, Kip Kiley wrote an account of this mission, adding that he was still in touch with Simon Fleming's mother who 'constantly wears an LRDG brooch'.

contrast to that of another member of the eight-man patrol, Lance Corporal Frank Lord. He had been one of the men recruited after the New Zealand squadron was withdrawn, having arrived in the Middle East a few months earlier with the Royal Sussex Regiment. Lord enjoyed the LRDG training in Syria, and then in Rodi. 'There was no bull,' he recalled. 'You went out as a fighting force and used your own initiative and you worked as a team. You weren't told to do this and do that, you did it automatically as trained soldiers.'

M1's mission was codenamed Jump and its objective was stated in the orders issued to Greenwood on 9 June:

> To obtain fullest information of roads and tracks, enemy troop movements, concentrations, possible Ops [Observation Posts], types and numbers of transport, in the area from Umbertide [20 miles north of Perugia] to Cittadi Castello [Città di Castello] and report to signals LRDG.

Two hours after departing Foggia, the patrol jumped from a Dakota aircraft having first despatched the containers holding their arms and equipment. Lord carried a pistol tucked into the waistband of his battledress, a Mk1 carbine (a lighter version of the standard Lee Enfield rifle designed for parachute troops) with 100 rounds, and a small haversack containing hard rations and a water bottle full of rum 'because you had to have something to warm you up'.

Each man had seven days' rations and in one of the containers was a further ten days' rations per man, which were to be buried at the DZ for use in an emergency. Captain Greenwood had been issued with some Italian lira and a Union flag, and on his own initiative carried a cowbell to round up his troops on the DZ. Harrison boarded the plane proudly wearing the baseball cap he had been given by an American airman in exchange for his jump hat. Highly irregular, said Greenwood, with mock solemnity.

Greenwood was the first to exit the aircraft, Lord followed soon after and Harrison, as sergeant, was the last out. 'As soon as I got out [of the aircraft] I knew something was dreadfully wrong,' he recalled. 'On the DZ picked there was a river and a road, side by side for miles, and it opened up onto a meadow and then closed up again, and we were supposed to drop in this meadow. It was a perfect DZ, no river or road.'

But as Harrison floated down he could see no river running parallel to a road, no meadow, nothing that vaguely resembled the DZ. What he did see was a village, and a church spire, and one of their number floating perilously close to it. Harrison focused on his own landing, bracing himself as he dropped into a vineyard. 'I walked up against the vines trying to pick up rest of the stick but I kept going into all the wires,' remembered Harrison. 'This was getting me nowhere so I turned and followed the vines down.'

One of the first men Harrison collected was Frank Lord, who had also come down among the vines. 'We gradually found one another just by wandering around,' he said. One man emerged from a pond, another from a hedge, but of Captain Greenwood and Fusilier Ford there was no sign.

Ford, a Mancunian, had been the sixth man out of the aircraft, jumping immediately before Gordon Harrison. He had landed in a tree and for several interminable minutes struggled to cut himself free. 'Having done that I crossed the road and made for where I had seen No. 5 [Corporal Burgess] land,' recollected Ford. 'I saw signs of him having been there as the corn was trampled down.'

Ford then heard the sound of vehicles, more vehicles than there should have been for three o'clock in the morning. He dropped into the corn and waited.

Captain Greenwood had 'landed on the roof of a small church' and for several seconds silently cursed the American pilots for dropping them in the wrong place. Wherever they had landed it was not the planned DZ. His position was dire. Dawn was already starting to bring a purple tint to the sky and the silk of his parachute drooped over the edge of the church. Using a cowbell to summon his men was clearly out of the question. With the utmost caution, Greenwood managed to cut himself out of his harness and scramble across the roof of the church into the belfry. Descending from the belfry he slipped out of the church and straight into a startled villager on his way to work. 'He asked why I had come because it was full of Germans,' recalled Greenwood. Ignoring the question, Greenwood asked where he was. The village of Lama, replied the man, who also said he had seen three other paratroopers land. Greenwood told the man to stay where he was while he buried his parachute. He was interrupted twice while doing this by Germans, each time leaping into the graveyard to avoid detection.

When Greenwood returned to the front of the church the Italian had vanished. 'At that moment I heard orders in German of men beginning to form up so there was nothing to do but get out.'

Creeping out of the north end of the village, Greenwood scoured the surroundings for signs of his men but without success. 'Walked along road to Montione and enquired at cottage and was told that Germans were next door,' he wrote in his operation report. 'Getting very light now, so turned NE into hills and at 0500 hours lay up in a wood all day. Sporadic firing all round all day.'

Sergeant Gordon Harrison, having found his way out of the vineyard, failed to locate the rest of the patrol. 'It was getting near dawn and so I decided to make for the hills,' he remembered. 'I was doing quite well, walking along quite happily, and I got clear of the town. I came over the brow of the hill and on the other side of hill it was all terraced. As I came over, on the other side of me as far as the eye could see was a string of German soldiers. I had a carbine, a revolver, a knife, and I thought "Gordon, really, you have two choices, you can shoot one or two of them and die in a blaze of bullets and glory, or you can put your hands up." So being a sensible fellow I put my hands up.'

Before the Germans reached their prisoner, Harrison had surreptitiously discarded his carbine and Colt revolver among the vines. 'The Germans never found them, they were so pleased to get me they never searched,' he remembered.

Frank Lord had rendezvoused with four of his comrades, including Preston, the signaller, and Corporal Burgess, the section navigator. 'We started to reconnoitre a bit and the navigator was going to check where we were and then we spotted the Germans right round us, coming in droves,' recalled Lord. 'We said the best thing was to disperse and hide up, and bury your weapons. So we did that, crawled away from it, and hoped for the best.'

Lord didn't get far. The Germans had encircled the area and as the net tightened the British paratroopers were caught one by one. 'It was hopeless,' said Lord. 'There was no shooting. Just "*raus*" and up go your hands.'

The four men were marched into the village and 'bundled into a building all together and then they brought the rest of the gear in . . . they let us undo the haversacks and they took the cigarettes.' The quartet were joined by Harrison and they were soon being transported to Verona. En route Harrison told his comrades to say nothing other than that they were aircrew who had baled out of their stricken aircraft. The fact Harrison was wearing a USAAF cap would validate their claim. Sure enough, Harrison recorded, 'we were taken to Verona . . . and treated as aircrew.'

It was a prudent tactic, for in October 1942 Hitler had issued his Commando Order, instructing all captured Allied commandos or similar units to be handed over to the Sicherheitsdienst (SD, the intelligence service of the SS) so that they could be 'annihilated to the last man'. The Order was in retaliation for an instruction allegedly issued by Allied commanders prior to the ill-fated Canadian raid on Dieppe in August 1942 to 'bind prisoners' captured on the operation. An October raid on Sark in the Channel Islands during which four German soldiers were killed was also a factor.

For more than a year the Order remained a closely-guarded secret within the Germany military (a minority of senior officers, among them Rommel, ignored Hitler's Decree), and Jimmy Patch recalled that when he and Ron Hill were captured in October 1943 they had not the slightest doubt they would be treated in accordance with the Geneva Convention. It was not until an SAS operation in January 1944 that the Allies got wind of the Order.

One of the officers on Operation Pomegranate, Lieutenant Jimmy Hughes, was captured as he and his men attempted to destroy aircraft at Sant Egidio airfield, close to Perugia. During his interrogation Hughes was informed that as a special forces soldier 'you are not a prisoner of war, you are a political prisoner. Under the Commando Order issued by our Führer all saboteurs, whether in uniform or not, are to be shot.'

With the connivance of a sympathetic German doctor, Hughes managed to escape and eventually he made his way to Britain whereupon he informed his superiors of the Commando Order. Initially Hughes' testimony was treated with scepticism by the HQ of 1st Airborne Corps. Nothing more than an 'interrogation technique' was the prevailing view among the higher echelons of the Airborne staff, commented Barkworth. 'Reference to other men of the Regiment who had neither returned, nor had been reported as casualties, was explained away by the fact that the enemy probably wished to keep us in the dark about the success of operations.'

In fact nearly a dozen SAS soldiers had already been executed by the end of 1943, and in April 1944 an SBS patrol was captured in the Dodecanese. After days of brutal torture, during which they revealed nothing of importance, the four soldiers were sent for 'special treatment', a chilling euphemism for execution.

Harrison, Lord and the three other LRDG men were well treated at first, housed in 'a nice room with sheets and lighting'. It was too good to be true. 'We put two and two together and we surmised . . . that the place was bugged,' recalled Lord. 'They wanted us to talk, but we didn't. We just put our fingers up to mouths and so we talked about anything bar the LRDG.'

Realizing that the prisoners had guessed their motives, the Germans reverted to more traditional forms of interrogation. 'It was one at a time,' said Lord. 'They tore your clothes off you, and made you stand in front of about six officers who spoke fluent English and they asked you questions but all they got was name, rank and number.' The Germans found the silk map of the area and the button-sized compass (the patrol weren't carrying miniature hacksaws) and declared this was proof they were special forces soldiers. The men denied it, saying such kit was standard issue to all aircrew in the event of being shot down over enemy territory. Lord remembered that he came in for special attention because of his surname. 'They saw in my pay book that I was "Lord, Frank" so I was grilled a couple of times because they thought I was a member of the aristocracy.'

Eventually the prisoners had their clothes returned and soon found themselves on their way to a POW camp in Germany.

Fusilier Ford had avoided the Germans in the hours after the patrol's drop by hiding deep in the woods, but now had to decide upon his best course of action. Captain Greenwood had told his men that once the operation was complete the patrol would extricate by one of three means, as stated in his operational instructions:

(a) By the advance of our armies.
(b) By the help of local guides.
(c) By its own initiative.

In his predicament, Ford knew he had no option other than 'C'. At nightfall on 14 June, nearly twenty-four hours after the start of the operation, Ford emerged from the woods and stole back into the village of Lama in the hope of finding some of his comrades. Realizing he was engaged in a fruitless task, Ford struck out west along a river and carried on walking the whole night. The next morning he turned south and for five days and nights trekked up hills, over fields, through woods and across rivers. Then disaster. Walking across what appeared to be an innocuous stretch of countryside at night Ford fell into what, sticking to his desert vernacular, he described as a deep wadi, probably a dry riverbed. Before he knew what had happened he was lying on the ground with a damaged ankle and back. 'I crawled back up the side of the wadi and lay down,' he recalled. 'Some people found me, took me to a house, and gave me food.'

Ford's ankle was so painful that he remained immobile for more than a week, during which time word reached him through his hosts that the rest of his friends had been captured at Lama. When his ankle had healed, Ford attempted to continue his trek south, but the enemy forces were too numerous and he returned to the house. A couple of days later a man arrived at the house seeking shelter. He said he was an Italian deserter but Ford 'suspected [him] of being a German'. The fact he carried some British-issue Italian lira first aroused Ford's suspicion, and then he heard the 'Italian' curse in German when he thought no one was around. Ford decided he could take no chances, so he shot the man and 'disposed of the body in the hills'.

Two days later the Germans pulled back further north and Ford was able to head in the other direction, finally reaching Allied lines on 19 July.

Ashley Greenwood passed the whole of 14 June concealed in the woods near the village of Montione. At dusk he headed back towards Lama and knocked on a house three-quarters of a mile from the village. 'Inhabitants terrified and turned me out quickly, but gave me food and water' he wrote in his diary. 'They said 6 or 7 parachutists captured.'

Nourished by the food, Greenwood trekked south with the intention of reaching the pre-arranged RV with Captain Gordon Rowbottom's 'W1' Patrol at Volterrano. He also reasoned that while he was walking it might be an idea to make a note of everything he saw, so the operation would not be a complete waste. As he crossed the Tiber valley Greenwood 'stopped by main road for half an hour to observe enemy traffic. It was continuous and mostly horse-drawn'.

Ploughing on, Greenwood forded the Tiber river and by dawn on 16 June was fast asleep in a wood. That night – the eve of his thirty-second birthday – he continued, reaching the Marcignano valley, approximately fifteen miles north-west of Umbertide

As he skirted around a farm Greenwood was accosted by a cry of '*Chi va la?*' (Who goes there?). 'Before I had time to reply, a shot rang out from a farm building, and they turned out to be Italian partisans,' he recalled. 'Thinking I was a German they treated me fairly roughly until I convinced them I was British. I spoke a bit of Italian and told them I was a British parachutist and they were all over me.'

It was only when Greenwood noticed the sentry's weapon that he realized how lucky he was to still be alive. 'The reason the chap missed me from such a short range was his rifle barrel was bent away from the rifle.'

There were about thirty partisans in the group; poorly dressed, poorly equipped but rich in courage and enthusiasm. The Italian peasants and the upper-class British Army officer made for an odd coupling but in Greenwood the partisans recognized a man who could help them coordinate attacks on the Germans. Nonetheless Greenwood initially disappointed them by insisting he had to reach a rendezvous with some of his comrades. He departed the next night, reaching the RV point at Volterrano, four miles south-west over the hills. He was guided by a 'beautiful partisaness accompanied, unfortunately, by her partisan boyfriend'. At a house belonging to a partisan sympathizer, Greenwood and his escort waited for the rest of his men. No one turned up, wrote Greenwood in his diary, but on the plus side the wait in a house full of books and pictures 'provided an unexpected taste of civilisation'. He tried again the next night but the RV was uninhabited. Back at the partisan HQ Greenwood discovered they had ambushed a German truck on a mountain road, killing the occupants but bringing back alive a despatch rider. 'We spent the whole evening questioning him, plying him with wine, and getting him very merry,' recalled Greenwood. The merrier the German became, the more he talked. He had been posted to the supposedly quiet backwater of central Italy after surviving the Russian Front. Greenwood listened as the German 'disburdened himself of his war weariness' but a little after 1 a.m. he decided to turn in for the night. He didn't want to be present when the inevitable happened. Sure enough, when Greenwood woke the next morning there was no sign of the German. He didn't enquire as to his whereabouts, he knew there was no point because the partisans 'were in no position to keep prisoners'.

Greenwood used his time in the mountains to gather as much intelligence as possible about the strength and disposition of the German forces in the region. On 21 June he and the leader of his partisan band met with the head of another group, who passed on everything he knew. The following day Greenwood wrote in his diary: 'Decided to walk back to British lines with information so far collected.' He set out a few hours later in the morning, accompanied by two Partisan guides, who escorted him into the neighbouring valley from where Greenwood continued alone.

When the opportunity arose Greenwood cut telephone cables and spied on German troop movements. He teamed up with an Italian who had deserted from a German labour battalion and was endeavouring to return to his home further south. Eventually they came within sight of Lake Trasimeno, a few miles west of Perugia, very close to the German frontline. 'We got to a farm around evening and the Italian went ahead to reconnoitre and came back to say it was impossible to get through because there were too many Germans.'

Greenwood decided to see for himself, and soon realized the Italian had not been exaggerating. 'I found myself among German batteries,' he recalled. 'Fortunately they were preparing the evening meal and were occupied, so I was able to dart from olive tree to olive tree. I decided to go down to the lake and get a rowing boat and row across the lake. When I got near the lake, there was some tall reeds and marshy country, separated by ditches, so I was able to go along quite safely.'

At Le Piagge, on the south-east corner of Lake Trasimeno (the lake is six miles long), Greenwood ducked into a barn to shelter from the torrential rain. 'I looked in the barn and it was full of German equipment, evidently a forward patrol of Germans,' he remembered. 'I took a German haversack, and peeped into the farm and as I did I could hear snores and at that moment two sentries came out wearing capes. I circumspectly went round the other way and went on with my walk.'

Greenwood peered inside the haversack hoping to discover some food but to his disappointment it was stuffed full of cigars and cigarettes. At dawn the next day, 25 June, Greenwood stopped at a small cottage in the woods and asked the woman inside if there were any Germans nearby. No, she replied, but there are some English just up the road. The woman, with the hospitality characteristic of the Italian peasant, insisted that Greenwood have something to eat before he departed. The eggs, roasted in embers, fortified Greenwood for the final stage of his odyssey and he soon encountered the 'English' soldiers. In fact they turned out to be a detachment of South African troops who, in exchange for some cigarettes, plied Greenwood with strong coffee before giving him a lift to Perugia.

CHAPTER TWENTY-THREE

'Ineffective but quite fun'

Ashley Greenwood's report was a masterpiece of intelligence, invaluable to the Allies as they planned the next phase of their advance. In Appendix A he conveyed information on the surface of roads, pinpointed destroyed bridges (and the fording places used by the Germans as a result), described the terrain – and where it was not suitable for armour. Appendix B concerned enemy movements and dispositions and identification, including the locations of a fuel and ammunition dump and enemy gun emplacements. Appendix C described the local partisans, praising their bravery and belligerence, and stating that 'arms, ammunition and boots are the chief requirements'.

Of the other two patrols, Lieutenant Gordon Rowbottom's stick landed safely but ran into a German unit the following day. All but Corporals Buss and Rod Matthews were caught. Rowbottom was separated from his men and transported for questioning aboard a truck. But the truck failed to negotiate a tight bend on one of the rural lanes and ended up in a ditch.

Rowbottom was out of the truck before his guards had time to recover their senses, and headed off with the aim of reaching the same RV point at Volterrano that Greenwood was making for. Partisans intercepted him, however, as they had Buss and Matthews, and the three chose to remain with them. The partisans, recalled Matthews, were brave but volatile, and easily scared by the firepower the Germans had at their disposal. 'We went down one day to shoot at some German trucks going along the road,' recalled Matthews. 'We were halfway up the mountain and had a few pot shots. Then the Germans had pot shots back and we were soon being run over by these Italians [as they fled].'

Unlike Greenwood's patrol, Rowbottom had collected his equipment on the DZ, so he called in a drop of arms and explosives for his band of partisans. By early July Rowbottom was leading the Italians on sabotage operations, mining roads with plastic explosives, and then shooting the survivors as they emerged from the wreckage. On 10 July the LRDG men mined another road, using 10 lbs of plastic explosive and double-pressured time switches. The lorry blown up was carrying ammunition and petrol 'and burned for an hour and a half'. The Germans responded by executing fourteen males from the nearby village of Castiglion Fibocchi, including an old man of seventy and a boy of twelve.

The one patrol that met without mishap was that of Lieutenant John Bramley, who landed without incident and then spent a week radioing back information to Allied Armies in Italy (AAI) HQ. When the radio died he led his men back safely having provided information of 'considerable value to our advancing troops'.

Lloyd Owen had to shoulder much of the blame for the failure of the parachute operations. He should have known from his time in the desert that inserting troops just behind the enemy frontline is fraught with danger; as Lofty Carr had said, 500 miles inside enemy territory is far safer than fifty miles.

Gordon Harrison, a desert veteran, had plenty of time to ponder the failure of his patrol as he rotted in a German POW camp. 'The role of the LRDG in Italy was completely different [to Africa],' he said. 'It finished up like a commando unit. We were trained really for the desert and we were experts in the desert. We could drive better in the desert, live in the desert . . . If you're going to fight a war the desert is a perfect place. No civilians to get mixed up in it, no cities to bomb, vast open spaces where you can manoeuvre.'

Jim Patch and Ron Hill also had time on their hands up in the mountains of Macedonia to mull over the reasons for their unenviable predicament. Both agreed that John Olivey 'had a streak of madness in him and was a very brave man' but he had planned for Levitha as if they had still been in the desert. 'We were used to getting about in fast vehicles where we could get away from any trouble,' reflected Patch. 'On Levitha it was an entirely different kettle of fish and I suppose there were other ways he could have looked at things and used the very minimum forces that he had at disposal. But one can't blame him for that. It was an entirely different situation to the desert.'

Early August 1944 found Patch and Hill still marooned in Macedonia and more downcast than ever. 'Are almost under arrest,' Hill had written in his diary on 18 July. The reason for the Chetniks' hostility was the betrayal they felt as it became clear that the Allies looked to Tito and his communist partisans as the men to help drive the Germans from Yugoslavia. Patch and Hill tried to persuade the Chetniks to join with the partisans but they refused. Gradually, however, the pressure to be amalgamated into the partisans became too strong to resist, culminating in a warning that Chetniks refusing to join the partisans would be considered as enemies. 'With the partisan takeover – as the Yugoslav Army of National Liberation – we now had to relearn our greetings procedures,' recorded Hill. 'From "*Jivili Kralj Petr Drugi*" (Long Live King Peter the Second) to "*Smrt za Fascis mo*" (Death to the Fascists).' The standard reply to the partisan communist greeting was 'And Victory to the People'. Hill and Patch found it all a bit earnest and came up with their own response in English: 'And Joe [Stalin] for king.' The partisans nodded their heads in solemn appreciation, oblivious to what the pair were actually saying.

The volatile and unpredictable political situation in Yugoslavia that Hill and Patch had endured for nearly a year would become all to apparent to David Lloyd Owen in the early autumn of 1944. 'Infuriating, gallant, devious' was how he described the Yugoslav partisans who 'were only too anxious to take all that we could give but they offered little in return'. Typical of the attitude of the partisans was the experience of Lieutenant Mike Reynolds and his Rhodesian patrol when he arrived in Fiume (present day Rijeka on the Croatian coast) in late August to carry out a shipping watch in Istria between Fiume and Pola. After two weeks of collecting valuable intelligence, Reynolds and his three men were attacked by a German unit sent to the area to hunt down and kill them. The four Rhodesians withdrew and were chased fifteen miles by the Germans into Istria. No sooner had they set foot in Istria they 'they were ordered out again by the Partisans'.

Fortunately throughout the summer of 1944 and for their operations in the Dalmatian Islands, the LRDG had no need to ask the Partisans for assistance, nor even the Royal Navy. Wishing to have the self-sufficiency and independence that the LRDG had enjoyed in North Africa, Lloyd Owen procured the unit's very own vessel – the motor fishing vessel *Palma*. This allowed them to operate without having to rely on the Royal Navy, who might not always be able to meet the LRDG's requirements. Lloyd Owen appointed as skipper of the *Palma* Captain Alan Denniff, his navigator from the desert days. There was only ever one man capable of fulfilling the bosun's duties, and that was Sergeant Tich Cave, while the engineer was called Danny and the gunner behind the Oerlikon 20 mm cannon was Ron Cryer.

The *Palma*'s maiden voyage was to the island of Vis in June, her crew of nine taking seven and a half hours to cover the seventy miles. It was the first of many such trips, the aim of which were to either report on enemy shipping so that the RAF or Royal Navy could launch an attack, or so small raiding-parties could attack enemy shipping or installations on lightly-held islands.

On one such raid, Ashley Greenwood and Curly Armstrong were taken by the *Palma* to within sight of Drvenik island near Split on which was situated a German gun battery. 'We had carrier pigeons as the means of communication and were to find out the positions of the German batteries,' recalled Greenwood. 'We landed in a rubber canoe, and then tried to hide it on a sharp rocky coast in a little cave. We went off, there was not much vegetation on this island, and as it got light we were not far from the hill on which the German battery was. We sat there watching the German battery and in the afternoon decided to send the pigeons off with messages . . . I released these pigeons and to my dismay, instead of flying off straight away, they stayed around this bush, I imagine trying to find some food, and then flew off in entirely the wrong direction.' Greenwood and Armstrong remained on Drvenik for three days gathering what the LRDG war diarist described as 'detailed information'. In Greenwood's mind the mission was 'ineffective but quite fun'.

As had been the case in the desert it was the LRDG's patient, meticulous reconnaissance that earned them the admiration of their peers. By September, as the unit war diary noted, the 'Royal Navy had begun to appreciate the value of our shipping intelligence and now requested us to establish a watch on enemy shipping around the coast of Istria.'

One such operation was led by Captain Gordon Rowbottom, recently returned to the LRDG from his escapades with the Italian partisans. On 7 September Rowbottom and five men (including Corporal Buss – one of his men from the parachute drop – and a partisan interpreter) left on the *Palma* to conduct a shipping watch from the island of Vrgada, two and a miles off the Croatian coast. The mission began well. Rowbottom found the thirty partisans on the island cooperative, pugnacious and well armed.

On 8 September the LRDG commenced its watch on the Vela Arta Channel, the narrow strip of water between the mainland and their island of Vrgada, and soon radio reports abundant with intelligence were being sent to HQ. On the night of 11–12 September Rowbottom and his men, together with four partisans, rowed the mile east to the island of Vela Arta to carry out a night watch. Half way across three German E-boats on a routine patrol intercepted the rowing boat. 'We were ordered on board and placed aft covered by a sentry with a Sten gun after being searched for weapons,' wrote Rowbottom. They were transported to Split and asked the standard question of 'name, rank and number'. Wishing the Germans to believe he was nothing more than an ignorant member of the rank and file, Rowbottom gave his rank as private. 'We were taken in transport to a local prison and placed in the same cell,' he explained. 'The four partisans, whom we said were fishermen, hired by us to row, were placed in a cell alongside. [Sergeant] Morley managed to get his escape map through, tied round his ankle.'

The next day the men were interrogated one by one. Sergeant Morley was first, as the most senior among the four prisoners, or so the Germans thought. The German officer remarked to Morley that he saw from his paybook that his trade in civilian life was a gardener. He made a quip about the English growing roses for Uncle Joe Stalin. Morley retorted that the only country frightened of Russia was Germany. The officer flew into a rage and threatened Morley with execution for being a saboteur. His humour did not improve when he questioned 'Private' Rowbottom, who resolutely refused to join in his condemnation of the United States. When he compared the German officer's drivel to Josef Goebbels the interrogation was terminated, and Rowbottom returned to his cell with more vague threats of being shot. But they were only threats. On 18 September the four LRDG and three partisan prisoners were taken from the prison and marched into Split, where they were loaded into three-ton trucks, one vehicle in a convoy that Rowbottom estimated to be 100-strong. The convoy departed at 1700 hours and made its first stop at 1915; the four men got out, stretched their legs, and quietly agreed that at the first opportunity they would escape.

Back on board, they began to deftly undo the cords of the tarpaulin cover, and a short while later the convoy came under attack from a group of partisans. 'Lights extinguished, terrific firing from column, 20 mm, mortars, machine guns and rifles, all firing blindly into hills east of road' wrote Rowbottom. When the four German guards jumped from the truck to join in the firefight, so the LRDG men seized the moment, squirming under the tarpaulin and vanishing into the night. Four days later they were back with their unit, Rowbottom being heartily congratulated by Lloyd Owen for his second successful escape from a German lorry in three months. 'This was not entirely due to his good fortune,' assessed Lloyd Owen. 'It was also because he was not the kind of man to suffer a prisoner's status lightly. He grasped every opportunity to escape in his big hands and he succeeded where others, less determined, might have failed.'

CHAPTER TWENTY-FOUR

'It was with profound regret'

By September 1944 the Third Reich was on its way to defeat. Squeezed on two fronts, Germany began recalling its troops from the Balkans to defend its border from the Soviet army rampaging westwards, who had already captured the Ploieşti airfields, entered Bucharest and made the first push into Yugoslavia.

As German soldiers streamed north from Greece, up through Albania and Yugoslavia, Winston Churchill demanded his chiefs of staff act quickly to ensure British troops beat their Soviet allies into Greece. The problem faced by Britain was a lack of resources; with so many soldiers fighting their way up Italy or across France, there simply were not enough troops in the Mediterranean theatre to meet Churchill's insistence that a force of 5,000 march on Athens. The Americans were not interested in helping, either, so instead the British turned to its air force and its special forces to seize a series of key objectives while they waited for additional troops to arrive from elsewhere.

While Churchill was pressing for swift action in Greece, David Lloyd Owen saw 'great opportunities' for the LRDG in Yugoslavia and particularly Albania. 'Once the German withdrawal began in earnest I wanted to be able to drop every possible man into Albania to strike across the enemy's routes,' he wrote. 'I argued that the Germans' static defences along these roads must became disorganized, and the retreating enemy less vigilant in their desire to get on hastily to the north.'

Lloyd Owen took his plan to Brigadier George Davy, commanding Land Forces Adriatic and to whom the LRDG answered after they ceased to fall under the auspices of Allied Armies in Italy in early August.

Davy was all for it, instructing Lloyd Owen to begin planning for a series of parachute insertions into Albania, but then the partisans raised some objections about the likelihood of increased casualties were such an operation to be launched. While negotiations continued, on 18 September, some 10,000 Germans broke out of Greece and began streaming up into Albania; Lloyd Owen urged the partisans to agree to the operation and they did. On 24 September the first LRDG patrols parachuted into Albania.

Already on the ground were units from the SBS, commanded by Major David Sutherland, as well as members of the SOE. 'We were stepping into a full-blown Balkan Civil War,' reflected Sutherland, 'with Royalists and Communists fighting each other to the death in Albania and Yugoslavia.'

Sutherland based himself initially just south of the town of Përmet, close to the border with Greece, but soon most of the Germans had passed through, so he gave chase but neither the SBS nor the LRDG could do much to inconvenience the massive German withdrawal.

The bountiful food in Albania was one of the few pleasures of the squadron's operations in the Balkans that autumn. The men, Sutherland remembered, 'longed for the sound of Greek voices again, and for the feeling of trust and cooperation' which they had experienced in the Dodecanese.

In Greece the LRDG was one of several units that formed 'Foxforce', under the command of Lieutenant-Colonel Ronnie Tod of No. 9 Commando. As well as the LRDG, Foxforce comprised the SBS, Commandos, Greek Sacred Squadron and the Raiding Support Regiment. Tod was answerable to the 2nd Special Service Brigade which came under overall control of Brigadier Davy's Land Forces Adriatic.

On 15 September Foxforce occupied the island of Kythira, six miles south of the Peloponnese, the large peninsula in southern Greece. The island was a good place from which to launch operations on the Greek mainland and the British established a naval base on the south of the island. From here the SBS and LRDG began reconnoitring the islands in the Bay of Athens, clearing out the last pockets of resistance, before, on 24 September, it was deemed the Peloponnese was sufficiently clear of the enemy to land a 450-strong force – codenamed 'Bucket Force' – at Araxos airfield in a fleet of Dakotas.

Lloyd Owen was asked to provide an LRDG patrol to act as Bucket Force's eyes and ears as they advanced east from Araxos, so he called on John Olivey and his Rhodesian 'Z1' Patrol. Olivey had rejoined the unit after an epic adventure, even by his brazen standards. After his capture on Leros in November 1943 Olivey had been loaded onto a German vessel along with 1,500 other prisoners and transported to Athens. Once in the Greek capital they were marched through the streets by their captors, an attempt by the Germans to humiliate their prisoners and demonstrate to the natives that the British were no match for the Third Reich. The stunt backfired, to the delight of Olivey, who described the trek through Athens as 'like a victory march' with Greeks throwing oranges, apples and cigarettes to the prisoners and the British blowing kisses to the women in the crowd. The column was still marching after six miles but had now become strung out with some of the guards – many of whom were older soldiers as well as those deemed not fit for active service – struggling to keep up. Olivey glimpsed out of the corner of his eye his own guard wheezing with the effort of the march

One of the LRDG men marching behind Olivey, Signalman Toity du Toit, gasped in astonishment as his officer 'whipped off his hat and chucked it to the ground, then quickly stepped into the crowds on the pavement'. A Greek saw the impudent act and reacted with equal alacrity, helping Olivey wriggle out of his rucksack so he could run unimpeded. 'John yelled at me to break out,' remembered du Toit. 'But I was too dumbstruck and indecisive at the time to react quickly!'

Olivey sprinted down a side street and turned into the first house he saw. 'A few moments later two Greek women followed me having seen me escape,' he recounted. 'They removed me from the house, which they said contained Germans, and took me to a house next door, where lived a tinsmith and his Maltese wife and three children.'

Within minutes Olivey, decked out as a local, was tucking into some hot food. It was to be four months before members of the Greek Underground smuggled him out of Athens on a fishing boat, but the hospitality he received throughout his stay had left him with a deep affection for the country.

Olivey's reward for his escape was a month's leave in southern Rhodesia, a sort of Busman's Holiday. Yes, he had instructions to select twenty new recruits for A Squadron, but in between interviewing volunteers for the LRDG Olivey married the woman who had been waiting for him since 1939.

Olivey's eleven jeeps arrived in Greece by Landing Craft on 26 September, roaring ashore at Katakolon, forty miles south of Araxos. The patrol soon became bogged down, however, Olivey noting as they drove north that 'the roads [are] very bad after the recent rain.' Four of the jeeps in the patrol pulled trailers, on each of which was 1,000 lbs of equipment for Bucket Force, and within a day of landing Olivey began to doubt that all the vehicles would stand the ordeal if the condition of the roads did not improve. Fortunately, there were two fitters in the patrol, James Heys and Alf Tighe, part of the LRDG's Light Aid Detachment, skilled mechanics whose efforts in keeping the unit mobile wrote Lloyd Owen, 'were seldom recognized as they should have been'.

'We were supposed to look after the jeeps if they went wrong,' recalled Heys, who had joined the LRDG at the end of 1943. He and Tighe were good friends, a couple of Lancastrians who both had a passion for vehicle maintenance. Tighe, a corporal, was the senior of the two, not just in rank but also in experience, being one of the very few members of the LRDG in 1944 whose lineage stretched back to the early days in the desert.

The 25-year-old had been one of the four men immortalized in 'Moore's March', the epic trek through the desert after Pat Clayton's patrol had been ambushed by the Italians in January 1941. Subsequently awarded a Military Medal for his actions with the LRDG, the citation praising his 'utmost devotion to duty', Tighe was on his last patrol before returning to England for an automatic home leave of six weeks after nearly five years of unbroken service overseas.

On 30 September Olivey's patrol arrived at Bucket Force's Forward HQ, a few miles west of Patras. L Squadron of the SBS were positioned on the high ground overlooking the port and their commander, Major Ian Patterson was endeavouring to persuade the garrison of 900 Germans and 1,600 Greeks from a collaborationist security battalion to surrender.

LRDG used the lull to repair the jeeps, several of which needed the attention of Tighe and Heys after the pounding they had been put through in the previous five days. Then Heys was ordered by Olivey to collect Major George Jellicoe, CO of the SBS, who had arrived at Araxos by aircraft. Jellicoe was there to help in the negotiations with the enemy force in Patras. In the company of a local Red Cross representative, Jellicoe and Patterson entered the port under a white flag to parley with the German commander. Patterson had the impression the Germans was 'playing for time', trying to stall the British while they organized a withdrawal from the city, so the SBS focused their efforts on the 1,600 Greek collaborators. Giving them his word that if they capitulated they would not be handed over to their left-wing compatriots, Jellicoe issued the Greeks with an ultimatum: surrender by 0600 hours on 2 October or else answer to the communists. Jellicoe was pessimistic about the chances of their success, but at the appointed hour '1,600 Greeks presented themselves to a man and laid down their arms.'

The LRDG and the SBS oversaw the disarming of the collaborationist security battalion, a chore that was tedious, and ended in tragedy when a weapon went off accidentally as Sergeant 'Ginger' Van Rensberg loaded it onto the back of a truck. 'He got one straight in the chest,' recalled Heys. 'He was dead in about five minutes.'

The sergeant's funeral was at 0900 hours the following day, his patrol gathered around the graveside as the padre from the RAF Regiment conducted the burial service. During the night of 3–4 October word reached Bucket Force HQ that the Germans had started withdrawing from Patras; at first light a patrol of the SBS, travelling on the LRDG jeeps, raced into the port and discovered that all but a German rearguard had indeed sailed out of Patras, heading east up the Gulf of Corinth towards the Corinth Canal. On the plus side, noted Captain Walter Milner-Barry, one of the SBS officers, they received a 'terrific reception . . . carpet on the streets, flowers and lovely girls on balconies.'

A sizeable press corps followed the SBS and the LRDG into Patras, one American correspondent writing that it was hoped that the fall of the port 'might clear the way for a major Allied operation in Greece that could result in the liberation of the entire country within two weeks'.

The SBS and the LRDG now set off in pursuit of the Germans. In a convoy of jeeps they roared along the headland overlooking the gulf, a captured 75 mm German field gun hitched to the back of one of the jeeps. 'Chased the enemy who were withdrawing by boat,' wrote Olivey in his log, 'firing with .5 Browning and 75 mm Gun, from positions on the Corinth Road.'

They reached Corinth on 7 October, exchanged desultory fire with the Germans on the other side of the canal and then accepted the surrender of another battalion of Greek collaborators. From Corinth Olivey received instructions to push on to the town of Megara, several miles to the north-east over a mountain road, but to leave two jeeps' worth of men in Corinth to help in the clearance of German mines. 'It came to a point where one of us had to carry on with the patrol and one stayed behind,' remembered James Heys. 'John Olivey told Tighe to stay behind.'

Olivey knew that Tighe was due for home leave; he had done his bit and Olivey didn't want to expose a fellow desert veteran to any unnecessary danger as they pursed the enemy north.

Olivey's patrol reached Megara on 9 October and at dawn the next day assisted an SBS unit to 'blow the escape road that the enemy were using'. With that done they set about clearing a landing strip in the town and preparing to set off after the Germans on the road to Athens.

Back at Corinth Alf Tighe was acting as a driver for the Royal Engineers as they began constructing a pontoon bridge over the Corinth Canal to replace the main bridge that had been destroyed. On the morning of 10 October Tighe was transporting Sapper Reg Grey and Lance Sergeant Robert Lee along the south bank of the Corinth Canal when the jeep drove over a mine. One of the first to reach the scene was a Rhodesian LRDG soldier called Alf Page. 'Corporal Tighe . . . was sitting there, to all intents OK,' he reflected. 'He said to check the others, but when the lads came back to him he'd died – with not a mark on him, it was very sad.'

The death of Tighe depressed the spirits of everyone in the LRDG. It was not just that he was unflaggingly cheerful, but to have survived so much only to die in such a mundane way seemed grievously unfair; proof that fate could play the cruellest of tricks when you least expected it. Olivey noted the death of Tighe in the war diary, writing that he was laid to rest by the SBS in the British military cemetery at Corinth.*

Instead of welcoming back their son after five years' overseas service, Tighe's parents received a letter from his commanding officer. Explaining the circumstances of their son's death, Lloyd Owen wrote:

> It was with profound regret that we all heard of the tragic death of your son. To me personally it was the loss not only of a magnificently gallant and able soldier, but a most charming and loyal friend. We had several patrols together, and for two of them I was his patrol officer in the desert. We all knew him as a quiet and courageous person, and he won the Military

* Tighe and the two sappers killed with him were later reinterred in Phaleron war cemetery to the south-east of Athens.

> Medal with me as the result of repeated acts of bravery in actions behind the lines. None of us who knew him ever ceased in our admiration of his historic walk. The episode is always known as one of the greatest in the history of the Long Range Desert Group. A more loyal and likeable person I would never have wished for.

Major Jellicoe arrived at Megara with a company from the 4th Independent Parachute Brigade on 12 October and the next day he was ordered by Land Forces Adriatic HQ to reconnoitre Athens. Bumping himself up to a brigadier with the 'necessary emblems' he and Captain Milner-Barry (masquerading as a lieutenant colonel) set off for Athens accompanied by three SBS bodyguards, arriving on the late afternoon of Friday 13 October. 'Tears, shouts, kisses, handshakes, blows on the back, dragged into the houses and nearly suffocated,' wrote Milner-Barry in his diary. 'Made a speech from a balcony, shouting "Zeto to ELAS", when I ought to have said "Helas", meaning "Up with Greece", rather than "Up with ELAS". I don't think the loss of an "H" was remarked on in the excitement.'

The rest of L Squadron, SBS, followed a few hours later and Olivey led his LRDG patrol into the Greek capital on 17 October where they remained for five days, billeted in the Ford workshops on Syngros Avenue. It was an ideal location, considering all the maintenance work that the jeeps required, but there was still time to celebrate the city's liberation with Athenians. Anyone in a British uniform was a target for well-wishers, more often than not finding themselves dragged off to a party where they were plied with kisses and wine. 'We felt like cinema stars,' wrote Milner-Barry in his diary. On the day Olivey arrived in Athens, Milner-Barry took tea with Princess Andrew of Greece, sister of Louis Mountbatten (and mother of the Duke of Edinburgh).

The festivities soon ended and Olivey's 'Z1' Patrol was subsumed into 'Pompforce', a 1,000-strong amalgamation of the SBS, the 4th Independent Parachute Battalion, a unit from the RAF Regiment and a battery of 75 mm guns under the command of Jellicoe, no longer a 'brigadier' but recently promoted – officially – to colonel.

'Pompforce' headed north towards Larissa, driving past the detritus of a large-scale retreat without ever catching sight of their enemy. Finally they made contact with their quarry just south of the town of Kozani. Jellicoe split his force in two, the paratroopers skirting around Kozani and pushing on to Florina, which lay close to the borders with Yugoslavia and Albania, while the rest of 'Pompforce' crushed German resistance at Kozani.

Olivey's patrol 'proceeded south of Florina and harassed the withdrawing enemy and proceeded to the flat country . . . firing at a range of 2,000 yards, at the enemy force withdrawing up the Florina–Havrokhoma Road. Florina was occupied/captured at 1600 hours.'

Hours after the capture of Florina Jellicoe received a signal 'instructing us not to go into Yugoslavia or Albania, presumably as a result of a pact with the Russians'.

The LRDG and the SBS returned to Athens on 12 November to find that the carefree days of the previous month were but a distant memory. There was trouble brewing between the government of 'National Unity', who were pro-monarchy, and EAM, the predominantly communist National Liberation Front, whose military wing was ELAS, the Greek People's Liberation Army. At first it was assumed that the trouble could be easily contained by the Greek authorities and so Major Stormonth Darling led his B Squadron (who had also been in Greece) back to Italy on the same day Olivey's 'Z1' Patrol arrived back in Athens, the men all looking forward to the ten days leave they had been promised.

On 13 November leave was cancelled because of 'trouble, which was expected from ELAS' and six days later the LRDG were placed under the command of 23 Armoured Brigade. A short while later they moved their base to Osiphoglion Orphanage, on the main road to Athens, but they rarely ventured out, their presence more symbolic than practical. James Heys recalled that initially, despite being caught up in an incipient Civil War, the LRDG encountered little hostility from Athenians. 'I never came across any hostility from any Greeks,' he reflected. 'They were very sociable. John Olivey had been a prisoner in Greece and had escaped, and he had contacts.'

It was even suggested at the end of November that the LRDG should sail to Crete to corral the large number of Germans on the island who had surrendered. But as this proposal was being discussed the situation in Athens deteriorated. The LRDG were asked to send out patrols, their jeeps stripped of weapons, but a reminder to the warring factions that the British were still in the city. The patrols only served to inflame tensions, to the dismay of many of the LRDG who were unhappy at the prospect of fighting men who a few weeks ago had welcomed them with open arms. 'I made some Greek friends in Athens,' recalled James Swanson, one of a number of men sent to reinforce Olivey's patrol. 'The ones who were against the king asked us why we were doing it [supporting the king]. They felt we were turning against them after we had fought together against Germans. I understood that but told them it was our government not us.'

On 11 December Swanson and Corporal Buss were detailed to drive two men suffering from dysentery to the 97 General Hospital for an examination. On their way back they were ambushed by ELAS. 'We were driving along the street . . . and these bullets come flying over like nobody's business,' recalled Swanson. 'I was wounded in the shoulder and hand, it wasn't too bad. The driver wasn't hit and immediately turned into this place where there was a British HQ with medical orderlies.' ELAS claimed later it was a mistake and that they had thought it was a pro-Royalist vehicle, but the LRDG men were in a British truck, wearing British uniform. 'Pity after all we had been through to have bullets flying around,' said Swanson, 'Some of others were fairly badly wounded but no one killed.'

An hour or so later John Olivey and his driver, Artie Botha, nicknamed 'Ape' by his fellow patrol members, popped into Athens on a supply run. As they turned up a quiet side street a machine gun opened up from an overhead window. Botha was shot in the head and Olivey hit as he dragged his wounded driver to cover. The pair were rushed to the 97 General Hospital but nothing could be done to save Botha's life. Olivey was evacuated to Italy by air and eight days later the LRDG left the orphanage for their long-awaited spell of Rest and Recuperation. They had completed what Captain Bill Armstrong, who had replaced Olivey as OC, described as a a 'non-spectacular and tiring job extremely well'. Their reward was to be put up in the Carlton Hotel, in Omonia Square, and they were still there a week later. Christmas Dinner for the officers was a lavish affair, the menu consisting of crème Marie Louise soup for starters, then roast turkey and all the trimmings, followed by two desserts – a plum pudding and a Sherry cream trifle – and finished with cheese fingers and coffee. No shortage of drinks, either, with a choice of wines and spirits, including whisky, gin, sherry and port.

Christmas Day for the men was not quite as extravagant, but it was enjoyable in its own way. For weeks they had been husbanding their rum ration, and come 25 December they could wait no longer. 'We all stayed in bed and sipped this rum,' recalled James Hey. 'It was a very nice day.'

CHAPTER TWENTY-FIVE

'The bomb was ticking'

Captain Ashley Greenwood spent the Christmas period in Nikšić, the second largest city in Montenegro, on the liaison staff of Brigadier Joseph O'Brien-Twohig, commander of the 183 Infantry Brigade. O'Brien-Twohig was utterly fearless and utterly 'fiery', though he had nothing but admiration for the LRDG. 'The brigadier was tickled pink with the LRDG, these young chaps he could just send off to miles away, make reconnaissance and come back to report to him personally,' explained Greenwood. 'I was with him one time and he was giving absolute hell to his staff captain, who'd done something wrong. The door opened and an LRDG lance-corporal poked his head round and the brigadier said "Oh, come in, Ralph [Aspden], what have you discovered now?" Then he had a long chat with him.'

Evelyn Waugh, who, with Randolph Churchill, had been sent on a military mission to Yugoslavia in the summer of 1944, was a frequent visitor to Nikšić during this period. 'I had one of the most amusing dinners I've ever had, with the brigadier and Waugh, who was very frightfully funny,' said Greenwood. 'He wasn't a particularly nice man, not at all helpful to the LRDG, but his stories were very funny.'*

---

* Randolph Churchill had first encountered the LRDG in 1942 when he and Fitzroy MacLean flew in to Siwa. Guy Prendergast detailed Lofty Carr and Tich Cave to greet the pair and drive them to HQ. 'So we collected them, and they glared at us and waited for us to carry their luggage and when they realized we weren't going to

Evelyn Waugh was not alone in being uncooperative to the LRDG at this time. 'The Yugoslav partisans were most unhelpful,' said Greenwood. 'At that stage they knew the Germans were getting out, they didn't want to get involved and they wanted to retain arms to take control of the country and if anything they hindered us when we were trying to do what we were doing.'

By January 1945 the partisans were preparing for war with the pro-Nazi Ustaše, who for nearly four years had ruled the Independent State of Croatia. General Tito had reached out a hand of reconciliation to the Ustaše in 1944, declaring a general amnesty for any of their number who joined the partisans before 31 December 1944: after that date all Ustaše would be hunted down and killed.

Many did change allegiance but there were still a lot of Ustaše who melted into the countryside to begin a campaign of terrorism under the command of Ante Pavelić. It was a volatile time and the LRDG, as they had in Athens, became caught up in the internecine warfare.

As well as liaising with Brigadier O'Brien-Twohig, Greenwood's other task at Nikšić was to visit the LRDG patrols scattered among the Dalmatian islands. One such patrol was situated on the sparsely populated island of Ist, just three and three-quarter miles square. Codenamed Kickshaw, the fourteen-man patrol drew from both 'Y1' and 'Y2' and was led by Captain Archie Gibson, a maverick Scot who had joined the LRDG at the tail end of the war in North Africa. His orders were to report on the movement of enemy shipping and any other relevant information, but at this stage of the war it was an uninspiring task. 'We had various look-out points on the tops of rocks,' recalled Gibson. 'And these would be manned pretty regularly in daylight hours and the information sent back. You'd just sit there, wearing the arse out of your pants. It was a rather tedious sort of occupation.'

At the end of December Gibson injured his back and was

help they lugged it themselves,' remembered Carr. 'When we got up to Prendergast, Randolph's first words were "These two men didn't salute me." Prendergast said "I can't get them to salute me and I'm a colonel. You're only a major." '

evacuated to hospital in Zara. Greenwood visited in the first week of January to see how the men were faring in his absence, but he need not have worried; Sergeant Tich Cave had assumed command and the veteran had matters in hand.

He and four men were billeted in a room on the first floor of a house 400 yards from the jetty. A room on the ground floor was used as their office and the rest of the house was occupied by a couple, Stanko Babajko and his wife, and their five children. The house next door contained the wireless transmitter room and 200 yards up the road a house had been converted into a makeshift hospital, a local midwife tending Sergeant Gilbert Jetley and Trooper Hutchinson, both of whom were under the weather.

The radio room was the domain of the patrol signaller, Ken Smith, who had celebrated his twenty-fourth birthday on Ist in December. Born in Lincolnshire, Smith had joined the Royal Signals in 1939 before volunteering for the LRDG in North Africa. Gibson had specially asked for Smith to accompany him to Ist, having been impressed with his cool efficiency during a summer operation in Mostar. He had a dry sense of humour, an unflappable nature and a habit, so Gibson remarked, of wearing 'his beret on the back of his head so that it looked as though it must fall off'. Smith's cheerful nature made him a favourite with the five Babajko children, who liked his impish sense of fun and his generosity with the ration chocolate bars.

On the evening of 10 January most of the patrol were in their billet playing cards. It was 2115 hours and Cave was about to turn in for the night. Suddenly he heard four shots. Thinking it might be the MFV *Palma* arriving at the jetty, Cave went outside but saw no lights in the sea, nor did he notice anything untoward coming from the radio room where he knew Ken Smith and Jock Watson to be. He returned to the billet and went upstairs to bed. A couple of minutes later Watson knocked on the door. He was calm but there was an urgency to his voice all the same. A bomb had just been left outside the radio room. Cave 'at first treated the matter as a jest'. Who would leave a bomb outside the radio room? Watson insisted it wasn't a joke. Cave, noticing the concern in his face, instructed Watson to return to the house and tell Smith to evacuate the radio room. Smith was putting on his shirt when Watson reappeared. 'I told him to hurry and get out,' recalled Watson, who popped his head round the door to check on the bomb, which resembled a large shoebox. 'I heard it ticking. I shouted to Smith that the bomb was ticking and he must get out.' By now four partisans had arrived, explaining that they had fired the shots at some men they had seen creeping around the houses. Smith 'pushed them aside and endeavoured to get the bomb away'.

As Watson ran from the house Cave and Trooper Taylor emerged from the billet. Smith appeared holding the bomb and coolly explained 'that his intention was to place it behind a wall nearby'.

He had gone five yards when the bomb exploded. Cave and Taylor were blown back into their billet and Watson threw himself flat among the grass. 'I ran to the scene of the explosion to render any assistance I could,' said Watson. 'I then found two legs each blown off below the knee. There was no further sign of Sgm. Smith at all.'

There were several other explosions on Ist that night, including an ammunition dump and the partisan bathhouse destroyed, all attributed to a Ustaše raiding party. The next day 'Y' Patrol was withdrawn from Ist and a week later Major Tim Heywood, the LRDG officer in charge of the Signal Section, wrote to Smith's mother, telling her his son 'undoubtedly saved the lives of his comrades and of many allied troops and troops in a nearby house'. He added: 'It is very difficult to express this sort of thing adequately on paper. But I do want you to believe that all those who knew your son are full of sympathy for you. We all miss him, I and other officers who came into contact with him, because he always did his job conscientiously and with a smile. The men because he was always cheerful and never complained of anything. I can assure you we were all very fond of him.' Back at LRDG HQ, Sergeant Gilbert Jetley returned the patrol's radio equipment to the signals section, among which were wristwatches issued to each signaler. The sergeant in charge asked for Smith's watch. A look of contempt spread across Jetley's face. 'There wasn't any wristwatch,' he explained. There wasn't any wrist. We buried his boots.'

Signalman Smith was awarded a posthumous George Cross, which was presented to his mother by King George VI in 1946.* Outside Buckingham Palace she told reporters: 'It was just typical of him to do what he did . . . he was a grand boy and never caused me any trouble. He always wanted to go into the army from a boy, and joined up at the age of eighteen for twelve years' service. He was never happier than when he could get his dad to talk about his experiences in the Great War but his dad said: "My boy, when you have been through what I have you won't be so keen." But he went all the same.'

* Mrs Smith kept her son's medal by her side until her death in 1968. It was subsequently sold, but in 1998 was auctioned in London and bought for £7,000 by the Royal Signals Museum.

CHAPTER TWENTY-SIX

'I say farewell and good luck to you all'

In February it was decided to establish a small Combined Operations HQ at Zara, a town on the Croatian coast, 200 miles north of Dubrovnik. Known as the Land Forces Northern Adriatic, it comprised A Squadron LRDG, the SBS and a unit called the Raiding Support Regiment. They were commanded by Lieutenant-Colonel David Sutherland, who had recently replaced George Jellicoe as the new CO of the SBS, but they received a cold reception from the Yugoslavs, many of whom were now openly hostile to the presence of British soldiers in their country.

Without the cooperation of the partisans, the British conducted a series of reconnaissance patrols and raids throughout the spring on islands such as Olib, Cherso, Lussino, Rab and Pag. Towards the end of March David Lloyd Owen returned from a conference in England and assumed command of the Combined Operations HQ. By now relations with the partisans had deteriorated to a dangerous level and on 13 April Lloyd Owen received a signal saying that Mike Reynolds had been arrested in Istria at gunpoint, along with another LRDG officer, Stan Eastwood. 'The whole trouble was caused by Tito's desire to have an indisputable claim to Istria,' reflected Lloyd Owen. 'He feared that too many British troops were gaining an influence, and that we were poised ready to enter Trieste before he could enter it.'

Reynolds and Eastwood were released on the night of 16 April but just a few hours later the partisans tried to take John Olivey into custody. Since 8 March the Rhodesian – fully recovered from the wounds he had sustained in Athens – and his 'Z1' Patrol had been on a long-range reconnaissance in Istria. Having suffered at the hands of one lot of partisans, Olivey was damned if he was going to be victimized by another bunch. Warned by Lloyd Owen that he might be arrested, Olivey was waiting for the partisans when they arrived with orders for his return. He informed the partisans what they could do with their arrest warrant, and then 'moved camp after they had left, slightly closer to the enemy, thereby using the enemy as protection from the Ptzns [partisans]'.

Olivey subsequently received an apology from the partisans, who realized that in the nuggety Rhodesian they had more than met their match. 'Z1' Patrol continued with their road watch north of Fiume, observing an adversary in his death throes: 'I remember seeing the retreating Jerries and what a pitiful sight they were too,' recalled Alf Page. 'If we saw any tanks or trucks amongst them we'd radio through and the RAF would come over and blast them.'

On 4 May Olivey deemed it safe enough to radio in a resupply by air, and two days later a cornucopia of delicacies floated down from the sky: tea, sugar, milk and best of all, whisky.

'We gave the food to the partisans and their thanks was to disarm us and lock us up in a machine shop in a village down the mountain,' said Alf Page, who recalled that Olivey, denied access to a lavatory by the guard, 'peed on his candle!' Olivey had reached the end of his tether – but so fortunately had the war. On 8 May Europe celebrated VE Day. The LRDG and the SBS threw a joint party, a riotous affair with a funfair and a water cart full to the brim with wine.

Olivey was not there. Having handed over his Patrol to the British Liaison Officer in Trieste, Lieutenant-Colonel Clarke, to ensure there would be no further trouble with the partisans, Olivey travelled back to Italy alone, hitchhiking the last few miles on a truck. He had missed the party, but as Olivey proudly noted at the conclusion of his operational report: 'Z1 Patrol last to operate in Europe for LRDG.'

* * *

The war was over in Europe, but not in the Far East, and David Lloyd Owen was quietly confident that the LRDG would now have a role to play in that conflict. Since July 1944 he had 'been trying to get the authorities interested' in deploying the unit to that theatre, writing a series of papers that earned noises of approval from Combined Operations in London, but little else. So in March 1945 Lloyd Owen had flown to London to argue his case in person. 'He was informed that SEAC (South East Asia Command) had asked for the unit in November', but that Allied Forces Headquarters (AFHQ) in the Mediterranean refused on the grounds that the LRDG were required in their sphere of operations. Lloyd Owen had returned to the LRDG from London no nearer to knowing if the unit would be sent to the Far East at the conclusion of the European War, so he pestered Combined Operations again on 2 May, but it was not until seventeen days later that AFHQ discussed the future of the LRDG. The results of the conference looked encouraging for Lloyd Owen. He had already recruited 300 men from the LRDG – including some who had been released from captivity and were eager to rejoin the fray – and was able to tell them on 25 May that the War Office was studying a proposal to transfer the unit to the Far East. Three weeks later, on 16 June, AFHQ told Lloyd Owen that 'the War Office had definitely asked for us . . . to regroup and have some leave before going on to Asia'.

Within a week the War Office had changed its mind and it was Lloyd Owen's sorry task to inform the men that the Long Range Desert Group was to be disbanded. The news devastated Lloyd Owen, who had invested so much of himself, physically, spiritually and emotionally, into the unit in the past four years. Seeking solace, suffering understandable pangs of self-pity, he immediately wrote a plaintive letter to Field Marshal The Hon. Sir Harold Alexander, who replied on 26 June:

Dear Lloyd Owen
The news of the war office decision to disband the Long Range Desert Group must have come to you as a great shock – as it did to me. Long before I first went to the Middle East I had heard

of the exploits of the LRDG in your original hunting grounds in Tripolitania and Cyrenaica, and it was with great pride that I first took you under my command in August 1942.

Since then you have continued your fine work with undiminished skill and enthusiasm and it is indeed with great reluctance that I say farewell and good luck to you all.

A touching tribute from the field marshal, a letter Lloyd Owen could read again and again during the six weeks it took him and his faithful adjutant, Captain Leo Capel, to disband the unit and organize the transportation home of men, paperwork and equipment.

In that time the LRDG formed its Association and published its inaugural newsletter, reprinting Alexander's letter – and one in a similar vein from General Freyberg* and boasting that already membership of the Association was running at 381. From 1946 there would be an annual dinner, added the LRDG newsletter, and the first 'should be held on the night of the Wembley Cup Final'.

And then the men began to leave the base, for England, Scotland, Wales, Ireland, Rhodesia, New Zealand. For home.

Twenty-six years later, in the 1971 edition of the LRDG Newsletter, Leo Capel reminisced about those long sultry summer days in Italy as the unit gradually, gently, disintegrated. 'On the last night of all we sat and talked,' he recalled in his letter, adding that by now there were only himself and a dozen others still left in Italy. 'Next morning we all shook hands and went our various ways.' They left in a small convoy of trucks, heading first to Benevento where they returned the last few LRDG trucks to an adjutant, and then on to AFHQ in Caserta. 'There I handed in a wad of certificates stating that all had been accounted for and that I and my driver were verily the last of the LRDG . . . what that adjutant said in Benevento was true, you know. The men of the LRDG *were* "sort of different", and thank God they were.'

---

* Describing the news as 'sad', Freyberg added: 'Nobody realizes better than I do the extent to which their work contributed to the success of the North African campaign, and it will always be a source of pride and satisfaction in 2 NZEF that New Zealanders were able to play a part in your long series of brilliant operations.'

EPILOGUE

'It was a family'

On 9 December 2013 a memorial to the Long Range Desert Group was dedicated in the west cloister of Westminster Abbey. The Dean of Westminster, the Very Reverend Dr John Hall, conducted the service and he said in his Bidding: 'We stand beside a monument commemorating officers and men of the Submarine Service of the Royal Navy, the Commandos, and all ranks of the Airborne Forces and Special Air Service. It was designed by the sculptor Gilbert Ledward and unveiled by Winston Churchill on 21 May 1948. It commemorates mighty men of valour.

'Today we honour the debt the SAS has always owed to the Long Range Desert Group as we add to the monument a memorial to the commitment and expertise of the LRDG. The memorial . . . adds to the monument an evocation of the desert.'

The memorial had been a long time coming, and among the four LRDG veterans gathered in the west cloister of Westminster Abbey the irony had not escaped them that their unit, the first British special forces unit of the Second World War, was the last to be honoured.

The speed with which the LRDG had been disbanded in the summer of 1945 always rankled with David Lloyd Owen. Unseemly haste, in his opinion. It was not until October 1945 that the SAS and SBS suffered a similar fate. The SAS – which by the end of the war had expanded to a brigade comprising two British regiments, two French regiments and a Belgian regiment

– paraded for the last time on 8 October and four days later Brigadier Michael Calvert sent the twelve most senior officers of the three defunct units a memo entitled 'Future of SAS Troops'. Among the men to receive the memo were Lloyd Owen, David Stirling and George Jellicoe. Calvert had been instructed by the War Office to 'investigate all the operations of the Special Air Service with a view to giving recommendations for the future of SAS in the next war and its composition in the peace-time army'.

Calvert, who had made his name fighting the Japanese with the Chindits in the Burmese jungle in 1943–4, believed that Britain must retain its elite units at a time when the world faced a nebulous future; this would only happen if the War Office looked beyond the immediate peace to the years ahead when the British Empire was likely to come under threat from countries seeking independence from the Mother Country. 'We all have the future of the SAS at heart,' Calvert wrote in the memo, 'not merely because we wish to see its particular survival as a unit but because we have believed in the principles of its method of operations.' Therefore he urged all the twelve recipients of the memo to cooperate fully with Major-General Rowell, the Director of Tactical Investigation (DTI), when their views were canvassed.

The verdict of the impartial tribunal came as no surprise to Calvert nor to any other recipient of his memo – there was no place for a special forces unit in post-war Britain. Politicians wished to look forward to decades of peace, to rebuilding the world, and that world would have no room for a force of guerrilla fighters. With Winston Churchill no longer prime minister (replaced by Labour's Clement Attlee) the special forces had lost their closest ally.

Despite the disappointment felt by Lloyd Owen at the shortsightedness of the War Office, he remained in the army, commanding the 1st Battalion of The Queen's Royal Regiment from 1957 to 1959. He was appointed OBE in 1954, CB in 1971 and he also wrote two best-selling books about his time in the LRDG. He died in 2001 aged eighty-three. Lofty Carr remembers Lloyd Owen as a 'thoroughly good officer, very clever and [with] the guts of a lion'.

The man whom Lloyd Owen replaced in 'Y' Patrol in 1941, Captain Pat McCraith, survived the war and returned home to his firm of solicitors. He died in 1998. Frank Simms, another of 'Y' Patrol's officers from the desert days escaped from his POW camp, and rejoined the Royal Warwickshire Regiment, winning a Military Cross in 1944. After the war he became British military attaché in Turkey and in 1952 was killed in a car accident. The rumour in LRDG circles was that his car was deliberately forced off a mountain road by persons unknown. Of the other LRDG officers who fought in North Africa, two didn't survive the war. Gus Holliman of the Rhodesian Patrol was killed in January 1945 serving with the Royal Tank Regiment, and Anthony Hunter fell a month later, also in Holland, fighting with the Royal Scots Fusiliers. Shortly before he left the LRDG in 1943, Hunter was awarded the MC for displaying 'great personal bravery' when his patrol was attacked by ten enemy aircraft. In August 1944 Hunter had married twenty-year-old Mildred, a member of the Women's Royal Naval Service. Carr only learnt of Hunter's death in October 2014. 'He was an exceptionally nice person, self-effacing and not at all brutal,' he remembered.

Pat Clayton died in 1962 aged sixty-five having remained in the army until retirement in 1953. Michael Crichton-Stuart died in 1981, Don Steele, the gallant New Zealander, in 1983, Martin Gibbs – who was captured at Tobruk in 1942 but escaped from his POW camp the following year – in 1994; Tim Heywood in 2006 (for many years the president of the Country Landowners' Association), Rupert Harding-Newman in 2007. Ashley Greenwood died in 2003, aged ninety-one, after a distinguished career in the Colonial Service, including a three-year appointment as Attorney-General of Gibraltar. His love of climbing never left him and Greenwood celebrated his eightieth birthday by scaling a 6,000-metre peak in the Himalayas.

Richard Lawson was a regular contributor to the LRDG newsletter in the post-war years, always signing off as 'Doc'. In 1981 he wrote an article entitled 'Holiday in the Dodecanese', an account of his return to the scene of his capture thirty-eight years earlier.

It was a wonderful couple of weeks, an exploration of the islands by boat and bike, burning off all the good food and fine wine with which his hosts plied him. But Lawson was not just there to make hay; he visited Leros war cemetery and stood in front of Jake Easonsmith's gravestone, and those of Alan Redfern and the other LRDG men at rest on the island. 'It is beautifully designed and kept,' he said of the cemetery in his article. 'The ground rises and is covered with pink and white oleanders and between the graves are red geraniums and hibiscus.' Doc Lawson died in 2005 aged ninety-one.

Bill Kennedy Shaw died in 1979 aged seventy-seven and Guy Prendergast wrote his eulogy in the next edition of the LRDG newsletter: 'His life and soul were tied up entirely in the LRDG,' said Prendergast. 'And his knowledge of the method of functioning in the desert helped to bring the original Patrols to the state of efficiency which was the hallmark of the Unit.'

Prendergast, the father of five children, died in 1985, mourned by all who served under him in the desert, though few could claim they had ever been close to him. He was not the type. Jim Patch, a mere private, never had any direct contact with his commanding officer during the war, but in subsequent years – in his capacity as secretary of the LRDG Association – he was fortunate enough to glimpse the warmth beneath the cool exterior. 'After the war my wife and I went to stay with him in northern Scotland and he went out on the loch and caught some salmon for dinner,' remembered Patch. 'He was a quiet man, not a bit of a showman, who didn't forcibly declare his beliefs.' Carr retains a great affection for Prendergast, a leader who, though he never showed it, suffered terribly from the loneliness of command. 'Whenever he gave me instructions for a job, he would do so in a rather laconic way, adding at the end: "You'll think of something,"' said Carr. 'That almost became his catchphrase. It was only later that his clerk told me that often he would drop his head onto his desk when I had left and cry his eyes out because of what he was asking us to do.'

Teddy Mitford ended the war in command of the 3rd Royal Tank Regiment, fighting their way through the Ardennes and over the Elbe into Germany. He remained in the army after the war, retiring in 1966, and four years later he took over the 4,000-acre family estate which he ran until 2002, gaining a reputation among locals for his 'considerable charm' and charity work. Married twice, but with no children, Mitford sold the estate in 1993 and he died in 2002 aged ninety-three.

Another man of ineffable charm was John Olivey. He returned home to his farm in Melsetter, south-eastern Rhodesia, and his new wife Mickey. Over the next few years they produced five children – including twin sons and daughters – and Olivey also found time to lead a successful campaign to build the Melsetter Anglican Church. He never forgot his days as a soldier, however, and always attended the Rhodesian reunion of the LRDG in his beret and polished cap badge. He died in 1968 at the age of sixty-two. David Lloyd Owen recalled some of his favourite memories of Olivey in the LRDG newsletter. He was an officer who inspired his men not just by his courage and resilience but also his irrepressible spirit. Lloyd Owen finished his eulogy thus: 'About twelve of his old friends drove throughout the night to be at his funeral. Many of the crowd, which included Africans, had to stand outside the church where John had been a Lay Reader. His wife Mickey wrote and told me that his coffin was covered with a Union Jack – the flag he had served so faithfully and well. He was a happy man.'

There was a similar outpouring of grief among LRDG veterans when Ralph Bagnold died in 1990, a month after his ninety-fourth birthday. Having retired from the army in 1944, aged forty-eight with the honorary rank of brigadier and the Order of the British Empire (OBE) for his work in raising the LRDG, Bagnold married a year after the war and for the rest of his life devoted himself to his scientific studies. Among the papers he authored were 'Motion of waves in shallow water', published by the Royal Society of London, (1946) and 'Flow resistance in sinuous or irregular channels' by the United States Geological Survey in 1960. His work was recognized with a string of awards, including the Founders' Gold Medal of the Royal Geographical Society, the Wollaston Medal of the Geological Society of London and the Penrose Gold Medal of the Geological Society of America.

With his stammer and shy nature, Bagnold was not a man who relished the spotlight. Self-promotion was anathema and public speaking an ordeal. But in 1977 Bagnold was asked to give the keynote address at a North American Space Agency conference on the desert landscapes of Earth and Mars, an invitation he gladly accepted. The NASA scientists hung on his every word.

The esteem in which Bagnold was held by the men with whom he had served in the desert endured to the end. In 1986 David Lloyd Owen, chairman of the LRDG Association, wrote to Bagnold on the occasion of his ninetieth birthday. 'All of us who served in the Long Range Patrols or the Long Range Desert Group are proud to have been members of a unit which has such a very distinguished war record,' declared Lloyd Owen. 'That you were the driving force behind its formation in June 1940 is a historical fact which we hope gives you much satisfaction. That your inspired leadership in the early days of the unit had a profound effect throughout its five wartime years is recognized as a major contribution to the successful outcome of the Second World War. We hope you can be happy to accept my assurance that this is so.'

Bagnold was deeply touched by the declaration, replying with a letter that was published in the 1986 edition of the LRDG Association newsletter. As modest and unassuming as ever, Bagnold said he believed General Wavell deserved an equal share of the credit for the unit's formation. It was, he wrote 'astonishing' that the commander-in-chief had given him carte blanche to raise the LRDG, 'especially when others had ridiculed any such idea as utterly impossible . . . he alone grasped the possibilities and implications. A very great and many-sided man; yet homely and, I think, rather shy. The LRDG was due to him as much to me.'

Six months after Bagnold's death, David Stirling died aged seventy-four, a Knight Bachelor, the subject of two biographies and revered throughout the world as the father of the Special Air Service, in the eyes of the British public the greatest fighting force in history. These were the superheroes who had abseiled down the Iranian Embassy in May 1980 to spectacularly end the siege in front of the world's television cameras. Within weeks the SAS was the most famous regiment in the world.*

Just as Mike Calvert had foreseen, the end of the Second World War brought peace to Europe – for a while at least – but in the far-flung corners of the British Empire, from Malaya to Borneo to Aden, there were rebellions against British rule. In 1947 a territorial SAS regiment (21 SAS) was raised and five years later came a regular regiment, 22 SAS, continuing from where Stirling had left off, even down to the same sand-coloured beret and regimental motto, 'Who Dares Wins.'

The SAS were therefore very much of the time when Stirling died; not so the LRDG, who remained a romantic part of the Second World War, that distant conflict when gallant men trundled over the desert dunes in rickety old trucks.

But Stirling never forgot the contribution of the LRDG in nurturing the suckling SAS. In 1984, in opening the refurbished SAS base in Hereford, named Stirling Lines in his honour, the regiment's founder addressed the hundreds of serving and ex-members of the SAS present: 'In those early days we came to owe the Long Range Desert Group a deep debt of gratitude,' said Stirling. 'The LRDG were the supreme professionals of the desert and they were unstinting in their help. Here among us today is David Lloyd Owen, a wartime commanding officer of this magnificent unit. We are proud to regard the Long Range Desert Group as honorary members of our SAS family.'

In 2000 the veterans of the Long Range Desert Group celebrated the unit's Diamond Jubilee and with none of them getting younger

* One might argue that the mythical status of the SAS began as early as August 1944 when a series of articles about the regiment appeared in the British press. One such piece, in *The Times* of London, so irritated Colonel F.S. Kennedy Shaw, father of Bill, he felt obliged to write to the editor, pointing out: 'During the African campaign the S.A.S. men were, as you say, 'fed and equipped by secret patrols', but these patrols were furnished throughout by the Long Range Desert Group, to whom much of the success of the S.A.S. troops in Africa was due'.

it seemed an appropriate moment to wind up the Association. They met for the last time in London and those veterans unable to attend for whatever reasons sent their best wishes by letter. There was a very special message as well, one read out to the veterans and their families by Jim Patch, for twenty-four years the secretary of the LRDG Association. It was from Elizabeth R:

> I have received with much pleasure the message of loyalty and goodwill from the LRDG Association, meeting today at your final reunion. Your Association has since its foundation kept alive the memories of those who served with such courage and distinction in the LRDG during the last war. I send my warmest good wishes to you all as you gather together for the last time and wish to express my confidence that the remarkable exploits of the LRDG will never be forgotten.

With the LRDG Association no more, the SAS paid back their wartime debt by adopting the LRDG and amalgamating their remaining veterans into their own thriving Regimental Association.

It was the initiative of the SAS Regimental Association to honour the LRDG in Westminster Abbey, and they were also responsible for installing a memorial to the LRDG in Scotland in the autumn of 2014, a commemoration that was attended by, amongst others, the children of Guy Prendergast, David Lloyd Owen and Jake Easonsmith. The memorial is in the shadow of David Stirling's statue, which was inaugurated in 2002 and stands on the land David roamed as a young boy.

Mike Sadler, Jim Patch and Lofty Carr were all present at the ceremony in Scotland as they were in Westminster Abbey in December 2013 when the memorial was dedicated in the west cloister. Between them they boasted 279 years, and a fund of wonderful memories.

After transferring from the LRDG to the SAS in the summer of 1942, Sadler was commissioned and later served as intelligence officer in 1 SAS in Europe, parachuting into France shortly after the invasion. He finished the war with an MM and an MC, and a few months later went on an expedition to the Antarctic. Most of his post-war life, however, was spent in the Foreign Service and he now lives in the south-west of England. Reflecting on the legacy of the LRDG, Sadler says: 'Their main contribution to the winning of the war in North Africa was that they opened up the desert with their knowledge of the terrain and showed the possibility of moving through remote areas that had otherwise been considered inaccessible. Once into these areas they provided intelligence on enemy movements. They were a pioneer in reconnaissance.'

Lofty Carr is the last of 'Bagnold's Blue-eyed Boys', that select band of men recruited to 'Y' Patrol at the start of 1941. Carr was reunited with Tich Cave in the spring of 1945 when he returned to the UK having escaped from captivity in Germany. 'We were being marched from one camp to another and at the end of one day's march, I managed to wriggle through a hole in the barn we were in.' Carr eventually ran into the Americans advancing east and was put on a plane back to England, the country he had last seen more than five years earlier. 'When I got out of the train at Stoke station, my parents were there and my brother, and my sixteen-year-old sister,' he recalled. 'She walked towards me and shook my hand, and in a very British way, said "Hello, how are you?"'

Carr and Cave were among those LRDG personnel who answered Lloyd Owen's call for volunteers for the Far East. Nonetheless, they were all mightily relieved when they learned their services wouldn't be required in the war against Japan. Within weeks the pair were demobbed. Like many dumped back on civvy street in 1945–46, Carr found the adjustment painful. 'I hated those who had dodged the column [contemporary slang for shirkers] and, as we saw it, pinched all the best jobs.'

Carr worked in insurance for many years, married, got divorced, and then married again, to Barbara. In the late 1960s Carr decided that he needed a fresh challenge, so he became 'one of the oldest full-time students in captivity'. First he passed his A-levels, then he spent three years at university, and finally he graduated from teacher training college as a fully-qualified art teacher. Explaining to the LRDG newsletter in 1969 why he'd decided on such a radical departure from his previous life, Carr wrote: 'Don't let's live in the past too much. Let's start something rather than wait for the end; and if I drop dead during a physical education lecture, I'll say it for you: "I told you so." Anyway, you can have thrombosis doing anything.'

He and Tich Cave remained the best of friends after the war, the pair 'getting up to monkey business' whenever they met up. In 1947 Cave 'walked through France and down into Italy', trying to put some distance between him and his wartime memories. He settled in Jersey, tried to forge a career in market gardening, but that didn't work out. He chafed at the pettiness of post-war Britain, the silly social mores and the re-imposition of class divides that had been so blissfully eroded in the LRDG. Eventually he found contentment in Africa, where 'there were no Joneses to keep up with.' He lived first in Kenya, then Rhodesia, Malawai, and finally South Africa. Cave and his wife spent the last years of their lives managing a farm with 400 pigs in Gonubie, Eastern Cape Province. In one of his last letters to the LRDG newsletter, he quoted Walt Whitman in describing his happiness: 'I think I could turn and live with animals, they are so placid and self-contained.' He died in 2009.

This book is the first time Carr has publicly discussed his years in the LRDG. He was never really one for reunions, nor did he read the memoirs of former comrades. The war was over, and he had other priorities, though there were times when the past caught up with him. Of his conversations with Bagnold on the meaning of courage – discussions in which Bagnold had never offered a solution – Carr found an answer of sorts. 'I relate it [courage in battle] to a hit and run driver, which I came across in my insurance days,' says Carr. 'In those split seconds after an accident, a driver can run or he can stay. And the same with a soldier, he can flee or he might stay and win the VC. It's an imponderable.'

It has been only recently, in the twilight of his life, that Carr has truly appreciated what the LRDG represented in his life. 'We were regarded as an undisciplined and wild rabble,' he reflects. 'Anyone who didn't fit in, didn't meet the LRDG etiquette, was gone. For those of us who did serve in the unit, it was a privilege. The camaraderie was magnificent, it was a family.'

Jim Patch shares Carr's sentiments. The LRDG was a family, a tight-knit one that had an indefinable pull. When Patch and Ron Hill finally got out of Yugoslavia in February 1945, they immediately returned to the LRDG, then based in Rodi, and were greeted by David Lloyd Owen in his inimitable style: 'You've been a bloody long time getting back! What the hell have you been up to?' However, their hopes of seeing some action in the Dalmatians were dashed by the Red Cross, which reminded Lloyd Owen of the directive that former POWs were forbidden from fighting in the theatre in which they had been initially captured. 'We were compulsorily repatriated,' explained Patch. 'I was most unhappy and after six weeks' leave I was sent back to the Royal Artillery and put through basic training.'

Patch left the army in 1946 and spent the rest of his working life with the Post Office. When he retired in 1980 he threw himself into the LRDG Association for the next twenty years as their diligent and dedicated secretary. It was fitting, therefore, that it was Patch who was asked to read the lesson at the dedication of the LRDG memorial in Westminster Abbey in 2013. The passage Patch read was Isaiah 35:

The desert and the parched land will be glad;
  the wilderness will rejoice and blossom.
Like the crocus, it will burst into bloom;
  it will rejoice greatly and shout for joy.
And a highway will be there;
  it will be called the Way of Holiness;
  it will be for those who walk on that Way.
The unclean will not journey on it;
  wicked fools will not go about on it.
No lion will be there,
  nor any ravenous beast;
  they will not be found there.

But only the redeemed will walk there,
  and those the Lord has rescued will return.
They will enter Zion with singing;
  everlasting joy will crown their heads.
Gladness and joy will overtake them,
  and sorrow and sighing will flee away.

Bibliography

Books

Bagnold, Ralph, *Sand, Wind and War* (University of Arizona Press, 1991)
Bierman, John and Smith, Colin, *Alamein* (Penguin, 2003)
Cowles, Virginia, *The Phantom Major* (Collins, 1958)
Crichton-Stuart, Michael, *G Patrol* (William Kimber, 1958)
Dimbleby, Richard, *The Frontiers Are Green* (Hodder & Stoughton, 1943)
Feebery, David (ed.), *Guardsman and Commando* (Pen & Sword Military, 2008)
James, Malcolm, *Born of the Desert* (Greenhill Books, 1991)
Kelly, Saul, *The Hunt for Zerzura* (John Murray, 2003)
Kennedy Shaw, Bill, *Long Range Desert Group* (Collins, 1945)
Liddell-Hart, Basil, *The Rommel Papers* (DaCapo Press, 1982)
Lewin, Ronald, *The Life and Death of the Afrika Korps* (Pen & Sword, 2003)
Lloyd Owen, David, *The Desert my Dwelling Place* (Cassell, 1957)
——, *The Long Range Desert Group* (Pen & Sword, 2001)
Maclean, Fitzroy, *Eastern Approaches* (Penguin, 1991)
Moorehead, Alan, *The Desert War* (Hamish Hamilton, 1965)
Morgan, Mike, *The Sting of the Scorpion* (The History Press, 2003)
Mortimer, Gavin, *Stirling's Men* (Weidenfeld, 2004)
——, *The Daring Dozen* (Osprey, 2011]
——, *The SAS in World War II* (Osprey, 2012)

——, *The SBS in World War II* (Osprey, 2013)
O'Carroll, Brendan, *The Kiwi Scorpions* (Token Publishing Ltd, 2000)
Peniakoff, Vladimir, *Popski's Private Army* (Harper & Collins, 1975)
Pitt, Barrie, *Special Boat Squadron* (Corgi, 1985)
Pittaway, Jonathan, *Long Range Desert Group* (Les Martens, 2006)
Public Record Office, *Special Forces in the Desert War 1940–1943* (PRO Publications, 2001)
Schmidt, Heinz, W. *With Rommel in the Desert* (Constable, 1998)
Smith, Peter C., *Massacre at Tobruk* (Stackpole Books, 2008)
Smith, Peter C. and Walker, Edwin R., *War in the Aegean* (Stackpole Books, 2008)
Timpson, Alistair, *In Rommel's Backyard* (Pen & Sword, 2010)
Young, Desmond, *Rommel* (Fontana Press, 1989)

Websites

http://www.lrdg.org
http://www.popski.org

Articles and Journals

Dundee Courier & Advertiser, October 1970
The Egyptian Mail, February 1941
'The Oasis of Siwa' by W.B. Kennedy-Shaw, in *Geographical Magazine*, Vol. 22, 1944
The Household Brigade Magazine, summer 1941
The Times, February 1941, August and September 1944
West Sussex County Times, December 1943

Author interviews

Mike 'Lofty' Carr, February to October 2014
Jim Patch, March 2014
Mike Sadler, August and December 2013
Rudolf Schneider, February 2014
Albert Youngman, December 2013

Imperial War Museum interviews
Arthur Arger
Ron Cryer
Ashley Greenwood
Rupert Harding-Newman
James Heys
Frank Lord
Rod Matthews
Teddy Mitford
James Patch
Spencer Seadon
Alexander Stewart
Les Sullivan
James Swanson
Lawrence Thompson
Peter Upcher

IWM documents
Diary of Walter Milner-Barry
David Lloyd-Owen papers
PJ Hurman papers

NZ SOUND ARCHIVES, Christchurch
'A Talk by the LRDG Commander', February 1941
'Further Talks on the "LRDG"', February 1941

SAS Archives
Papers of Ron Hill
LRDG Newsletters, 1941–2000
Mars & Minerva, regimental journal of the SAS, 1960–2010
Diary of Cyril Richardson

Churchill Archives, Cambridge
Bagnold Papers

National Archives, Kew

File numbers: WO 373/8/500
WO201/807
HS 9/1036/1
WO 201/810
WO 208/5582-5583
WO 208/3326/2920
WO 201/799
WO 201/797
INF 2/44/87
WO 201/817
WO 201/818
WO 201/813
WO 201/729
WO 204/8495
WO 204/8492
WO 201/816
WO 201/817
WO 201/818
WO 201/813
WO 204/8459
WO 204/8500
DO 35/1696
WO 201/812
WO 201/738
WO 204/8460
T 161/1436/6
HW 1/1261
WO 218/90
WO 218/92
WO 201/2201
WO 218/94
WO 218/89
HW 1/648

Index